Taste of Home
Make it!
TAKE IT

TASTE OF HOME BOOKS • RDA ENTHUSIAST BRANDS, LLC • MILWAUKEE, WI

PAGE 253

PAGE 96

PAGE 141

PAGE 132

CONTENTS

LIKE US
facebook.com/tasteofhome

FOLLOW US
pinterest.com/taste_of_home

SHOP WITH US
shoptasteofhome.com

TWEET US
@tasteofhome

SHARE A RECIPE
tasteofhome.com/submit

PAGE 250

PAGE 116

PAGE 12

PAGE 93

Cover Photography:
Photographer: Grace Natoli Sheldon
Food Stylist: Kathryn Conrad
Set Stylist: Stacey Genaw

Pictured on cover: Berry Cream Pie, p. 221;
Garlic Pepper Corn, p. 148; Colorful Corn Bread Salad, p. 146

Pictured on title page: Orange Gelatin Pretzel Salad, p. 118

Pictured on back cover: Strawberry-Rhubarb Cream Dessert,
p. 248; Roasted Balsamic Sweet Potatoes, p. 144; Peach Melba
Trifle, p. 248; Slow Cooker Meatball Sandwiches, p. 200

© 2019 RDA Enthusiast Brands, LLC
1610 N. 2nd St., Suite 102, Milwaukee WI 53212-3906

International Standard Book Number: 978-1-61765-797-9
Library of Congress Control Number: 2017963394
Component Number: 118100019H

Printed in China
3 5 7 9 10 8 6 4 2

A GUIDE TO MAKE-IT, TAKE-IT SUCCESS

BRING YOUR "A" GAME TO POTLUCKS WITH THESE EASY IDEAS

You know who they are: the mom who takes the perfect casserole to the church supper; the neighbor who contributes the best dessert to the block party; the guy whose appetizer receives cheers at the barbecue. Yeah...those people. Well, at *Taste of Home* we think it's about time you start counting yourself among them!

With the **303 crowd-pleasing recipes** in **Make It Take It,** bring-a-dish success is always at your fingertips. Simply follow these potluck practices, prepare a recipe from this book and become the life of the party.

PAGE 169

PLAN AHEAD

Who has time to set a dinner on the table, let alone whip up dozens of cupcakes for a bake sale? You do...with a little planning, that is. Be realistic about the time you have available, and choose a recipe that best fits your schedule. Look for **MAKE AHEAD** throughout this book, and consider those recipes first if time is tight.

USE YOUR SLOW COOKER

When it comes to making and taking a dish to a get-together, slow cookers are ideal travel partners. Not only do they simmer large-yield recipes on their own, but they also keep food warm on buffets. See page 184 for an entire chapter of slow-cooker greats.

PAGE 238

THINK OUTSIDE THE BOX

Salads, dips and brownies are welcome at shared-dish events, but why not wow the crowd with a change-of-pace item? Consider something like Slow Cooker Spiced Poached Pears (page 193), Bacon Cheeseburger Buns (p. 109) or Zesty Marinated Shrimp (page 181).

TRAVEL SAFELY

All the recipes in **Make It Take It** travel well, but plan accordingly. A four-layer cake may not be the best option for a long drive. Sturdy cardboard boxes prevent slow cookers and casserole dishes from sliding around in car trunks, so ask your grocer for any clean boxes you could have. Secure lids with rubber bands.

Rise to the Top of the Guest List

* Ask the host if guests have any food allergies.
* Tell the host what you're bringing.
* Pack an extension cord for buffets.
* Share extra copies of the recipe.
* Bring food on/in a decorative serving piece. Leave that piece as a hostess gift.
* Bake and pack extra baked goods for the host to enjoy the day after.
* No time to cook? Offer to bring beverages, plates, napkins, condiments or even a centerpiece.
* Volunteer to help set up, tear down or do dishes.

FOR A CLASSIC CROWD-PLEASER, CHECK OUT GERI'S **MAKE ONCE, EAT TWICE LASAGNA** ON PAGE 176.

POTLUCK DO'S AND DON'TS

✔ **Do bring a dish that's ready to serve or requires minimal assembly. Don't bring something that requires a lot of prep time, effort or space to put together in the host's kitchen.**

✔ **Do bring the item you planned. Don't go rogue. If you're asked to bring a specific item or if you signed up for a certain course, bring it.**

✔ **Do bring your contribution intact. Don't arrive with a slice of cake missing because your husband wanted to sample it first.**

✔ **Do leave leftovers at the party. Don't pack a to-go plate for home; take food home with you only if the host asks you to do so.**

Focaccia Barese
page 26

Appetizers & Dips

Invited to a holiday party or a game-day get-together? Find the perfect nibble, bite and nosh among these tasty and totable appetizers, snacks, dips and spreads!

PARTY APPETIZER MEATBALLS

These are a favorite at parties and other gatherings. The recipe is easy, and the meatballs can be made ahead of time and frozen until needed. What makes them so good? The sauce!
—Nathalie Guest, Caledon, ON

Prep: 15 min. • **Bake:** 40 min.
Makes: 8 dozen

- 2 pounds lean ground beef
- 2 large eggs, lightly beaten
- 1 cup shredded part-skim mozzarella cheese
- ½ cup dry bread crumbs
- ¼ cup finely chopped onion
- 2 tablespoons grated Parmesan cheese
- 1 tablespoon ketchup
- 2 teaspoons Worcestershire sauce
- 1 teaspoon Italian seasoning
- 1 teaspoon dried basil
- 1 teaspoon salt
- ¼ teaspoon pepper

SAUCE
- 1 bottle (14 ounces) hot or regular ketchup
- 2 tablespoons cornstarch
- 1 jar (12 ounces) apple jelly
- 1 jar (12 ounces) currant jelly

1. In a large bowl, combine the first 12 ingredients. Shape into 1-in. balls. Place meatballs on a greased rack in a shallow baking pan.
2. Bake at 350° for 10-15 minutes; drain. Combine ketchup and cornstarch in roasting pan. Stir in the jellies; add the meatballs. Cover and bake for 30 minutes.

SEASONED CRAB CAKES

These scrumptious crab cakes won First Place at the National Hard Crab Derby in Crisfield, Maryland. I entered them on a whim after trying a few different crab cake recipes to serve my family.
—Betsy Hedeman, Timonium, MD

Prep: 20 min. + chilling • **Cook:** 10 min.
Makes: 8 crab cakes

- 3 cans (6 ounces each) crabmeat, drained, flaked and cartilage removed
- 1 cup cubed bread
- 2 large eggs
- 3 tablespoons mayonnaise
- 3 tablespoons half-and-half cream
- 1 tablespoon lemon juice
- 1 tablespoon butter, melted
- 1½ teaspoons seafood seasoning
- 1 teaspoon Worcestershire sauce
- 1 teaspoon salt
- ½ cup dry bread crumbs
- ½ cup canola oil

1. In a large bowl, combine crab and bread cubes. In another bowl, whisk the eggs, mayonnaise, cream, lemon juice, butter, seafood seasoning, Worcestershire sauce and salt. Add to crab mixture and mix gently (mixture will be moist).
2. Place bread crumbs in a shallow dish. Drop crab mixture by ⅓ cupfuls into crumbs; shape each into a ¾-in.-thick patty. Carefully turn to coat. Cover and refrigerate for at least 2 hours.
3. In a large skillet, cook crab cakes in oil for 4-5 minutes on each side or until golden brown and crispy.

SPINACH TURNOVERS

The flaky cream cheese pastry adds a sensational texture to these hot appetizers—and just wait until you taste the wonderful filling. I usually fix a double batch and freeze some to have on hand in case unexpected guests drop by.
—Jean von Bereghy, Oconomowoc, WI

Prep: 30 min. + chilling • **Bake:** 10 min.
Makes: about 4 dozen

- 2   packages (8 ounces each) cream cheese, softened
- ¾   cup butter, softened
- 2½ cups all-purpose flour
- ½   teaspoon salt

FILLING

- 5   bacon strips, diced
- ¼   cup finely chopped onion
- 2   garlic cloves, minced
- 1   package (10 ounces) frozen chopped spinach, thawed and well drained
- 1   cup 4% cottage cheese
- ¼   teaspoon salt
- ¼   teaspoon pepper
- ⅛   teaspoon ground nutmeg
- 1   large egg, beaten
     Salsa, optional

1. In a bowl, beat cream cheese and butter until smooth. Combine the flour and salt; gradually add to creamed mixture (dough will be stiff). Turn onto a floured surface; gently knead the dough 10 times. Cover and refrigerate at least 2 hours.
2. In a skillet, cook the bacon until crisp. Remove bacon; reserve 1 tablespoon drippings. Saute the onion and garlic in drippings until tender. Remove from heat; stir in bacon, spinach, cottage cheese and seasonings. Cool.
3. On a lightly floured surface, roll dough to ⅛-in. thickness. Cut into 3-in. circles; brush edges with egg. Place 1 heaping teaspoon of filling on each circle. Fold over; seal edges. Prick tops with a fork. Brush with egg.
4. Bake at 400° for 10-12 minutes or until golden brown. Serve with salsa if desired.

SMOKY GRILLED CORN SALSA

The backyard grill is the perfect place to cook up the ingredients for homemade corn salsa. It's yummy with tortilla chips or as a topping for meat, poultry or fish.
—Alicia Dewolfe, Gloucester, MA

Start to Finish: 30 min.
Makes: 6 cups

- 6   plum tomatoes, halved
- 4   medium ears sweet corn, husks removed
- 2   medium sweet yellow peppers, halved
- 2   medium green peppers, halved
- 3   jalapeno peppers, halved and seeded
- 1   medium red onion, cut into ½-inch slices
- ¼   cup minced fresh cilantro
- 3   tablespoons olive oil
- 3   tablespoons red wine vinegar
- 5   garlic cloves, minced
- 1   teaspoon salt
- ½   teaspoon sugar
- ½   teaspoon pepper

1. Grill the tomatoes, corn, peppers and onion, covered, over medium heat for 10-12 minutes or until tender, turning occasionally. Allow vegetables to cool slightly. Remove corn from cobs; transfer to a large bowl. Chop the remaining vegetables and add to corn.
2. In a small bowl, whisk the cilantro, oil, vinegar, garlic, salt, sugar and pepper. Pour over vegetables; toss to coat. Serve warm or cold.
Note: Wear disposable gloves when cutting hot peppers; the oils can burn skin. Avoid touching your face.

SLOW COOKER CHEDDAR BACON ALE DIP

My tangy, smoky dip won the top prize at our office party recipe contest. Other beers will work in this recipe, too, but steer clear of the dark varieties.
—Ashley Lecker, Green Bay, WI

Prep: 15 min. • **Cook:** 3 hours
Makes: 4½ cups

18 ounces cream cheese, softened
¼   cup sour cream
1½ tablespoons Dijon mustard
1   teaspoon garlic powder
1   cup amber beer or
    nonalcoholic beer
2   cups shredded cheddar cheese
1   pound bacon strips, cooked
    and crumbled, divided
¼   cup heavy whipping cream
1   green onion, thinly sliced
    Soft pretzel bites

1. In a greased 3-qt. slow cooker, combine the cream cheese, sour cream, mustard and garlic powder until smooth. Stir in the beer, cheese and all but 2 tablespoons bacon. Cook, covered, on low, stirring occasionally, until heated through, about 3-4 hours.
2. In last 30 minutes, stir in heavy cream. Top with the onion and remaining bacon. Serve with pretzel bun bites.

TEST KITCHEN TIP Party foods left out for too long are at risk for bacteria growth, so it's important to keep an eye on them. The USDA says foods shouldn't sit at room temperature more than 2 hours. Discard foods that have been left out longer. Hot foods should be held at 140 degrees or warmer. Serve hot appetizers in chafing dishes, slow cookers or warming trays.

CHEESY CHICKEN TACO DIP

We're huge college football fans (go Irish!), and my chicken taco dip hasn't missed a season opener in 14 years and counting. A slow cooker makes easy work of keeping the dip warm throughout the entire game—if it lasts that long!
—Deanna Garretson, Yucaipa, CA

Prep: 15 min.
Cook: 4 hours 10 min.
Makes: 8 cups

1   **jar (16 ounces) salsa**
1   **can (30 ounces) refried beans**
1½ **pounds boneless skinless chicken breasts**
1   **tablespoon taco seasoning**
2   **cups shredded cheddar cheese**
3   **green onions, chopped**
1   **medium tomato, chopped**
¼   **cup chopped fresh cilantro**
    Tortilla chips

1. In a greased 3- or 4-qt. slow cooker, mix salsa and beans. Top with chicken; sprinkle with taco seasoning. Cook, covered, on low until chicken is tender, 3-4 hours.

2. Remove the chicken; shred finely using two forks. Return to slow cooker; stir in the cheese. Cook, covered, on low until the cheese is melted, 10-15 minutes, stirring occasionally.

3. To serve, top with green onions, tomato and cilantro. Serve with chips.

Health Tip: Skip the chips and serve with crunchy celery sticks for a lighter bite.

HOT CHEESE DIP

When a colleague brought this cheesy dip to school for a teachers' potluck, I immediately gave it an A+. I had to have this irresistibly creamy recipe!
—Ardyce Piehl, Poynette, WI

Start to Finish: 30 min.
Makes: 3 cups

- 2 cups shredded part-skim mozzarella cheese
- 2 cups shredded cheddar cheese
- 2 cups mayonnaise
- 1 medium onion, minced
- 1 can (4 to 4½ ounces) chopped green chilies, drained
- ½ cup sliced ripe olives
- 1½ ounces sliced pepperoni
  Assorted crackers and fresh vegetables

Preheat oven to 325°. Combine the first five ingredients; spread into a greased shallow baking dish or pie plate. Top with olives and pepperoni. Bake until bubbly, about 25 minutes. Serve with crackers and fresh vegetables.

SAUSAGE WONTON STARS

These fancy-looking appetizers are ideal when entertaining large groups. The cups are stuffed with a cheesy pork sausage filling. We keep a few in the freezer so we can easily reheat them for snacking.
—Mary Thomas, North Lewisburg, OH

Start to Finish: 30 min.
Makes: about 4 dozen

> 1 **package (12 ounces) wonton wrappers**
> 1 **pound bulk pork sausage**
> 2 **cups shredded Colby cheese**
> ½ **medium green pepper, chopped**
> ½ **medium sweet red pepper, chopped**
> 2 **bunches green onions, sliced**
> ½ **cup ranch salad dressing**

1. Lightly press wonton wrappers onto the bottom and up the sides of greased miniature muffin cups. Bake at 350° for 5 minutes or until edges are browned.
2. In a large skillet, cook sausage over medium heat until no longer pink; drain. Stir in the cheese, peppers, onions and ranch salad dressing. Spoon a rounded tablespoonful into each wonton cup. Bake for 6-7 minutes or until heated through.

ARTICHOKE, SPINACH & SUN-DRIED TOMATO DIP

This creamy, robust artichoke dip boasts the colorful addition of sun-dried tomatoes. It's great served with tortilla, pita or bagel chips. If you prefer to omit the tomatoes, follow the variation below.
—Lorilyn Tenney, Boise, ID

Prep: 10 min. • **Bake:** 30 min.
Makes: 5 cups

- 2 packages (8 ounces each) cream cheese, softened
- ½ cup mayonnaise
- 2 shallots, finely chopped
- 3 garlic cloves, minced
- 1 package (10 ounces) frozen chopped spinach, thawed and squeezed dry
- 1 jar (7½ ounces) marinated quartered artichoke hearts, drained and chopped
- 1 cup sun-dried tomatoes (not packed in oil), chopped
- ¾ cup grated Asiago cheese Tortilla chips

1. Preheat oven to 350°. In a large bowl, combine cream cheese, mayonnaise, shallots and garlic. Stir in the spinach, artichokes, tomatoes and Asiago cheese. Transfer to a greased 11x7-in. baking dish.
2. Bake 30-35 minutes or until golden brown. Serve with tortilla chips.
Artichoke Spinach Dip: Omit sun-dried tomatoes. Substitute one (14-oz.) can water packed artichokes for the marinated artichokes. Rinse, drain and chop artichokes. Stir in the Asiago cheese and, if desired, 2 teaspoons dried basil to the cream cheese mixture. Sprinkle ½ cup shredded mozzarella cheese over top. Bake as directed.

BUFFALO WING BITES

The Buffalo wing fans in my family were more than happy to taste test when I invented these. We love them anytime!
—Jasey McBurnett, Rock Springs, WY

Prep: 25 min. • **Bake:** 15 min.
Makes: 2 dozen (2 cups dressing)

- 2 tablespoons grated Parmesan cheese
- 1 envelope ranch salad dressing mix, divided
- 1 cup mayonnaise
- 1 cup 2% milk
- ¼ cup crumbled blue cheese, optional
- 1¼ cups finely chopped cooked chicken breast
- 1¼ cups shredded cheddar-Monterey Jack cheese
- ¼ cup Buffalo wing sauce
- 1 tube (13.8 ounces) refrigerated pizza crust
- 2 tablespoons butter, melted

1. Preheat oven to 400°. In a small bowl, combine the Parmesan cheese and 1 teaspoon dressing mix. In another bowl, mix the mayonnaise, milk and remaining dressing mix. If desired, stir in blue cheese. Refrigerate until serving.
2. In a large bowl, mix chicken, cheddar-Monterey Jack cheese and wing sauce. On a lightly floured surface, unroll pizza crust dough and pat into a 14x12-in. rectangle. Cut into 24 squares.
3. Place 1 rounded tablespoon of chicken mixture on the center of each square. Pull corners together to enclose filling; pinch to seal. Place 1 in. apart on greased baking sheets, seam side down. Brush the tops with butter; sprinkle with the Parmesan cheese mixture.
4. Bake 15-17 minutes or until golden brown. Serve with dressing.

ONION BRIE APPETIZERS

Guests will think you spent hours preparing these pretty appetizers, but puff pastry makes them easy to assemble. And the combination of Brie, caramelized onions and caraway is delicious.

—Carole Resnick, Cleveland, OH

Prep: 25 min. + chilling • **Bake:** 15 min.
Makes: 1½ dozen

- 2 medium onions, thinly sliced
- 3 tablespoons butter
- 2 tablespoons brown sugar
- ½ teaspoon white wine vinegar
- 1 sheet frozen puff pastry, thawed
- 4 ounces Brie cheese, rind removed, softened
- 1 to 2 teaspoons caraway seeds
- 1 large egg
- 2 teaspoons water

1. In a large skillet, cook the onions, butter, brown sugar and vinegar over medium-low heat until onions are golden brown, stirring frequently. Remove with a slotted spoon; cool to room temperature.

2. On a lightly floured surface, roll puff pastry into an 11x8-in. rectangle. Cut Brie into thin slices; distribute evenly over pastry. Cover with the onions; sprinkle with caraway seeds.

3. Roll up one long side to the middle of the dough; roll up the other side so the two rolls meet in the center. Using a serrated knife, cut into ½-in. slices. Place on parchment paper-lined baking sheets; flatten to ¼-in. thickness. Refrigerate for 15 minutes.

4. In a small bowl, beat egg and water; brush over slices. Bake at 375° for 12-14 minutes or until puffed and golden brown. Serve warm.

BOURBON CANDIED BACON DEVILED EGGS

At our house, it doesn't get any better than deviled eggs with bacon—bourbon candied bacon, that is. See if you can resist them. We can't!
—Colleen Delawder, Herndon, VA

Prep: 20 min. • **Bake:** 25 min.
Makes: 2 dozen

- 2 tablespoons brown sugar
- ¾ teaspoon Dijon mustard
- ½ teaspoon maple syrup
- ⅛ teaspoon salt
- 2 teaspoons bourbon, optional
- 4 thick-sliced bacon strips

EGGS
- 12 hard-boiled large eggs
- ¾ cup mayonnaise
- 1 tablespoon maple syrup
- 1 tablespoon Dijon mustard
- ¼ teaspoon pepper
- ¼ teaspoon ground chipotle pepper
  Minced fresh chives

1. Preheat oven to 350°. In a small bowl, mix brown sugar, ¾ teaspoon mustard, ½ teaspoon syrup and salt. If desired, stir in bourbon. Coat bacon with brown sugar mixture. Place on a rack in a foil-lined 15x10x1-in. baking pan. Bake 25-30 minutes or until crisp. Cool completely.
2. Cut eggs in half lengthwise. Remove yolks, reserving whites. In a small bowl, mash yolks. Add mayonnaise, 1 tablespoon syrup, 1 tablespoon mustard and both types of pepper; stir until smooth. Chop bacon finely; fold half into egg yolk mixture. Spoon or pipe into egg whites. Sprinkle with remaining bacon and chives. Refrigerate, covered, until serving.

MARINATED OLIVE & CHEESE RING

We love to turn our Italian meals into celebrations, and an antipasto always kicks off the party. This one is almost too pretty to eat, especially when sprinkled with pimientos, fresh basil and parsley.
—Patricia Harmon, Baden, PA

Prep: 25 min. + chilling
Makes: 16 servings

- 1 package (8 ounces) cream cheese, cold
- 1 package (10 ounces) sharp white cheddar cheese, cut into ¼-inch slices
- ⅓ cup pimiento-stuffed olives
- ⅓ cup pitted Greek olives
- ¼ cup balsamic vinegar
- ¼ cup olive oil
- 1 tablespoon minced fresh parsley
- 1 tablespoon minced fresh basil or 1 teaspoon dried basil
- 2 garlic cloves, minced
- 1 jar (2 ounces) pimiento strips, drained and chopped
  Toasted French bread baguette slices

1. Cut cream cheese lengthwise in half; cut each half into ¼-in. slices. On a serving plate, arrange cheeses upright in a ring, alternating cheddar and cream cheese slices. Place olives in center.
2. In a small bowl, whisk vinegar, oil, parsley, basil and garlic until blended; drizzle over cheeses and olives. Sprinkle with pimientos. Refrigerate, covered, at least 8 hours or overnight. Serve with baguette slices.

SAVORY BLT CHEESECAKE

Tomato and green onions mixed with cream cheese is like an irresistible form of gazpacho. Served on lettuce, the BLT version is great on its own, but it's also a tasty appetizer when served with crackers. This is a versatile recipe, so feel free to use other cheese in place of the Gruyere. Or add olives, crab meat, cooked mushrooms—whatever strikes your fancy!
—Joni Hilton, Rocklin, CA

Prep: 35 min. • **Bake:** 45 min. + chilling
Makes: 24 servings

¾ cup dry bread crumbs
½ cup grated Parmesan cheese
3 tablespoons butter, melted
FILLING
4 packages (8 ounces each) cream cheese, softened
½ cup heavy whipping cream
1½ cups crumbled cooked bacon
1 cup oil-packed sun-dried tomatoes, patted dry and chopped
1 cup shredded Gruyere or Swiss cheese
2 green onions, sliced
1 teaspoon freshly ground pepper
4 large eggs, lightly beaten
Optional toppings: shredded iceberg lettuce, chopped cherry tomatoes and additional crumbled cooked bacon
Assorted crackers, optional

1. Preheat oven to 325°. Place a greased 9-in. springform pan on a double thickness of heavy-duty foil (about 18 in. square). Securely wrap foil around pan.
2. In a small bowl, combine the bread crumbs, Parmesan cheese and butter. Press onto the bottom of prepared pan.

Place the pan on a baking sheet. Bake for 12 minutes. Cool on a wire rack.
3. In a large bowl, beat cream cheese and cream until smooth. Beat in the bacon, tomatoes, Gruyere cheese, onions and pepper. Add eggs; beat on low speed just until combined. Pour over crust. Place springform pan in a large baking pan; add 1 in. of boiling water to larger pan.
4. Bake 45-55 minutes or until center is just set and top appears dull. Remove springform pan from water bath; remove foil. Cool cheesecake on a wire rack for 10 minutes; loosen the edges from the pan with a knife. Cool 1 hour longer. Refrigerate overnight.
5. Remove the rim from the pan. Serve the cheesecake with the toppings and crackers if desired.

BUFFALO CHICKEN DIP

Buffalo wing sauce, cream cheese and ranch or blue cheese dressing make a great party dip. Everywhere I take it, people ask for the recipe.
—Belinda Gibson, Dry Ridge, KY

Start to Finish: 30 min.
Makes: about 2 cups

1 package (8 ounces) cream cheese, softened
1 cup cooked chicken breast
½ cup Buffalo wing sauce
½ cup ranch or blue cheese salad dressing
2 cups shredded Colby-Monterey Jack cheese
French bread baguette slices, celery ribs or tortilla chips

1. Preheat the oven to 350°. Spread the cream cheese into an ungreased shallow 1-qt. baking dish. Layer with the chicken, wing sauce and salad dressing. Sprinkle with cheese.
2. Bake, uncovered, 20-25 minutes or until the cheese is melted. Serve dip with baguette slices.

SUNNY ASPARAGUS TAPENADE

I use fresh asparagus from the farmers market for this healthy tapenade, which can also be served as a dip. It's one of my standbys for family gatherings.
—Kathy Patalsky, New York, NY

....

Start to Finish: 30 min.
Makes: 2 cups

- ¾ pound fresh asparagus, chopped
- ¾ cup packed fresh parsley sprigs
- ⅓ cup unsalted sunflower kernels
- ¼ cup lemon juice
- ¼ cup orange juice
- 1 tablespoon olive oil
- 2 teaspoons maple syrup
- 1 small garlic clove, chopped
- ½ teaspoon salt
- ½ teaspoon crushed red pepper flakes
- 1 teaspoon pepper
  Additional sunflower kernels, optional
  Assorted fresh vegetables, crackers and/or toasted French bread baguette

1. In a large saucepan, bring ½ in. of water to a boil. Add asparagus; cover and cook for 3-5 minutes or until tender. Drain and immediately place asparagus in ice water. Drain and pat dry.
2. Place in a food processor; add the parsley, sunflower kernels, lemon juice, orange juice, oil, syrup, garlic, salt, pepper flakes and pepper. Cover and process until desired consistency.
3. Transfer to a small bowl; sprinkle with additional sunflower kernels if desired. Serve at room temperature or chilled with the dippers of your choice.

REUBEN ROUNDS

Fans of the classic reuben sandwich will go crazy for baked pastry spirals of corned beef, Swiss and sauerkraut. They're a breeze to make, and bottled Thousand Island dressing makes the perfect dipping sauce.
—Cheryl Snavely, Hagerstown, MD

....

Start to Finish: 30 min.
Makes: 16 appetizers

- 1 sheet frozen puff pastry, thawed
- 6 slices Swiss cheese
- 5 slices deli corned beef
- ½ cup sauerkraut, rinsed and well drained
- 1 teaspoon caraway seeds
- ¼ cup Thousand Island salad dressing

1. Preheat oven to 400°. Unfold puff pastry; layer with cheese, corned beef and sauerkraut to within ½-in. of edges. Roll up jelly-roll style. Trim the ends and cut crosswise into 16 slices. Place on greased baking sheets, cut side down. Sprinkle with caraway seeds.
2. Bake 18-20 minutes or until golden brown. Serve with salad dressing.

FIVE-SPICE CHICKEN WINGS

These wings are baked to a perfect golden brown and shine with mild Asian spices. Thanks to an overnight marinade, the chicken stays tender while the skin maintains that signature crunch everyone loves.

—Crystal Jo Bruns, Iliff, CO

Prep: 20 min. + marinating
Bake: 25 min.
Makes: about 3 dozen

- 3½ pounds chicken wings
- 3 green onions, chopped
- 2 tablespoons sweet chili sauce
- 2 tablespoons reduced-sodium soy sauce
- 2 tablespoons fish sauce or additional soy sauce
- 4 garlic cloves, minced
- 1 tablespoon sugar
- 1 tablespoon Chinese five-spice powder
- 2 medium limes, cut into wedges

1. Cut chicken wings into three sections; discard wing tip sections. Combine the onions, chili sauce, soy sauce, fish sauce, garlic, sugar and five-spice powder in a large resealable plastic bag. Add wings; seal bag and toss to coat. Refrigerate 8 hours or overnight.
2. Drain chicken, discarding marinade. Place the wings in a greased 15x10x1-in. baking pan.
3. Bake at 425° for 25-30 minutes or until no longer pink, turning every 10 minutes. Squeeze lime wedges over wings.
Note: Uncooked chicken wing sections (wingettes) may be substituted for whole chicken wings.

CHILE RELLENO SQUARES

A friend gave me this recipe for a simple variation of chile rellenos, and now my family requests it often. It makes a tasty appetizer on its own or a nice addition to a Mexican-style meal.

—Fran Carll, Long Beach, CA

Prep: 10 min. • **Bake:** 25 min.
Makes: 16 servings

- 3 cups shredded Monterey Jack cheese
- 1½ cups shredded cheddar cheese
- 2 cans (4 ounces each) chopped green chilies, drained
- 2 large eggs
- 2 tablespoons whole milk
- 1 tablespoon all-purpose flour

1. Preheat oven to 375°. Sprinkle half of each of the cheeses onto bottom of a greased 8-in. square baking dish. Layer with chilies and remaining cheeses.
2. Whisk together eggs, milk and flour; pour over the top. Bake, uncovered, until set, 25-30 minutes. Cool 15 minutes before cutting.

MAKE AHEAD
HAM & BRIE PASTRIES

I loved pocket pastries growing up. Now as a busy mom with a hungry family to feed, I need quick bites. My spin on the classic ham and cheese delivers at snack or supper time.
—Jenn Tidwell, Fair Oaks, CA

Start to Finish: 30 min.
Makes: 16 pastries

1 sheet frozen puff pastry, thawed
⅓ cup apricot preserves
4 slices deli ham, quartered
8 ounces Brie cheese,
    cut into 16 pieces

1. Preheat oven to 400°. On a lightly floured surface, unfold puff pastry. Roll pastry to a 12-in. square; cut into sixteen 3-in. squares. Place 1 teaspoon preserves in center of each square; top with ham, folding as necessary, and cheese. Overlap two opposite corners of pastry over the filling; pinch tightly to seal.
2. Place on a parchment paper-lined baking sheet. Bake 15-20 minutes or until golden brown. Cool on pan 5 minutes before serving.
Freeze option: Freeze cooled pastries in a freezer container, separating layers with waxed paper. To use, reheat pastries on a baking sheet in a preheated 400° oven until heated through.

SALMON PARTY SPREAD

We're proud to serve our delicious Alaskan salmon to guests. Set out some crackers, and this slightly smoky spread will be gone in no time!
—Kathy Crow, Cordova, AK

Prep: 10 min. + chilling
Makes: 2 cups

1 package (8 ounces) cream
    cheese, softened
1 can (7½ ounces) pink
    salmon, drained, flaked
    and cartilage removed
3 tablespoons chopped
    fresh parsley
2 tablespoons finely
    chopped green pepper
2 tablespoons finely chopped
    sweet red pepper
2 teaspoon lemon juice
1 teaspoon prepared horseradish
½ teaspoon Liquid Smoke, optional
    Finely chopped pecans or
    additional parsley
    Crackers

In a large bowl, combine the first eight ingredients; stir until well blended. Cover and chill 2-24 hours. Transfer to a serving bowl; sprinkle with pecans or parsley. Serve with crackers.

FOCACCIA BARESE

This recipe has been in my mom's family for several generations, and now it's one of my most requested items. Whenever I'm invited to a party, I am not allowed to attend unless I bring it!
—Dora Travaglio, Mount Prospect, IL

Prep: 30 min. + rising • **Bake:** 30 min.
Makes: 8 servings

1⅛ teaspoons active dry yeast
¾ cup warm water (110° to 115°), divided
½ teaspoon sugar
⅓ cup mashed potato flakes
1½ teaspoons plus 2 tablespoons olive oil, divided
¼ teaspoon salt
1¾ cups bread flour
TOPPING
2 medium tomatoes, thinly sliced
¼ cup pitted Greek olives, halved
1½ teaspoons minced fresh or dried oregano
½ teaspoon coarse salt

1. In a large bowl, dissolve yeast in ½ cup warm water. Add the sugar; let stand for 5 minutes. Add the potato flakes, 1½ teaspoons oil, salt, 1 cup flour and the remaining water. Beat until smooth. Stir in enough of the remaining flour to form a soft dough.
2. Turn onto a floured surface; knead until smooth and elastic, about 6-8 minutes. Place in a greased bowl, turning once to grease the top. Cover and let rise in a warm place until doubled, about 1 hour. Punch dough down. Cover and let rest for 10 minutes.
3. Place 1 tablespoon olive oil in a 10-in. cast-iron or other ovenproof skillet; tilt pan to evenly coat. Add dough; shape dough to fit pan. Cover and let rise until doubled, about 30 minutes.

4. With fingertips, make several dimples over top of dough. Brush with remaining tablespoon of oil. Blot tomato slices with paper towels. Arrange tomato slices and olives over dough; sprinkle with oregano and salt.
5. Bake at 375° for 30-35 minutes or until golden brown.

CUCUMBER FRUIT SALSA

We always have more cucumbers and tomatoes from our garden than we can consume. This recipe is a delightful way to use them up. If making the salsa ahead, stir in the chopped banana and peach right before serving.
—Anna Davis, Springfield, MO

Prep: 25 min. + chilling
Makes: 24 servings (¼ cup each)

1 large cucumber, finely chopped
2 medium green peppers, finely chopped
2 medium tomatoes, finely chopped
1 small red onion, finely chopped
1 small navel orange, segmented and chopped
2 tablespoons lemon juice
1 tablespoon minced fresh cilantro
1 tablespoon minced fresh parsley
1 garlic clove, minced
¼ teaspoon salt
¼ teaspoon hot pepper sauce
⅛ teaspoon pepper
1 medium peach, peeled and finely chopped
1 small banana, finely chopped

In a large bowl, combine the first 12 ingredients. Refrigerate at least 30 minutes to allow flavors to blend. Just before serving, stir in peach and banana.

MARINATED ANTIPASTO MEDLEY

Every year during the winter holiday season, the faculty and staff at my school bring treats to share on a designated "Goodies Day." One time, these tasty marinated bites were gone before the first lunch period!
—Laurie Hudson, Westville, FL

Prep: 20 min. + chilling
Makes: 9 servings

- 8 ounces Colby-Monterey Jack cheese, cut into ½-inch cubes
- 1 jar (10 ounces) pimiento-stuffed olives, drained
- 1 jar (16 ounces) cocktail onions, drained
- 1 cup grape tomatoes
- 6 ounces pepperoni, cut into ½-inch cubes

DRESSING
- ¼ cup olive oil
- 2 tablespoons cider vinegar
- ½ teaspoon sugar
- ¼ teaspoon salt
- ¼ teaspoon dried basil
- ¼ teaspoon dried oregano
- ⅛ teaspoon garlic powder
- ⅛ teaspoon pepper
- ⅛ teaspoon Louisiana-style hot sauce

In a large bowl, combine the first five ingredients. In a small bowl, whisk the dressing ingredients; pour over vegetable mixture and toss to coat. Cover medley and refrigerate for at least 3 hours. Stir before serving. Serve with a slotted spoon.

HAM & CHEESE QUICHES

I reach for this recipe when I need a festive finger food. With cheese in both the crust and the filling, it's impossible to eat just one.
—Virginia Abraham, Oxford, MS

Prep: 15 min. + chilling • **Bake:** 30 min.
Makes: 2 dozen

- ½ cup butter
- 1 jar (5 ounces) process sharp cheese spread
- 1 cup all-purpose flour
- 2 tablespoons water

FILLING
- 1 large egg
- ½ cup milk
- ¼ teaspoon salt
- ½ cup finely chopped ham
- ½ cup shredded Monterey Jack cheese

In a small bowl, cut butter and cheese spread into flour until well blended. Add water and toss with a fork until a ball forms. Refrigerate for 1 hour. Press tablespoonfuls onto the bottom and up the sides of greased miniature muffin cups. In a bowl, beat the egg, milk and salt. Stir in ham and cheese. Spoon a rounded teaspoonful into each shell. Bake at 350° for 30 minutes or until golden brown. Let stand for 5 minutes before serving.

SAUSAGE PINWHEELS

These eye-catching spirals are simple to make but look special on a buffet. Guests eagerly help themselves—sometimes the pinwheels never make it to their plates!
—Gail Sykora, Menomonee Falls, WI

Start to Finish: 30 min.
Makes: 1 dozen

1   tube (8 ounces) refrigerated
     crescent rolls
½   pound uncooked bulk
     pork sausage
2   tablespoons minced chives

1. Preheat the oven to 375°. Unroll the crescent dough onto a lightly floured surface; press perforations to seal. Roll into a 14x10-in. rectangle.
2. Spread sausage to within ½ in. of edges. Sprinkle with chives. Roll up carefully jelly-roll style, starting with a long side; pinch the seam to seal. Cut into 12 slices; place them 1 in. apart in an ungreased 15x10x1-in. pan.
3. Bake until golden brown and sausage is cooked through, 12-16 minutes.

DUTCH MEATBALLS (BITTERBALLEN)

I host an annual Christmas party for some close friends. One year, I made a traditional dish that represented each person's heritage. Talk about a hit! These moist meatballs with a crispy coating were one of the favorites of the night.
—Tracey Rosato, Markham, ON

Prep: 30 min. + chilling
Cook: 5 min./batch
Makes: 2½ dozen

3   tablespoons butter
3   tablespoons all-purpose flour
½   cup beef broth
1   beef top sirloin steak (¾ pound),
     cut into ½-inch cubes
¼   cup minced fresh parsley
¼   teaspoon salt
¼   teaspoon ground nutmeg
⅛   teaspoon pepper
1⅓   cups dry bread crumbs
2   large eggs
1   teaspoon milk
1   teaspoon canola oil
     Oil for deep-fat frying
     Stone-ground mustard, optional

1. In a large saucepan, melt butter over medium heat. Stir in flour until smooth. Gradually add broth; bring to a boil. Cook and stir for 1 minute or until thickened. Carefully add meat and parsley; cook and stir for 2-5 minutes or until meat is no longer pink. Stir in the salt, nutmeg and pepper. Transfer to a bowl; refrigerate for 3-4 hours or until chilled.
2. Place bread crumbs in a small shallow bowl. In another bowl, whisk the eggs, milk and oil. Drop the meat mixture by tablespoonfuls into bread crumbs; shape into balls. Dip meatballs in egg mixture, then coat again with crumbs. In an electric skillet or deep fryer, heat oil to 375°.
3. Fry meatballs, a few at a time, for 2-4 minutes or until golden brown on all sides. Drain on paper towels. Serve hot with mustard if desired.

SAVORY PARTY BREAD

It's impossible to stop nibbling on warm pieces of this cheesy loaf. The bread fans out for a beautiful presentation.
—Kay Daly, Raleigh, NC

Prep: 10 min. • **Bake:** 25 min.
Makes: 8 servings

1   unsliced round loaf sourdough
     bread (1 pound)
1   pound Monterey Jack cheese

½   cup butter, melted
½   cup chopped green onions
2   to 3 teaspoons poppy seeds

1. Preheat oven to 350°. Cut the bread widthwise into 1-in. slices to within ½ in. of bottom of loaf. Repeat cuts in opposite direction. Cut cheese into ¼-in. slices; cut slices into small pieces. Place pieces of cheese in cuts.
2. In a small bowl, mix butter, green onions and poppy seeds; drizzle over the bread. Wrap in foil; place on a baking sheet. Bake 15 minutes. Unwrap; bake 10 minutes longer or until cheese is melted.

TEST KITCHEN TIP
The bread can be sliced and filled a day ahead. Right before company comes, melt the butter and add the green onions and poppy seeds.

JALAPENO HUMMUS

Hummus is an easy, tasty and nutritious snack or appetizer. Friends are often surprised at the uncommonly good taste, especially the nice kick from the jalapeno. Serve with vegetables, crackers or tortilla chips.
—Lisa Armstrong, Murray, KY

Start to Finish: 15 min.
Makes: 4 cups

- 2 cans (15 ounces each) garbanzo beans or chickpeas, rinsed and drained
- ⅔ cup roasted tahini
- ½ cup water
- ⅓ cup lemon juice
- ¼ cup olive oil
- 2 tablespoons minced garlic
- 2 tablespoons pickled jalapeno slices, chopped
- 1 tablespoon juice from pickled jalapeno slices
- ½ to 1 teaspoon crushed red pepper flakes
- ½ teaspoon salt
- ½ teaspoon pepper
- ⅛ teaspoon paprika
   Assorted fresh vegetables

Place first 11 ingredients in a food processor; cover and process until well blended. Garnish with paprika. Serve with assorted vegetables.

ASPARAGUS WITH BASIL PESTO SAUCE

Add zip to your appetizer platter with an easy asparagus dip that can also double as a flavorful sandwich spread.
—Janie Colle, Hutchinson, KS

Start to Finish: 15 min.
Makes: 12 servings

- ¾ cup reduced-fat mayonnaise
- 2 tablespoons prepared pesto
- 1 tablespoon grated Parmesan cheese
- 1 tablespoon minced fresh basil
- 1 teaspoon lemon juice
- 1 garlic clove, minced
- 1½ pounds fresh asparagus, trimmed

1. In a small bowl, mix first six ingredients until blended; refrigerate until serving.
2. In a Dutch oven, bring 12 cups water to a boil. Add asparagus in batches; cook, uncovered, until crisp-tender, 2-3 minutes. Remove and immediately drop into ice water. Drain and pat dry. Serve with sauce.

BLT BITES

These quick hors d'oeuvres may be small but their big bacon and tomato flavor make up for what they lack in size. I serve them at parties, brunches and picnics, and they're always a hit.
—Kellie Remmen, Detroit Lakes, MN

Prep: 25 min. + chilling
Makes: 16-20 appetizers

- 16 to 20 cherry tomatoes
- 1 pound sliced bacon, cooked and crumbled
- ½ cup mayonnaise
- ⅓ cup chopped green onions
- 3 tablespoons grated Parmesan cheese
- 2 tablespoons snipped fresh parsley

1. Cut a thin slice off each tomato top. Scoop out and discard pulp. Invert the tomatoes on a paper towel to drain.
2. In a small bowl, combine the remaining ingredients. Spoon into tomatoes. Refrigerate for several hours.

BACON-WRAPPED TATER TOTS

Indulge in just one of these sweet and savoy bacon-wrapped bites and you'll know why they elicit oohs and aahs. Try the recipe as directed or one of the tasty variations below.
—Joni Hilton, Rocklin, CA

Start to Finish: 25 min.
Makes: 32 appetizers

- 16 bacon strips, cut in half
- ½ cup maple syrup
- 1 teaspoon crushed red pepper flakes
- 32 frozen Tater Tots

1. Cook the bacon in a large skillet over medium heat until partially cooked but not crisp. Remove to paper towels to drain; keep warm.
2. Combine syrup and pepper flakes. Dip each bacon piece in the syrup mixture, then wrap around a Tater Tot. Secure with toothpicks.
3. Place appetizers on a greased rack in a 15x10-x1-in. baking pan. Bake at 400° for 12-15 minutes or until the bacon is crisp.

Bacon-Wrapped Shrimp: Substitute 1 pound shrimp (31-40 per pound) with ¼ cup creamy Caesar dressing (marinated for up to 1 hour) for Tater Tots. Omit maple syrup mixture. Assemble and bake as directed 8-12 minutes or until shrimp turn pink. Brush with additional dressing if desired.

Bacon-Wrapped Stuffed Jalapenos: Make a lengthwise slit down each of 32 small to medium jalapenos; remove the seeds. Mix 1 pound of uncooked chorizo and 2 cups of shredded cheddar cheese; stuff the peppers. Assemble and bake as directed 22-30 minutes or until a thermometer reads 160°.

GARBANZO-STUFFED MINI PEPPERS

Mini peppers are so colorful and they're the perfect size for a two-bite appetizer. They have all the crunch of a pita chip, without the extra calories.
—Christine Hanover, Lewiston, CA

Start to Finish: 20 min.
Makes: 32 appetizers

- 1 teaspoon cumin seeds
- 1 can (15 ounces) chickpeas, rinsed and drained
- ¼ cup fresh cilantro leaves
- 3 tablespoons water
- 3 tablespoons cider vinegar
- ¼ teaspoon salt
- 16 miniature sweet peppers, halved lengthwise
   Additional fresh cilantro leaves

1. In a dry small skillet, toast cumin seeds over medium heat 1-2 minutes or until aromatic, stirring frequently. Transfer to a food processor. Add chickpeas, cilantro leaves, water, vinegar and salt; pulse until they are blended.
2. Spoon the mixture into pepper halves. Top with additional cilantro. Refrigerate until serving.

GARLIC BREAD MINI MUFFINS

These savory muffins make a terrific addition to any party spread, or include them alongside your favorite Italian entree. They're best served warm.
—Kathy Yarosh, Apopka, FL

Prep: 25 min. • **Bake:** 20 min.
Makes: 2 dozen

- 6 ounces cream cheese, softened
- 1 teaspoon garlic powder
- 1 teaspoon onion powder
- ¾ cup shredded Colby-Monterey Jack cheese
- ¾ cup shredded Italian cheese blend
- 1 tube (11 ounces) refrigerated breadsticks
- 1 large egg, lightly beaten
- ½ cup shredded Parmesan cheese

1. Preheat oven to 375°. In a small bowl, beat cream cheese, garlic powder and onion powder until blended. In another bowl, toss Colby-Monterey Jack cheese with Italian cheese blend.
2. On a lightly floured surface, unroll breadstick dough; press perforations to seal. Roll dough to a 12x8-in. rectangle; cut dough lengthwise in half.
3. Spread each 12x4-in. rectangle with half of the cream cheese mixture to within ¼-in. of edges. Sprinkle each with half of the combined cheeses; roll up jelly-roll style, starting with a long side. Pinch seam to seal. Cut rolls into 1-in. slices.
4. Place beaten egg and Parmesan cheese in separate shallow bowls. Dip a cut side of each slice in the egg, then in Parmesan cheese; place in greased mini-muffin cups, cheese side up.
5. Bake until golden brown, 17-20 minutes. Serve warm.

LAYERED HUMMUS DIP

My love for Greece inspired this fast-to-fix Mediterranean dip. It's great for parties and is a delicious way to include garden-fresh veggies on your menu.
—Cheryl Snavely, Hagerstown, MD

Prep: 15 min.
Makes: 12 servings

- 1 carton (10 ounces) hummus
- ¼ cup finely chopped red onion
- ½ cup Greek olives, chopped
- 2 medium tomatoes, seeded and chopped
- 1 large English cucumber, chopped
- 1 cup crumbled feta cheese
  Baked pita chips

Spread hummus into shallow 10-in. round dish, then layer over it with the onion, olives, tomatoes, cucumber and cheese. Refrigerate until serving. Serve with chips.

★ ★ ★ ★ ★ **READER REVIEW**

"Super easy and always a hit!"

WSMITTY1961@YAHOO.COM
TASTEOFHOME.COM

FETA BRUSCHETTA

You won't believe the compliments you'll receive when you greet guests with these warm appetizers. Every crispy bite offers savory tastes of feta cheese, tomatoes, basil and garlic. The apps are terrific for holiday parties or most any gathering.
—Stacey Rinehart, Eugene, OR

Start to Finish: 30 min.
Makes: 10 appetizers

¼	cup butter, melted
¼	cup olive oil
10	slices French bread (1 inch thick)
1	package (4 ounces) crumbled feta cheese
2	to 3 garlic cloves, minced
1	tablespoon minced fresh basil or 1 teaspoon dried basil
1	large tomato, seeded and chopped

1. In a small bowl, combine butter and oil; brush onto both sides of bread. Place on a baking sheet. Bake at 350° for 8-10 minutes or until lightly browned on top.
2. Combine the feta cheese, garlic and basil; sprinkle over toast. Top with tomato. Bake 8-10 minutes longer or until heated through. Serve warm.

★ ★ ★ ★ ★ **READER REVIEW**

"Excellent and so easy. A little strong on the garlic but good if you like that."
DEBBIET TASTEOFHOME.COM

PARMESAN ASPARAGUS ROLL-UPS

Make the most of fresh asparagus and crispy phyllo dough with these roll-ups.
—Eleanor Froehlich, Rochester, MI

Start to Finish: 30 min.
Makes: 1 dozen

12 **fresh asparagus spears**
2 **sheets phyllo dough
(18 inches x 14 inches)**
4 **teaspoons olive oil**
¼ **cup grated Parmesan cheese
Dash pepper**

1. Cut asparagus spears into 4-in. lengths (discard stalks or save for another use). In a large saucepan, bring ½ in. of water to a boil. Add asparagus; cover and boil for 2 minutes. Drain and immediately place asparagus in ice water. Drain and pat dry.
2. Stack both sheets of phyllo dough on a work surface. Cut the stack in half lengthwise, then widthwise into thirds. Separate pieces and brush with some of the oil. Sprinkle each with 1 teaspoon cheese. Place one asparagus spear along one side of each piece of phyllo dough. Sprinkle lightly with pepper; roll up tightly.
3. Place seam side down on an ungreased baking sheet. Brush tops with oil. Bake roll-ups at 400° for 7-9 minutes or until golden brown.

LAYERED RANCH DIP

I found something similar to this in one of my cookbooks for kids. It looked delicious, so I decided to try my own version. It's easy to customize with your favorite toppings.
—Peggy Roos, Minneapolis, MN

Prep: 10 min.
Makes: 8 servings

2 **cups (16 ounces) sour cream**
1 **envelope ranch salad dressing mix**
1 **medium tomato, chopped**
1 **can (4 ounces) chopped green chilies, drained**
1 **can (2¼ ounces) sliced ripe olives, drained**
¼ **cup finely chopped red onion**
1 **cup shredded Monterey Jack cheese
Corn chips or tortilla chips**

In a small bowl, mix sour cream and dressing mix; spread into a large shallow dish. Layer with tomato, green chilies, olives, onion and cheese. Refrigerate until serving. Serve with chips.

MINI SAUSAGE BUNDLES

These savory hors d'oeuvres are baked instead of deep fried. This method trims some of the fat and eases cleanup. Tying them with chives adds a fancy touch.
—*Taste of Home* Test Kitchen

Prep: 25 min. **Bake:** 10 min.
Makes: 1 dozen

- ½ pound turkey Italian sausage links, casings removed
- 1 small onion, finely chopped
- ¼ cup finely chopped sweet red pepper
- 1 garlic clove, minced
- ½ cup shredded cheddar cheese
- 12 sheets phyllo dough (14x9-inch size) Cooking spray
- 12 whole chives, optional

1. Preheat oven to 425°. In a large skillet, cook and crumble sausage with onion, red pepper and garlic over medium-high heat until no longer pink, 4-6 minutes. Stir in cheese; cool slightly.
2. Place one sheet of phyllo dough on a work surface; spritz with cooking spray. Layer with two additional phyllo sheets, spritzing each layer. (Keep remaining phyllo covered with plastic wrap and a damp towel to prevent it from drying out.) Cut phyllo crosswise into three strips (about 4½-in. wide).
3. Place a rounded tablespoon sausage mixture near the end of each strip. Fold end of strip over filling, then fold in sides and roll up. Place on an ungreased baking sheet, seam side down. Repeat with the remaining phyllo and filling.
4. Bake until lightly browned, 8-10 minutes. If desired, tie bundles with chives. Serve warm.

★ ★ ★ ★ ★ **READER REVIEW**

"I made these for a tapas party, and they were fantastic! It was clumsy at first working with the phyllo dough and rolling up the bundles, but once I figured it out they went fast. They're super delicious little pockets of flavor!"

JUJUBEAN79 TASTEOFHOME.COM

SPINACH DIP PULL-APARTS

Even picky eaters who don't like spinach will dig into these tasty little bites. Set a small bowl of dipping sauce in the center for a pretty presentation.
—Kelly Williams, Forked River, NJ

Prep: 35 min. • **Bake:** 45 min. + cooling
Makes: 15 servings

- 1 package (8 ounces) cream cheese, softened
- 2 garlic cloves, minced
- ¼ teaspoon pepper
- 1 package (10 ounces) frozen chopped spinach, thawed and squeezed dry
- ½ cup shredded part-skim mozzarella cheese
- ¼ cup grated Parmesan cheese
- ¼ cup mayonnaise
- 2 tubes (one 6 ounces, one 12 ounces) refrigerated buttermilk biscuits
  Marinara sauce, warmed, optional

1. Preheat oven to 350°. In a small bowl, beat the cream cheese, garlic and pepper until blended. Stir in the spinach, cheeses and mayonnaise.

2. Separate the biscuit dough. Using a serrated knife, cut each biscuit in half horizontally. Wrap each biscuit half around 1 tablespoon spinach mixture, pinching to seal and forming a ball.

3. Layer dough balls in a greased 10-in. fluted tube pan. Bake 45 to 50 minutes or until golden brown. Cool in pan 10 minutes before inverting onto a serving plate. Serve warm with marinara sauce if desired.

PADDY'S REUBEN DIP

My slow-cooked dip tastes just like the popular Reuben sandwich. Even when I double the recipe, I come home with an empty dish.
—Mary Jane Kimmes, Hastings, MN

....

Prep: 5 min. • **Cook:** 2 hours
Makes: about 4 cups

- 4 packages (2 ounces each) thinly sliced deli corned beef, finely chopped
- 1 package (8 ounces) cream cheese, cubed
- 1 can (8 ounces) sauerkraut, rinsed and drained
- 1 cup (8 ounces) sour cream
- 1 cup shredded Swiss cheese
  Rye bread or crackers

In a 1½-qt. slow cooker, combine the first five ingredients. Cover and cook on low for 2 hours or until cheese is melted; stir until blended. Serve dip warm with bread or crackers.

BACON, CHEDDAR & SWISS CHEESE BALL

When it's time for a party, everyone requests this ultimate cheese ball. It's great spread on crackers or mini garlic toasts and makes a fabulous hostess gift.
—Sue Franklin, Lake St. Louis, MO

....

Prep: 20 min. + chilling
Makes: 4 cups

- 1 package (8 ounces) cream cheese, softened
- ½ cup sour cream

- 2 cups shredded Swiss cheese
- 2 cups shredded sharp cheddar cheese
- 1 cup crumbled cooked bacon (about 12 strips), divided
- ½ cup chopped pecans, toasted, divided
- ½ cup finely chopped onion
- 1 jar (2 ounces) diced pimientos, drained
- 2 tablespoons sweet pickle relish
- ¼ teaspoon salt
- ¼ teaspoon pepper
- ¼ cup minced fresh parsley
- 1 tablespoon poppy seeds
  Assorted crackers

1. In a large bowl, beat cream cheese and sour cream until smooth. Stir in shredded cheeses, ½ cup bacon, ¼ cup pecans, onion, pimientos, pickle relish, salt and pepper. Refrigerate, covered, for at least 1 hour.

2. In a small bowl, mix parsley, poppy seeds and remaining bacon and pecans. Spread half of parsley mixture on a large piece of plastic. Shape half of the cheese mixture into a ball; roll in parsley mixture to coat evenly. Wrap in plastic. Repeat. Refrigerate the ball for at least 1 hour. Serve with crackers.

Note: To toast nuts, bake in a shallow pan in a 350° oven for 5-10 minutes or cook in a skillet over low heat until lightly browned, stirring occasionally.

CHICKEN PARMESAN SLIDER BAKE

Sliders are the perfect finger food for any get-together, and this flavorful chicken Parmesan version won't disappoint.
—Nick Iverson, Milwaukee, WI

Prep: 20 min. • **Bake:** 25 min.
Makes: 1 dozen

24 ounces frozen breaded chicken tenders
1 package (18 ounces) Hawaiian sweet rolls
1 package (7½ ounces) sliced provolone and mozzarella cheese blend
1 jar (24 ounces) marinara sauce
TOPPING
½ cup butter, cubed
1 teaspoon garlic powder
1 teaspoon crushed red pepper flakes
¼ cup grated Parmesan cheese
2 tablespoons minced fresh basil

1. Preheat oven to 375°. Prepare chicken tenders according to package directions. Meanwhile, without separating rolls, cut horizontally in half; arrange roll bottoms in a greased 13x9-in. baking dish. Spread half of cheese slices over roll bottoms. Bake until cheese is melted, 3-5 minutes.
2. Layer rolls with half of sauce, chicken tenders, remaining sauce and remaining cheese slices. Replace top halves of rolls.
3. For topping, microwave butter, garlic powder and red pepper flakes, covered, on high, stirring occasionally, until butter is melted. Pour over rolls; sprinkle with Parmesan cheese.
4. Bake, uncovered, until golden brown and heated through, 20-25 minutes. Sprinkle with basil before serving.

BLUE CHEESE POTATO CHIPS

Game day calls for something bold. I top crunchy kettle chips with tomatoes, bacon, green onions and tangy blue cheese. I make two big pans, and they always disappear.
—Bonnie Hawkins, Elkhorn, WI

Start to Finish: 15 min.
Makes: 10 servings

1 package (8½ ounces) kettle-cooked potato chips
2 medium tomatoes, seeded and chopped
8 bacon strips, cooked and crumbled
6 green onions, chopped
1 cup crumbled blue cheese

1. Preheat broiler. In a 15x10x1-in. baking pan, arrange potato chips in an even layer. Top with remaining ingredients.
2. Broil 4-5 in. from heat 2-3 minutes or until the cheese begins to melt. Serve immediately.

MAKE AHEAD
BREADSTICK PIZZA

This hassle-free homemade appetizer pizza uses refrigerated breadsticks as the crust. Feeding kids? Slice pieces into small strips and let them dip each strip into marinara sauce. They'll love it!
—Mary Hankins, Kansas City, MO

Prep: 25 min. • **Bake:** 20 min.
Makes: 12 servings

- 2 tubes (11 ounces each) refrigerated breadsticks
- ½ pound sliced fresh mushrooms
- 2 medium green peppers, chopped
- 1 medium onion, chopped
- 1½ teaspoons Italian seasoning, divided
- 4 teaspoons olive oil, divided
- 1½ cups shredded cheddar cheese, divided
- 5 ounces Canadian bacon, chopped
- 1½ cups shredded part-skim mozzarella cheese
- Marinara sauce

1. Unroll the breadsticks into a greased 15x10x1-in. baking pan. Press onto the bottom and up the sides of pan; pinch the seams to seal. Bake at 350° until set, 6-8 minutes.
2. Meanwhile, using a large skillet, saute the mushrooms, peppers, onion and 1 teaspoon of Italian seasoning in 2 teaspoons oil until crisp-tender; drain.
3. Brush the crust with the remaining oil. Sprinkle with ¾ cup cheddar cheese; top with vegetable mixture and Canadian bacon. Combine the mozzarella cheese and remaining cheddar cheese; sprinkle over the top. Sprinkle with remaining Italian seasoning.
4. Bake until cheese is melted and crust is golden brown, 20-25 minutes. Serve with marinara sauce.

Freeze option: Bake crust as directed, add toppings and cool. Securely wrap and freeze unbaked pizza. To use, unwrap pizza; bake as directed, increasing time as necessary.

CUCUMBER CANAPES

I always get requests for the recipe whenever I serve these delicate finger sandwiches. They boast a creamy herb spread with red and green garnishes.
—Nadine Whittaker, South Plymouth, MA

Prep: 20 min. + chilling
Makes: 2 dozen

- 1 cup mayonnaise
- 3 ounces cream cheese, softened
- 1 tablespoon grated onion
- 1 tablespoon minced chives
- ½ teaspoon cider vinegar
- ½ teaspoon Worcestershire sauce
- 1 garlic clove, minced
- ¼ teaspoon paprika
- ⅛ teaspoon curry powder
- ⅛ teaspoon each dried oregano, thyme, basil, parsley flakes and dill weed
- 1 loaf (1 pound) white or rye bread
- 2 medium cucumbers, scored and thinly sliced
- Diced pimientos and additional dill weed

1. In a blender or food processor, combine the mayonnaise, cream cheese, onion, chives, vinegar, Worcestershire sauce, garlic and seasonings. Cover and process until blended. Cover and refrigerate mixture for 24 hours.
2. Using a 2½-in. biscuit cutter, cut out circles from bread slices. Spread the mayonnaise mixture over bread; top with cucumber slices. Garnish with pimientos and dill.

Jelly Doughnuts
page 56

Breakfast For a Bunch

Whether it's for Mother's Day, Christmas morning or the big church potluck on Easter Sunday, find the perfect dish to pass with these eye-opening breakfast and brunch delights.

4. Bake at 400° for 10 minutes or until lightly browned. For icing, combine sugar, milk, butter and extracts; spread over warm rolls. Sprinkle with nuts.

EASY BREAKFAST STRATA

I start this breakfast casserole the night before so it's ready for the oven the next day. That way, I don't have to deal with the prep and dirty dishes first thing in the morning!
—Debbie Johnson, Centertown, MO

Prep: 20 min. + chilling • **Bake:** 30 min.
Makes: 12 servings

- 1 **pound bulk pork sausage**
- 1 **large green pepper, chopped**
- 1 **medium onion, chopped**
- 1 **loaf (1 pound) herb or cheese bakery bread, cubed**
- 1 **cup shredded cheddar cheese**
- 6 **large eggs**
- 2 **cups 2% milk**
- 1 **teaspoon ground mustard**

1. In a large skillet, cook sausage, pepper and onion over medium heat until meat is no longer pink; drain.
2. Place bread in a greased 13x9-in. baking dish. Top with sausage; sprinkle with cheese. In a large bowl, whisk eggs, milk and mustard. Pour over top. Cover and refrigerate overnight.
3. Remove from refrigerator 30 minutes before baking. Preheat oven to 350°. Bake, uncovered, 30-35 minutes or until a knife inserted in the center comes out clean. Let strata stand 5 minutes before cutting.

FRENCH CRESCENT ROLLS

Layers of buttered dough will result in the richest sweet rolls you've ever tasted.
—Betty Ann Wolery, Joplin, MT

Prep: 25 min. + rising
Bake: 10 min. + chilling
Makes: 16 rolls

- 1 **package (¼ ounce) active dry yeast**
- ¼ **cup warm water (110° to 115°)**
- ¾ **cup warm milk (110° to 115°)**
- 1 **large egg**
- 2 **tablespoons sugar**
- 1 **tablespoon shortening**
- 1 **teaspoon salt**
- 3 **cups all-purpose flour**
- 3 **tablespoons butter, softened, divided**

ICING
- 1½ **cups confectioners' sugar**
- 2 **tablespoons milk**
- 3 **tablespoons butter**
- ½ **teaspoon almond extract**
- ½ **teaspoon vanilla extract**
- ½ **cup chopped walnuts**

1. Dissolve yeast in warm water. Add milk, egg, sugar, shortening and salt; mix well. Add flour; mix until smooth. Place in a greased bowl, turning once to grease top. Cover and refrigerate at least 1 hour.
2. Turn dough onto a floured surface; roll to ¼-in. thickness. Spread with 1 tablespoon softened butter. Fold corners to the middle and then fold in half. Wrap dough in waxed paper; chill for 30 minutes. Repeat rolling, buttering, folding and chilling steps twice.
3. Turn dough onto a floured surface; roll into a 34x5-in. rectangle. Cut into 16 triangles; roll up each triangle from wide edge to tip and pinch to seal. Place rolls, tip down, on greased baking sheets and curve to form crescents. Cover and let rise in a warm place until doubled, about 30 minutes.

PEPPERED BACON & CHEESE SCONES

Mmm! That's what you'll hear as you serve a big platter of these buttery, savory scones. The bacon and cheese combo is a welcome change of pace from most brunch's typical sweets.
—Janice Elder, Charlotte, NC

Prep: 20 min. • **Bake:** 20 min.
Makes: 8 scones

- 3 cups all-purpose flour
- 1 tablespoon baking powder
- 2 teaspoons coarsely ground pepper
- ¼ teaspoon salt
- ¼ teaspoon cayenne pepper
- ½ cup cold butter, cubed
- 1½ cups shredded Gouda cheese
- 4 bacon strips, cooked and crumbled
- 1 shallot, finely chopped
- 1 large egg
- 1 cup buttermilk

1. Preheat oven to 400°. In a large bowl, whisk the first five ingredients. Cut in butter until mixture resembles coarse crumbs. Stir in cheese, bacon and shallot.
2. In a bowl, whisk the egg and buttermilk until blended; reserve 1 tablespoon egg mixture for brushing scones. Stir the remaining mixture into crumb mixture just until moistened.
3. Turn onto a lightly floured surface; knead gently 10 times. Pat dough into an 8-in. circle. Cut into eight wedges. Place wedges on a greased baking sheet. Brush with reserved buttermilk mixture.
4. Bake 20-25 minutes or until golden brown. Serve warm.

MAKE AHEAD
WALNUT ZUCCHINI MUFFINS

Shredded zucchini adds moisture to these tender muffins dotted with raisins and chopped walnuts. If you have a surplus of zucchini in summer, as most of us do, this is a good way to use it up.
—Harriet Stichter, Milford, IN

Prep: 20 min. • **Bake:** 20 min.
Makes: 1 dozen

- 1 cup all-purpose flour
- ¾ cup whole wheat flour
- ⅔ cup packed brown sugar
- 2 teaspoons baking powder
- ¾ teaspoon ground cinnamon
- ½ teaspoon salt
- 2 large eggs
- ¾ cup 2% milk
- ½ cup butter, melted
- 1 cup shredded zucchini
- 1 cup chopped walnuts
- ½ cup raisins

1. Preheat oven to 375°. In a large bowl, whisk the first six ingredients. In another bowl, whisk eggs, milk and melted butter until blended. Add to flour mixture; stir just until moistened. Fold in zucchini, walnuts and raisins.
2. Fill greased muffin cups three-fourths full. Bake for 18-20 minutes or until a toothpick inserted in center comes out clean. Cool 5 minutes before removing from pan to a wire rack. Serve warm.
Freeze option: Freeze cooled muffins in resealable plastic freezer bags. To use, thaw at room temperature or, if desired, microwave each muffin on high for 20-30 seconds or until heated through.

CRANBERRY SCONES WITH ORANGE BUTTER

Tempting cranberry scones brighten up any holiday brunch or tea. The orange butter is simply irresistible.
—Joan Hallford, North Richland Hills, TX

Prep: 20 min. • **Bake:** 25 min.
Makes: 8 scones (½ cup orange butter)

- 2½ cups all-purpose flour
- ¼ cup sugar
- 3 teaspoons baking powder
- ½ cup cold butter, cubed
- 2 large eggs
- ½ cup heavy whipping cream
- ¾ cup dried cranberries

EGG WASH
- 1 large egg
- 1 tablespoon water

ORANGE BUTTER
- ½ cup butter, softened
- 1 tablespoon honey
- 1½ teaspoons grated orange peel
- 1 tablespoon orange juice

1. Preheat oven to 350°. In a large bowl, whisk flour, sugar and baking powder. Cut in butter until mixture resembles coarse crumbs. In another bowl, whisk eggs and cream until blended; stir into crumb mixture just until moistened. Stir in cranberries.

2. Turn onto a floured surface; knead gently 10 times. Transfer to a greased baking sheet. Pat into an 8-in. circle. Cut into eight wedges, but do not separate. In a small bowl, whisk egg with water; brush over dough.

3. Bake 22-25 minutes or until golden brown. For orange butter, in a small bowl, mix remaining ingredients until blended. Serve with warm scones.

CINNAMON-APPLE FRENCH TOAST

Serving this on Christmas morning is a tradition in our family. It's wonderful because I can make it the night before and pop it in the oven while we are opening gifts.
—Jill Peterson, Richfield, WI

Prep: 20 min. + chilling • **Bake:** 1 hour
Makes: 12 servings

- 1 cup packed brown sugar
- ½ cup butter, melted
- 3 teaspoons ground cinnamon, divided
- 3 medium tart apples, peeled and sliced (about 3 cups)
- ½ cup dried cranberries
- 12 slices day-old French bread (1 inch thick)
- 6 large eggs
- 1½ cups whole milk
- 3 teaspoons vanilla extract

1. In a small bowl, mix brown sugar, butter and 1 teaspoon cinnamon; pour into a greased 13x9-in. baking dish. Top with apples and cranberries. Arrange bread slices over fruit. In a small bowl, whisk eggs, milk, vanilla and remaining cinnamon; pour over bread. Refrigerate, covered, overnight.

2. Preheat oven to 350°. Remove French toast from refrigerator while oven heats. Bake, covered, for 40 minutes. Bake, uncovered, 20-25 minutes longer or until golden brown and a knife inserted in the center comes out clean. Let stand for 5-10 minutes before serving. To serve, invert onto a serving platter.

PUMPKIN-APPLE MUFFINS WITH STREUSEL TOPPING

My mother always made these tasty muffins whenever our family got together at her house. Now they're a family favorite at my house, and my in-laws love them, too!
—Carolyn Riley, Carlisle, PA

Prep: 20 min.
Bake: 30 min. + cooling
Makes: about 1½ dozen

- 2½ cups all-purpose flour
- 2 cups sugar
- 1 tablespoon pumpkin pie spice
- 1 teaspoon baking soda
- ½ teaspoon salt
- 2 large eggs, lightly beaten
- 1 cup canned pumpkin
- ½ cup vegetable oil
- 2 cups finely chopped peeled apples

TOPPING
- ¼ cup sugar
- 2 tablespoons all-purpose flour
- ½ teaspoon ground cinnamon
- 1 tablespoon butter or margarine

In a large bowl, combine flour, sugar, pumpkin pie spice, baking soda and salt. Combine eggs, pumpkin and oil; stir into dry ingredients just until moistened. Fold in apples. Fill greased or paper-lined muffin cups three-fourths full. For topping, combine sugar, flour and cinnamon. Cut in butter until mixture resembles coarse crumbs; sprinkle 1 teaspoon over each muffin. Bake at 350° for 30-35 minutes or until muffins test done. Cool in pan 10 minutes before removing to wire rack.

VEGGIE-PACKED STRATA

Folks are always eager to try this deliciously different casserole that features eggs, cheese and a rainbow of veggies. Baked in a springform pan and cut into wedges, it catches attention no matter where it's served. It's even great for dinner alongside a salad and rolls.
—Jennifer Unsell, Vance, AL

Prep: 15 min.
Bake: 1 hour + standing
Makes: 8-10 servings

- 2 medium sweet red peppers, julienned
- 1 medium sweet yellow pepper, julienned
- 1 large red onion, sliced
- 3 tablespoons olive oil, divided
- 3 garlic cloves, minced
- 2 medium yellow summer squash, thinly sliced
- 2 medium zucchini, thinly sliced
- ½ pound fresh mushrooms, sliced
- 1 package (8 ounces) cream cheese, softened
- ¼ cup heavy whipping cream
- 2 teaspoons salt
- 1 teaspoon pepper
- 6 large eggs
- 8 slices bread, cubed, divided
- 2 cups shredded Swiss cheese

1. In a large skillet, saute peppers and onion in 1 tablespoon oil until tender. Add garlic; cook 1 minute longer. Drain; pat dry and set aside. In the same skillet, saute the yellow squash, zucchini and mushrooms in remaining oil until tender. Drain; pat dry and set aside.

2. In a large bowl, beat the cream cheese, cream, salt and pepper until smooth. Beat in eggs. Stir in vegetables, half of the bread cubes and Swiss cheese. Arrange the remaining bread cubes in a greased 10-in. springform pan. Place on a baking sheet. Pour egg mixture into pan.

3. Bake strata, uncovered, at 325° for 60-70 minutes or until a knife inserted in the center comes out clean. Let stand for 10 minutes before serving. Run a knife around edge of pan to loosen; remove sides. Cut into wedges.

TEST KITCHEN TIP According to the American Egg Board, fresh eggs can be stored in their carton in the refrigerator for 4 to 5 weeks beyond the pack date. Some manufacturers stamp their cartons with a date 30 days beyond the pack date.

AUNT BETTY'S BLUEBERRY MUFFINS

My Aunt Betty bakes many items each Christmas, but I look forward to these muffins for brunch the most.
—Sheila Raleigh, Kechi, KS

Prep: 15 min. • **Bake:** 20 min.
Makes: about 1 dozen

- ½ cup old-fashioned oats
- ½ cup orange juice
- 1 large egg
- ½ cup canola oil
- ½ cup sugar
- 1½ cups all-purpose flour
- 1¼ teaspoons baking powder
- ½ teaspoon salt
- ¼ teaspoon baking soda
- 1 cup fresh or frozen blueberries

TOPPING
- 2 tablespoons sugar
- ½ teaspoon ground cinnamon

1. In a large bowl, combine oats and orange juice; let stand for 5 minutes. Beat in the egg, oil and sugar until blended. Combine the flour, baking powder, salt and baking soda; stir into oat mixture just until moistened. Fold in blueberries.

2. Fill greased or paper-lined muffin cups two-thirds full. Combine topping ingredients; sprinkle over batter. Bake at 400° for 20-25 minutes or until a toothpick inserted in the center comes out clean. Cool for 5 minutes before removing from pan to a wire rack. Serve muffins warm.

Note: If using frozen blueberries, use without thawing to avoid discoloring the batter.

RICOTTA SCONES WITH RHUBARB-ORANGE COMPOTE

These scones are a little piece of heaven, especially when served warm with a dollop of fruit compote. Be prepared to share the recipe!
—Marilyn Rodriguez, Sparks, NV

Prep: 30 min. • **Bake:** 15 min.
Makes: 1 dozen (¾ cup compote)

- ¾ cup sugar
- 2 tablespoons cornstarch
- ½ cup orange juice
- 1 cup finely chopped fresh or frozen rhubarb, thawed
- ½ small navel orange, peeled and pureed

SCONES
- 3 cups all-purpose flour
- ⅓ cup sugar
- 2 teaspoons baking powder
- ¾ teaspoon salt
- ½ teaspoon baking soda
- ½ cup cold butter
- 1 large egg, beaten
- 1 cup heavy whipping cream
- 1 cup ricotta cheese
- 2 teaspoons grated orange peel

TOPPING
- 2 tablespoons heavy whipping cream
- 2 tablespoons sugar
- ¼ teaspoon ground cinnamon

1. In a small saucepan, combine the sugar, cornstarch and orange juice until smooth. Stir in rhubarb and orange. Bring to a boil; cook and stir until thickened and rhubarb is tender. Remove from the heat; cool.

2. In a large bowl, combine the flour, sugar, baking powder, salt and baking soda. Cut in butter until mixture resembles coarse crumbs. Combine the egg, cream, cheese and orange peel; stir into crumb mixture just until moistened. Turn onto a floured surface; knead 10 times.

3. Divide dough in half; pat each into a 7-in. circle. Cut each into six wedges. Separate wedges and place on a greased baking sheet. Brush with cream; sprinkle with sugar and cinnamon. Bake at 375° for 15-20 minutes or until golden brown. Remove to a wire rack. Serve warm with compote.

Note: If using frozen rhubarb, measure the rhubarb while still frozen, then thaw it completely. Drain in a colander, but do not press liquid out.

2. In a large bowl, whisk eggs, milk, salt and pepper. Pour mixture over sausage and cheese.

3. Bake, uncovered, 35-40 minutes or until a knife inserted in the center comes out clean. Let casserole stand 5-10 minutes before serving.

To Make Ahead: Refrigerate unbaked casserole, covered, several hours or overnight. To use, preheat oven to 375°. Remove casserole from refrigerator while oven heats. Bake as directed, increasing time as necessary until a knife inserted in the center comes out clean. Let stand 5-10 minutes before serving.

ULTIMATE BACON-MAPLE FRENCH TOAST

A savory update on baked French toast, this is an easy make-ahead dish that is excellent for brunch or luncheons. The combination of maple syrup, bacon and nuts makes it impressive and satisfying.
—John Whitehead, Greenville, SC

....

Prep: 30 min. + chilling
Bake: 40 min. + standing
Makes: 10 servings

- 8 large eggs
- 2 cups half-and-half cream
- 1 cup 2% milk
- 1 tablespoon sugar
- 1 tablespoon brown sugar
- 1 teaspoon vanilla extract
- ½ teaspoon ground cinnamon
- ¼ teaspoon ground nutmeg
  Dash salt
  Dash cayenne pepper
- 1 loaf (1 pound) French bread, cut into 1-inch slices

TOPPING
- 6 thick-sliced bacon strips, cooked and crumbled
- 1 cup butter, melted
- 1 cup packed brown sugar
- ½ cup chopped pecans, toasted
- 2 tablespoons corn syrup
- 1 teaspoon ground cinnamon
- ½ teaspoon ground nutmeg
- ¼ teaspoon ground cloves
  Maple syrup

1. Grease a 13x9-in. baking dish; set aside.

2. In a large shallow bowl, whisk the first 10 ingredients. Dip each slice of bread into egg mixture. Arrange slices in prepared dish. Pour remaining egg mixture over top. Cover and refrigerate overnight.

3. Remove from refrigerator 30 minutes before baking. Preheat oven to 350°. In a small bowl, combine the first eight topping ingredients. Spread over top.

4. Bake, uncovered, 40-45 minutes or until a knife inserted in the center comes out clean. Let stand 10 minutes before serving. Drizzle with syrup.

SAUSAGE & CRESCENT ROLL CASSEROLE

I made this casserole when I hosted a baby shower. It turned out to be a lifesaver. Making it in advance gave me time to finish other party preparations.
—Melody Craft, Conroe, TX

....

Prep: 15 min. • **Bake:** 35 min.
Makes: 12 servings

- 1 pound bulk pork sausage
- 1 tube (8 ounces) refrigerated crescent rolls
- 2 cups shredded part-skim mozzarella cheese
- 8 large eggs
- 2 cups 2% milk
- ½ teaspoon salt
- ¼ teaspoon pepper

1. Preheat oven to 375°. In a large skillet, cook the sausage over medium heat 6-8 minutes or until no longer pink, breaking into crumbles; drain. Unroll crescent roll dough into a greased 13x9-in. baking dish. Seal seams and perforations. Sprinkle with sausage and cheese.

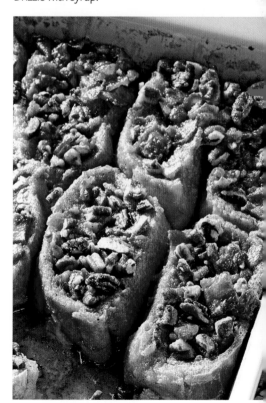

MAKE AHEAD
BRUNCH BUDDIES ENCHILADAS

I belong to a women's group, and we take turns making brunch. I grew tired of making the standard breakfast fare, so I invented this Mexican-style bake.
—Julia Huntington, Cheyenne, WY

Prep: 40 min. • **Bake:** 40 min. + standing
Makes: 12 servings

- 3 cups shredded Mexican cheese blend, divided
- 2 cups cubed fully cooked ham
- 1 small green pepper, chopped
- 1 small onion, chopped
- 1 medium tomato, chopped
- 12 flour tortillas (6 inches)
- 10 large eggs
- 2 cups half-and-half cream
- 2 tablespoons all-purpose flour
- ½ teaspoon salt
- ½ teaspoon onion powder
- ½ teaspoon pepper

TOPPINGS
- 4 green onions, thinly sliced
- ½ cup cherry tomatoes, quartered
- 1 can (2¼ ounces) sliced ripe olives, drained, optional

1. Preheat oven to 350°. Place 2 cups cheese, ham, green pepper, onion and tomato in a large bowl; toss to combine. Place ½ cup mixture off center on each tortilla. Roll up and place in a greased 13x9-in. baking dish, seam side down.
2. In another bowl, whisk eggs, cream, flour and seasonings until blended; pour over enchiladas. Sprinkle with remaining cheese; add toppings.
3. Bake, covered, 30 minutes. Uncover; bake 10-15 minutes longer or until cheese is melted and a knife inserted in egg portion comes out clean. Let stand for 10 minutes before serving.

Freeze option: Cover and freeze unbaked casserole. To use, partially thaw in refrigerator overnight. Remove from the refrigerator 30 minutes before baking. Preheat oven to 350°. Cover casserole with foil; bake as directed, increasing uncovered time to 25-35 minutes or until cheese is melted and a thermometer inserted in center reads 165°.

CHOCOLATE CHIP ELVIS PANCAKES

Growing up in a family with 13 children, finding a recipe that everyone liked was a challenge. This one was a Saturday-morning special that we all loved.
—Keenan McDermott, Springfield, MO

Prep: 15 min. • **Cook:** 5 min./batch
Makes: 16 pancakes

- 1¼ cups all-purpose flour
- 2 tablespoons brown sugar
- 3 teaspoons baking powder
- ½ teaspoon salt
- 1 large egg
- ¼ cup peanut butter
- 1½ cups 2% milk
- 3 tablespoons butter, melted
- 1 teaspoon vanilla extract
- ½ cup chopped ripe banana
- ½ cup semisweet chocolate chips

1. In a large bowl, whisk flour, brown sugar, baking powder and salt. In another bowl, whisk egg, peanut butter, milk, melted butter and vanilla until blended. Add to the flour mixture; stir just until moistened. Fold in the banana and chocolate chips.
2. Lightly grease a griddle; heat over medium heat. Pour batter by ¼ cupfuls onto griddle. Cook until bubbles on top begin to pop and bottoms are golden brown. Turn; cook until second side is golden brown.

HOME-FOR-CHRISTMAS FRUIT BAKE

Pop this special dish in the oven and mouths will water in anticipation—the cinnamony aroma is tantalizing! The fruit comes out tender and slightly tart while the pecan halves add a delightful crunch.
—Bonnie Baumgardner, Sylva, NC

Prep: 15 min. • **Bake:** 45 min.
Makes: 12 servings

1 medium apple, peeled and thinly sliced
1 teaspoon lemon juice
1 can (20 ounces) pineapple chunks
1 can (29 ounces) peach halves, drained
1 can (29 ounces) pear halves, drained
1 jar (6 to 8 ounces) maraschino cherries
½ cup pecan halves
⅓ cup packed brown sugar
1 tablespoon butter, melted
1 teaspoon ground cinnamon

1. Preheat oven to 325°. Toss apple slices with lemon juice. Arrange in a greased 2½-qt. baking dish. Drain pineapple, reserving ¼ cup juice. Combine pineapple, peaches and pears; spoon over apples. Top with cherries and pecans; set aside.
2. In a small saucepan, combine brown sugar, butter, cinnamon and reserved pineapple juice. Cook and stir over low heat until sugar is dissolved and butter is melted. Pour over fruit. Bake, uncovered, until apples are tender, about 45 minutes. Serve warm.

FRUITY BAKED OATMEAL

This is my husband's favorite breakfast treat and the ultimate comfort food. It's warm, filling and always a hit when I serve it to guests.
—Karen Schroeder, Kankakee, IL

Prep: 15 min. • **Bake:** 35 min.
Makes: 9 servings

3 cups quick-cooking oats
1 cup packed brown sugar
2 teaspoons baking powder
1 teaspoon salt
½ teaspoon ground cinnamon
2 large eggs, lightly beaten
1 cup fat-free milk
½ cup butter, melted
¾ cup chopped peeled tart apple
⅓ cup chopped fresh or frozen peaches
⅓ cup fresh or frozen blueberries
   Additional fat-free milk, optional

1. Preheat oven to 350°. In a large bowl, combine oats, brown sugar, baking powder, salt and cinnamon. Combine eggs, milk and butter; add to the dry ingredients. Stir in apple, peaches and blueberries.
2. Pour into an 8-in. square baking dish coated with cooking spray. Bake, uncovered, 35-40 minutes or until a knife inserted in center comes out clean. Cut into squares. Serve with milk if desired.
Note: If using frozen blueberries, use without thawing to avoid discoloring the batter.

JELLY DOUGHNUTS

There's no need to run to the bakery for your favorite jelly doughnuts. I've been fixing these homemade treats for years. They're lighter than air and disappear almost as fast as I make them.
—Kathy Westendorf, Westgate, IA

Prep: 30 min. • **Cook:** 10 min.
Makes: 16 doughnuts

- 2 packages (¼ ounce each) active dry yeast
- ½ cup warm water (110° to 115°)
- ½ cup warm 2% milk (110° to 115°)
- ⅓ cup butter, softened
- 1⅓ cups sugar, divided
- 3 large egg yolks
- 1 teaspoon salt
- 3 to 3¾ cups all-purpose flour
- 3 tablespoons jelly or jam
- 1 large egg white, lightly beaten
  Oil for deep-fat frying

1. In a small bowl, dissolve yeast in warm water. In a large bowl, combine milk, butter, ⅓ cup sugar, egg yolks, salt, yeast mixture and 3 cups flour; beat until smooth. Stir in enough remaining flour to form a soft dough (do not knead).
2. Place in a greased bowl, turning once to grease top. Cover and let rise in a warm place until doubled, about 45 minutes.
3. Punch dough down. Turn onto a lightly floured surface; knead about 10 times. Divide dough in half.
4. Roll each portion to ¼-in. thickness; cut with a floured 2½-in. round cutter. Place about ½ teaspoon jelly in the center of half of the circles; brush edges with egg white. Top with remaining circles; press edges to seal tightly.
5. Place on greased baking sheet. Cover and let rise until doubled, about 45 minutes.
6. In an electric skillet or deep-fat fryer, heat oil to 375°. Fry doughnuts, a few at a time, 1-2 minutes on each side or until golden brown. Drain on paper towels. Roll warm doughnuts in remaining sugar.

MINI HAM & CHEESE QUICHES

I bake mini quiches for breakfast or brunch with ham and cheddar in muffin pans. Salad croutons replace the need for a crust.
—Lois Enger, Colorado Springs, CO

Start to Finish: 30 min.
Makes: 1 dozen

- 1 cup salad croutons
- 1 cup shredded cheddar cheese
- 1 cup chopped fully cooked ham
- 4 large eggs
- 1½ cups 2% milk
- 1½ teaspoons dried parsley flakes
- ½ teaspoon Dijon mustard
- ¼ teaspoon salt
- ⅛ teaspoon onion powder
  Dash pepper

1. Preheat oven to 325°. Divide croutons, cheese and ham among 12 greased muffin cups. In a large bowl, whisk remaining ingredients until blended. Divide egg mixture among prepared muffin cups.
2. Bake 15-20 minutes or until a knife inserted in the center comes out clean. Let stand 5 minutes before removing from pan. Serve warm.

FIESTA BREAKFAST BAKE

I get a kick out of making breakfast for a crowd when I have weekend guests, and my family also loves breakfast for dinner. I created this dish by combining my family's favorite southwest flavors in an all-in-one-pan recipe.
—Whitney Gilbert, Smithville, MO

Prep: 15 min. • **Bake:** 35 min.
Makes: 8 servings

1	tube (16.3 ounces) refrigerated corn biscuits
3	cups frozen seasoning blend vegetables (about 14 ounces)
1½	cups shredded Monterey Jack cheese
8	large eggs
¾	cup 2% milk
⅛	teaspoon cayenne pepper
¼	teaspoon salt
¼	teaspoon black pepper
¼	teaspoon ground cumin
½	cup salsa
	Fresh cilantro leaves
	Additional salsa

1. Preheat oven to 350°. Cut biscuits into quarters; arrange evenly in a greased 13x9-in. baking dish. Layer with vegetables and shredded cheese. Whisk together eggs, milk and seasonings; pour evenly over layers. Top with salsa.
2. Bake, uncovered, until casserole is browned and middle set, 35-45 minutes. Let stand 10 minutes before serving. Top servings with fresh cilantro leaves and additional salsa.

HAM POTATO PUFFS

Here is a new, fun way to use up leftover mashed potatoes. These puffs were an instant hit with our teenagers. Serve with scrambled eggs or fresh fruit.
—Brad Eichelberger, York, PA

....

Prep: 20 min. • **Bake:** 20 min.
Makes: 10 puffs

- 1 **tube (12 ounces) refrigerated buttermilk biscuits**
- 1 **cup cubed fully cooked ham**
- 1 **cup leftover mashed potatoes**
- 1 **cup shredded cheddar cheese, divided**
- ½ **teaspoon dried parsley flakes**
- ¼ **teaspoon garlic powder**
    Minced fresh parsley, optional

1. Press each biscuit onto the bottom and up the sides of a greased muffin cup. In a large bowl, combine the ham, potatoes, ½ cup cheese, parsley and garlic powder.
2. Spoon ¼ cup into each prepared cup. Sprinkle with remaining cheese. Bake at 350° for 20-25 minutes or until lightly browned. If desired, sprinkle with minced fresh parsley. Serve warm. Refrigerate leftovers.

CROISSANT BREAKFAST CASSEROLE

Turn buttery croissants and orange marmalade into a classic overnight casserole. It makes a wonderful treat for family and guests the next morning.
—Joan Hallford, North Richland Hills, TX

Prep: 15 min. + chilling • **Bake:** 25 min.
Makes: 12 servings

- 1 jar (18 ounces) orange marmalade
- ½ cup apricot preserves
- ⅓ cup orange juice
- 3 teaspoons grated orange peel
- 6 croissants, split
- 5 large eggs
- 1 cup half-and-half cream
- 1 teaspoon almond or vanilla extract
  Quartered fresh strawberries

1. In a small bowl, mix marmalade, preserves, orange juice and peel. Arrange croissant bottoms in a greased 13x9-in. baking dish. Spread with 1½ cups marmalade mixture. Add croissant tops.
2. In another bowl, whisk eggs, cream and extract; pour over croissants. Spoon remaining marmalade mixture over tops. Refrigerate, covered, overnight.
3. Preheat oven to 350°. Remove casserole from refrigerator while oven heats. Bake, uncovered, 25-30 minutes or until a knife inserted in the center comes out clean. Let stand 5 minutes before serving. Serve with strawberries.

CINNAMON FRUIT BISCUITS

These sweet treats are so easy, I'm almost embarrassed when people ask me for the recipe. They're a snap to make with refrigerated buttermilk biscuits, sugar, cinnamon and your favorite fruit preserves.
—Ione Burham, Washington, IA

Prep: 15 min. • **Bake:** 15 min. + cooling
Makes: 10 servings

- ½ cup sugar
- ½ teaspoon ground cinnamon
- 1 tube (12 ounces) refrigerated buttermilk biscuits, separated into 10 biscuits
- ¼ cup butter, melted
- 10 teaspoons strawberry preserves

1. In a small bowl, combine sugar and cinnamon. Dip top and sides of biscuits in butter, then in cinnamon-sugar.
2. Place on ungreased baking sheets. With the end of a wooden spoon handle, make a deep indentation in the center of each biscuit; fill with 1 teaspoon preserves.
3. Bake at 375° for 15-18 minutes or until golden brown. Cool for 15 minutes before serving (preserves will be hot).

CREPE QUICHE CUPS

When it comes to trying new recipes, I'm always up for a challenge! Crepe cups have become one of my favorite items to serve when entertaining. These elegant bites are a nice addition to a special occasion brunch when the family is gathered around.

—Sheryl Riley, Unionville, MO

....

Prep: 40 min. + chilling • **Bake:** 25 min.
Makes: 16 crepe cups

2 large eggs
1 cup plus 2 tablespoons 2% milk
2 tablespoons butter, melted
1 cup all-purpose flour
⅛ teaspoon salt

FILLING
½ pound bulk pork sausage
¼ cup chopped onion
3 large eggs
½ cup 2% milk
½ cup mayonnaise
2 cups shredded cheddar cheese

1. For crepe batter, in a small bowl, beat the eggs, milk and butter. Combine flour and salt; add to egg mixture and mix well. Cover and refrigerate for 1 hour.

2. In a small skillet, cook sausage and onion over medium heat until meat is no longer pink; drain. In a large bowl, whisk the eggs, milk and mayonnaise. Stir in sausage mixture and cheese; set aside.

3. Heat a lightly greased 8-in. nonstick skillet. Stir the crepe batter; pour about 2 tablespoons into center of skillet. Lift and tilt pan to coat bottom evenly. Cook until top appears dry; turn and cook 15-20 seconds longer.

4. Remove to a wire rack. Repeat with remaining batter, greasing skillet as needed. When cool, stack crepes with waxed paper or paper towels in between.

5. Line greased muffin cups with crepes; fill two-thirds full with sausage mixture. Bake at 350° for 15 minutes. Cover cups loosely with foil; bake 10-15 minutes longer or until a knife inserted in the center comes out clean.

★ ★ ★ ★ ★ **READER REVIEW**

"Served this as part of my large Easter brunch and the only thing I regret was not making more! These will be a regular brunch item from now on."

MALVERNA BOSH TASTEOFHOME.COM

RHUBARB & STRAWBERRY COFFEE CAKE

Vanilla cake with a cream cheese filling and a strawberry-rhubarb sauce makes a grand finale for a Mother's Day brunch. It's great for other spring or summertime gatherings, too.
—Danielle Lee, Sewickley, PA

....

Prep: 50 min. • **Bake:** 50 min. + cooling
Makes: 12 servings

1½ teaspoons cornstarch
3 tablespoons sugar
¾ cup chopped fresh strawberries
¾ cup chopped fresh or frozen rhubarb
1 tablespoon water

FILLING
1 package (8 ounces) cream cheese, softened
¼ cup sugar
1 large egg, lightly beaten

CAKE
2 cups all-purpose flour
¾ cup sugar
½ cup cold butter, cubed
½ teaspoon baking powder
½ teaspoon baking soda
¼ teaspoon salt
1 large egg, lightly beaten
¾ cup fat-free sour cream
1 teaspoon vanilla extract

1. Preheat oven to 350°. Line bottom of a greased 9-in. springform pan with parchment paper; grease paper. In a small saucepan, mix cornstarch and sugar; stir in strawberries, rhubarb and water. Bring to a boil. Reduce heat; simmer, uncovered, 6-8 minutes or until thickened, stirring occasionally. For filling, in a small bowl, beat cream cheese and sugar until smooth. Beat in egg.

2. In a large bowl, combine flour and sugar; cut in butter until crumbly. Reserve ¾ cup for topping. Stir baking powder, baking soda and salt into remaining flour mixture. In a small bowl, whisk egg, sour cream and vanilla until blended; gently stir into flour mixture (do not overmix).

3. Spread batter onto bottom and ½ in. up sides of prepared pan. Spread filling over crust, leaving a ½-in. border around edge of pan. Spoon strawberry mixture over top; sprinkle with reserved crumb mixture.

4. Bake 50-60 minutes or until edges are golden brown. Cool on a wire rack for 20 minutes. Loosen sides from pan with a knife. Cool completely. Remove rim from pan. Refrigerate leftovers.

Freeze option: Securely wrap cooled cake in plastic wrap and foil, then freeze. To use, thaw in refrigerator.

✱

TEST KITCHEN TIP
Look for rhubarb stalks that are crisp and brightly colored. Tightly wrap in a plastic bag and store in the refrigerator for up to 3 days. Wash the stalks and remove the poisonous leaves before using. One pound of rhubarb yields about 3 cups chopped.

SCRAMBLED EGG HASH BROWN CUPS

These cuties pack all of your favorite breakfast foods—eggs, hash browns and bacon—in one single-serving-size cup. Grab one and get mingling.
—Talon DiMare, Bullhead City, AZ

....

Prep: 10 min. • **Bake:** 25 min.
Makes: 1 dozen

- **1 package (20 ounces) refrigerated Southwest-style shredded hash brown potatoes**

- **6 large eggs**
- **½ cup 2% milk**
- **⅛ teaspoon salt**
- **1 tablespoon butter**
- **10 thick-sliced bacon strips, cooked and crumbled**
- **1¼ cups shredded cheddar-Monterey Jack cheese, divided**

1. Preheat oven to 400°. Divide potatoes among 12 greased muffin cups; press onto bottoms and up sides to form cups. Bake 18-20 minutes or until golden brown.
2. Meanwhile, in a small bowl, whisk eggs, milk and salt. In a large nonstick skillet, heat butter over medium heat. Pour in egg mixture; cook and stir until eggs are thickened and no liquid egg remains. Stir in bacon and ¾ cup cheese. Spoon into cups; sprinkle with the remaining ½ cup cheese.
3. Bake 3-5 minutes or until cheese is melted. Cool 5 minutes before removing from pan.

ORANGE CHEESECAKE BREAKFAST ROLLS

These scrumptious citrus rolls with a cream cheese filling are a nice change of pace from the typical brown sugar-and-cinnamon kind.
—Hannah Cobb, Owings Mills, MD

....

Prep: 50 min. + rising • **Bake:** 25 min.
Makes: 2 dozen

- 2 packages (¼ ounce each) active dry yeast
- ¾ cup warm water (110° to 115°)
- 1¾ cups warm 2% milk (110° to 115°)
- 1 cup sugar
- 2 large eggs
- 3 tablespoons butter, melted
- 1½ teaspoons salt
- 7 to 8 cups all-purpose flour

FILLING
- 1 package (8 ounces) cream cheese, softened
- ½ cup sugar
- 1 tablespoon thawed orange juice concentrate
- ½ teaspoon vanilla extract

GLAZE
- 2 cups confectioners' sugar
- 3 tablespoons orange juice
- 1 teaspoon grated orange peel

1. In a large bowl, dissolve the yeast in warm water. Add milk, sugar, eggs, butter, salt and 5 cups flour. Beat until smooth. Stir in enough remaining flour to form a firm dough.

2. Turn onto a floured surface; knead until smooth and elastic, about 6-8 minutes. Place in a greased bowl, turning once to grease the top. Cover and let rise in a warm place until doubled, about 1 hour.

3. In a small bowl, beat cream cheese, sugar, orange juice concentrate and vanilla until smooth. Punch dough down. Turn onto a lightly floured surface; divide in half. Roll one portion into an 18x7-in. rectangle. Spread half of the filling to within ½ in. of edges.

4. Roll up jelly-roll style, starting with a long side; pinch seam to seal. Cut into 12 slices; place cut side down in a greased 13x9-in. baking pan. Repeat with remaining dough and filling. Cover and let rise until doubled, about 30 minutes.

5. Meanwhile, preheat oven to 350°. Bake 25-30 minutes or until golden brown. Combine confectioners' sugar, orange juice and peel; drizzle over warm rolls. Refrigerate leftovers.

To Make Ahead: Prepare, shape and place rolls in baking pans as directed. Cover and refrigerate overnight. Remove rolls from the refrigerator and let stand for 30 minutes. Bake and glaze as directed.

ALMOND APRICOT COFFEE CAKE

The nutty aroma and delicate fruit flavor make this tube cake special enough to serve to company. Use strawberry or raspberry preserves for a tasty variation.
—Sharon Mensing, Greenfield, IA

....

Prep: 20 min. • **Bake:** 55 min. + cooling
Makes: 12-16 servings

- 1 cup butter, softened
- 2 cups sugar
- 3 large eggs
- 1 cup (8 ounces) sour cream
- 1 teaspoon almond extract
- 2 cups all-purpose flour
- ½ teaspoon baking powder
- ½ teaspoon baking soda
- ¼ teaspoon salt
- ¾ cup slivered almonds, divided
- 1 jar (10 to 12 ounces) apricot preserves, divided
  Confectioners' sugar, optional

1. In a large bowl, cream butter and sugar until light and fluffy. Add the eggs, sour cream and extract; mix well. Combine the flour, baking powder, baking soda and salt; add to the creamed mixture and mix well.
2. Spread half of the batter in a greased and floured 12-cup fluted tube pan. Sprinkle with half of the almonds. Spread half of the preserves to within ½ in of the edges. Cover with remaining batter. Spoon remaining preserves over batter to within ½ in of edges. Sprinkle with remaining almonds.
3. Bake at 350° for 55-60 minutes or until toothpick inserted in the center comes out clean. Cool in pan for 15 minutes before inverting onto a serving plate. If desired, dust with confectioners' sugar.

FARMER'S STRATA

Give this hearty casserole a try the next time you need a dish that's both budget-friendly and easy to prepare. You can assemble it ahead and bake it just before leaving for a potluck. With homestyle ingredients like bacon, cheese and potatoes, it's one that will have folks going back for seconds!
—Pat Kuether, Westminster, CO

....

Prep: 25 min. + chilling • **Bake:** 65 min.
Makes: 16 servings

- 1 pound sliced bacon, cut into ½-inch pieces
- 2 cups chopped fully cooked ham
- 1 small onion, chopped
- 10 slices white bread, cubed
- 1 cup cubed cooked potatoes
- 3 cups shredded cheddar cheese
- 8 large eggs
- 3 cups milk
- 1 tablespoon Worcestershire sauce
- 1 teaspoon ground mustard
  Dash salt and pepper

1. In a large skillet, cook bacon over medium heat until crisp; add ham and onion. Cook and stir until onion is tender; drain.
2. In a greased 13x9-in. baking dish, layer half the bread cubes, potatoes and cheese. Top with all of the bacon mixture. Repeat layers of bread, potatoes and cheese.
3. In a large bowl, beat the eggs; add the milk, Worcestershire sauce, mustard, salt and pepper. Pour over all. Cover and chill overnight.
4. Remove from refrigerator 30 minutes before baking. Preheat oven to 325°. Bake, uncovered, for 65-70 minutes or until a knife inserted in the center comes out clean.

CARAMEL PECAN ROLLS

Soft and sweet, these rolls will get a lip-smacking smile from everyone. They rise nice and high, hold their shape and have a gooey caramel sauce that's scrumptious. There's no better way to start the day!
—Carolyn Buschkamp, Emmetsburg, IA

Prep: 40 min. + rising • **Bake:** 20 min.
Makes: 2 dozen

- 2   cups milk
- ½   cup water
- ½   cup sugar
- ½   cup butter
- ⅓   cup cornmeal
- 2   teaspoons salt
- 7   to 7½ cups all-purpose flour
- 2   packages (¼ ounce each) active dry yeast
- 2   large eggs

TOPPING
- 2   cups packed brown sugar
- ½   cup butter
- ½   cup milk
- ½   to 1 cup chopped pecans

FILLING
- ¼   cup butter, softened
- ½   cup sugar
- 2   teaspoons ground cinnamon

1. In a saucepan, combine the first six ingredients; bring to a boil, stirring frequently. Set aside to cool to 120°-130°. In a bowl, combine 2 cups flour and yeast. Add cooled cornmeal mixture; beat on low until smooth. Add eggs and 1 cup of flour; mix for 1 minute. Stir in enough remaining flour to form a soft dough.
2. Turn the dough onto a floured board; knead until smooth and elastic, about 6-8 minutes. Place in a greased bowl, turning once to grease top. Cover, let rise in warm place until doubled, about 1 hour.
3. Combine the first three topping ingredients in a saucepan; bring to a boil, stirring occasionally. Pour into two greased 13x9-in. baking pans. Sprinkle with pecans; set aside.
4. Punch dough down; divide in half. Roll each into a 12x15-in. rectangle; spread with butter. Combine sugar and cinnamon; sprinkle over butter. Roll up dough from one long side; pinch seams and turn ends under. Cut each roll into 12 slices. Place 12 slices, cut side down, in each baking pan. Cover and let rise in a warm place until nearly doubled, about 30 minutes.
5. Bake at 375° for 20-25 minutes or until golden brown. Let cool 1 minute; invert onto a serving platter.

BLUEBERRY KUCHEN

The warm summer months bring beautiful plump blueberries, which I use in this easy brunch dessert. I freeze extra berries so I have them available any time I want this treat.
—Anne Krueger, Richmond, BC

Prep: 10 min. • **Bake:** 40 min.
Makes: 12 servings

- 1½   cups all-purpose flour
- ¾   cup sugar
- 2   teaspoons baking powder
- 1½   teaspoons grated lemon peel
- ½   teaspoon ground nutmeg
- ¼   teaspoon salt
- ⅔   cup milk
- ¼   cup butter, melted
- 1   large egg, beaten
- 1   teaspoon vanilla extract
- 2   cups fresh or frozen blueberries

TOPPING
- ¾   cup sugar
- ½   cup all-purpose flour
- ¼   cup butter, melted

1. In a bowl, combine the first six ingredients. Add the milk, butter, egg and vanilla. Beat for 2 minutes or until well blended.
2. Pour into a greased 13x9-in. baking dish. Sprinkle with blueberries. In a bowl, combine sugar and flour; add butter. Toss with a fork until crumbly; sprinkle over blueberries. Bake at 350° for 40 minutes or until lightly browned.

CINNAMON DOUGHNUT MUFFINS

Back when my children were youngsters, they loved to have these muffins as part of Sunday brunch.
—Sharon Pullen, Alvinston, ON

Prep: 15 min. • **Bake:** 20 min.
Makes: 10 standard-size muffins

- 1¾ cups all-purpose flour
- 1½ teaspoons baking powder
- ½ teaspoon salt
- ½ teaspoon ground nutmeg
- ¼ teaspoon ground cinnamon
- ¾ cups sugar
- ⅓ cup canola oil
- 1 large egg, lightly beaten
- ¾ cup milk
- 10 teaspoons seedless strawberry or your favorite jam

TOPPING
- ¼ cup butter, melted
- ⅓ cup sugar
- 1 teaspoon ground cinnamon

1. In a large bowl, combine flour, baking powder, salt, nutmeg and cinnamon. In a small bowl, combine sugar, oil, egg and milk; stir into dry ingredients just until moistened.

2. Fill greased or paper-lined muffin cups half full; place 1 teaspoon jam on top. Cover jam with enough batter to fill muffin cups three-fourths full. Bake at 350° for 20-25 minutes or until a toothpick comes out clean.

3. Place melted butter in a small bowl; combine sugar and cinnamon in another bowl. Immediately after removing muffins from the oven, dip tops in butter, then in cinnamon-sugar. Serve warm.

OVERNIGHT CHERRY DANISH

These rolls with their cherry-filled centers melt in your mouth and store well, unfrosted, in the freezer.
—Leann Sauder, Tremont, IL

Prep: 1½ hours + chilling
Bake: 15 min. + cooling
Makes: 3 dozen

- 2 packages (¼ ounce each) active dry yeast
- ½ cup warm 2% milk (110° to 115°)
- 6 cups all-purpose flour
- ⅓ cup sugar
- 2 teaspoons salt
- 1 cup cold butter, cubed
- 1½ cups warm half-and-half cream (70° to 80°)
- 6 large egg yolks
- 1 can (21 ounces) cherry pie filling

ICING
- 3 cups confectioners' sugar
- 2 tablespoons butter, softened
- ¼ teaspoon vanilla extract
  Dash salt
- 4 to 5 tablespoons half-and-half cream

1. In a small bowl, dissolve yeast in warm milk. In a large bowl, combine flour, sugar and salt. Cut in butter until crumbly. Add yeast mixture, cream and egg yolks; stir until mixture forms a soft dough (dough will be sticky). Refrigerate, covered, overnight.

2. Punch down dough. Turn onto a lightly floured surface; divide into four portions. Roll each portion into an 18x4-in. rectangle; cut into 4x1-in. strips.

3. Place two strips side by side; twist together. Shape into a ring and pinch ends together. Place 2 in. apart on greased baking sheets. Repeat with remaining strips. Cover with kitchen towels; let rise in a warm place until doubled, about 45 minutes.

4. Preheat oven to 350°. Using the end of a wooden spoon handle, make a ½-in.-deep indentation in the center of each Danish. Fill each with about 1 tablespoon pie filling. Bake 14-16 minutes or until lightly browned. Remove from pans to wire racks to cool.

5. For icing, in a bowl, beat confectioners' sugar, butter, vanilla, salt and enough cream to reach desired consistency. Drizzle over Danish.

CANADIAN BACON ONION QUICHE

For more than 20 years, we sold our homegrown specialty onions at the farmers market. I handed out this favorite recipe for a classic quiche to all our customers.
—Janice Redford, Cambridge, WI

Prep: 30 min. • **Bake:** 40 min.
Makes: 8 servings

 1 cup all-purpose flour
 ¾ teaspoon salt, divided
 ½ cup plus 3 tablespoons
   cold butter, divided
 ½ cup 4% small-curd cottage cheese
 3 large sweet onions,
   sliced (about 6 cups)
 4 ounces Canadian bacon, diced
 ¼ teaspoon pepper
 3 large eggs, lightly beaten
 1 cup shredded cheddar cheese

1. Preheat oven to 350°. In a small bowl, mix flour and ¼ teaspoon salt; cut in ½ cup butter until crumbly. Gradually add cottage cheese, tossing with a fork until dough holds together when pressed. Shape into a disk.
2. On a floured surface, roll dough to a ⅛-in.-thick circle; transfer to a 9-in. pie plate. Trim pastry to ½ in. beyond rim of plate; flute edge.
3. In large skillet, heat remaining butter over medium heat. Add onions; cook and stir until golden brown. Stir in Canadian bacon, pepper and remaining salt. Remove from heat; add eggs and cheddar cheese. Pour into pastry shell.
4. Bake quiche on a lower oven rack 40-45 minutes or until a knife inserted in the center comes out clean. Let stand 10 minutes before cutting.

ORANGE MARMALADE BREAKFAST BAKE

When I host brunch, I select one item that can be prepared a day ahead so I have ample time to make other recipes the next morning. This French toast bake also works well with grapefruit or a mixed-fruit marmalade.
—Judy Wilson, Sun City West, AZ

Prep: 25 min. + chilling
Bake: 40 min.
Makes: 12 servings (1½ cups syrup)

 3 tablespoons butter, softened
 24 slices French bread (½ inch thick)
 1 jar (12 ounces) orange marmalade
 6 large eggs
 2¾ cups 2% milk
 ⅓ cup sugar
 1 teaspoon vanilla extract
 ¼ teaspoon ground nutmeg
 ⅓ cup finely chopped walnuts

SYRUP
 1¼ cups maple syrup
 ⅓ cup orange juice
 2 teaspoons grated orange peel

1. Spread butter over one side of each bread slice. Arrange half of the bread slices overlapping in a greased 13x9-in. baking dish, buttered side down. Spread marmalade over bread slices; top with remaining bread slices, buttered side up.
2. In a large bowl, whisk eggs, milk, sugar, vanilla and nutmeg until blended; pour over bread. Refrigerate, covered, several hours or overnight.
3. Preheat oven to 350°. Remove casserole from refrigerator while oven heats. Sprinkle with walnuts. Bake, uncovered, 40-50 minutes or until golden brown and a knife inserted in the center comes out clean.
4. Let stand 5-10 minutes before serving. In a small saucepan, combine maple syrup, orange juice and peel; heat through. Serve with casserole.

MAPLE MORNING GRANOLA

Salty and sweet ingredients combine for an easy, wholesome breakfast or snack. Hosting a kids' party? Pack the granola into treat bags and present them as take-home favors.
—Elizabeth Godecke, Chicago, IL

Prep: 15 min. • **Bake:** 35 min + cooling
Makes: 5 cups

- 3 **cups old-fashioned oats**
- ⅔ **cup chopped pecans**
- ⅓ **cup salted pumpkin seeds or pepitas**
- ½ **cup maple syrup**
- 4 **teaspoons butter, melted**
- 1½ **teaspoons ground cinnamon**
- ¼ **teaspoon salt**
- ¼ **teaspoon ground nutmeg**
- ½ **cup dried apples, chopped**
- ½ **cup dried cranberries**
  Plain yogurt

1. Preheat oven to 325°. In a large bowl, combine oats, pecans and pumpkin seeds. In a small bowl, mix maple syrup, butter, cinnamon, salt and nutmeg. Pour over oat mixture and toss to coat.
2. Transfer to a 15x10x1-in. baking pan coated with cooking spray. Bake for 35-40 minutes or until golden brown, stirring occasionally. Cool on a wire rack. Stir in dried fruits; serve with yogurt. Store granola in an airtight container.

HONEY BAGELS

Who has time to make from-scratch bagels? You do with this easy recipe from our Test Kitchen.
—*Taste of Home* Test Kitchen

Prep: 1 hour + standing • **Bake:** 20 min.
Makes: 1 dozen

- 1 **tablespoon active dry yeast**
- 1¼ **cups warm water (110° to 115°)**
- 3 **tablespoons canola oil**
- 3 **tablespoons sugar**
- 3 **tablespoons plus ¼ cup honey, divided**
- 1 **teaspoon brown sugar**
- 1½ **teaspoons salt**
- 1 **large egg**
- 4 **to 5 cups bread flour**
- 1 **tablespoon dried minced onion**
- 1 **tablespoon sesame seeds**
- 1 **tablespoon poppy seeds**

1. In a large bowl, dissolve yeast in warm water. Add the oil, sugar, 3 tablespoons honey, brown sugar, salt and egg; mix well. Stir in enough flour to form a soft dough.
2. Turn onto a floured surface; knead until a smooth firm dough forms, about 8-10 minutes. Cover and let rest for 10 minutes.
3. Punch dough down. Shape into 12 balls. Push thumb through centers to form a 1½-in. hole. Stretch and shape dough to form an even ring. Place on a floured surface. Cover and let rest for 10 minutes; flatten bagels slightly.
4. In a large saucepan or Dutch oven, bring 8 cups water and remaining honey to a boil. Drop bagels, one at a time, into boiling water. Cook bagels for 45 seconds; turn and cook 45 seconds longer. Remove bagels with a slotted spoon; drain, sprinkle with onion, sesame and poppy seeds.
5. Place bagels 2 in. apart on baking sheets lined with parchment paper. Bake at 425° for 12 minutes. Turn and bake 5 minutes longer or until golden brown.

★ ★ ★ ★ ★ **READER REVIEW**
"These are surprisingly easy to make, and my co-workers love them!"
KCRIHFIELD89 TASTEOFHOME.COM

CRANBERRY CREAM CHEESE FRENCH TOAST

A friend made this indulgent French toast with blueberries for brunch. I use the same recipe but with fresh cranberry sauce. Either way, it's divine.
—Sandie Heindel, Liberty, MO

Prep: 25 min. + chilling
Bake: 50 min. + standing
Makes: 12 servings

- 12 cups cubed French bread (about 12 ounces)
- 2 packages (8 ounces each) cream cheese, cubed
- 1 can (14 ounces) whole-berry cranberry sauce
- 12 large eggs, lightly beaten
- 2 cups 2% milk
- ⅓ cup maple syrup
- 2 teaspoons ground cinnamon
  Dash ground nutmeg
  Additional maple syrup, optional

1. Arrange half of the bread in a single layer in a greased 13x9-in. baking dish; top with cream cheese and spoonfuls of cranberry sauce. Top with remaining bread.
2. In a large bowl, whisk eggs, milk, ⅓ cup syrup, cinnamon and nutmeg until blended. Pour over casserole. Refrigerate, covered, overnight.
3. Remove casserole from refrigerator 30 minutes before baking. Preheat oven to 350°. Bake, uncovered, until a knife inserted in center comes out clean, 50-60 minutes. Let stand 10 minutes before serving. If desired, serve with additional maple syrup.

MAKE AHEAD
PIGS IN A POOL

My kids love sausage and pancakes, but making them for breakfast on a busy weekday is not a reality. My homemade version of pigs in a blanket is a great alternative to the packaged kind, and they freeze like a dream.
—Lisa Dodd, Greenville, SC

Prep: 45 min. • **Bake:** 20 min.
Makes: 4 dozen

- 1 pound reduced-fat bulk pork sausage
- 2 cups all-purpose flour
- ¼ cup sugar
- 1 tablespoon baking powder
- 1 teaspoon salt
- ½ teaspoon ground cinnamon
- ¼ teaspoon ground nutmeg
- 1 large egg, lightly beaten
- 2 cups fat-free milk
- 2 tablespoons canola oil
- 2 tablespoons honey
  Maple syrup, optional

1. Preheat oven to 350°. Coat mini-muffin cups with cooking spray.
2. Shape sausage into forty-eight ¾-in. balls. Place meatballs on a rack coated with cooking spray in a shallow baking pan. Bake 15-20 minutes or until cooked through. Drain on paper towels. In a large bowl, whisk flour, sugar, baking powder, salt and spices. In another bowl, whisk egg, milk, oil and honey until blended. Add to flour mixture; stir just until moistened.
3. Place a sausage ball into each mini-muffin cup; cover with batter. Bake for 20-25 minutes or until lightly browned. Cool 5 minutes before removing from pans to wire racks. Serve warm with syrup if desired.
Freeze option: Freeze cooled muffins in resealable plastic freezer bags. To use, microwave each muffin on high for 20-30 seconds or until heated through.

ROLLED BUTTERMILK BISCUITS

I scribbled down this recipe when our family visited the Cooperstown Farm Museum more than 25 years ago. I must have gotten it right, because these biscuits turn out great every time!
—Patricia Kile, Elizabethtown, PA

Prep: 20 min. • **Bake:** 15 min.
Makes: 8 biscuits

- 2 cups all-purpose flour
- 3 teaspoons baking powder
- ½ teaspoon baking soda
- ¼ teaspoon salt
- 3 tablespoons cold butter
- ¾ to 1 cup buttermilk
- 1 tablespoon fat-free milk

1. In a large bowl, combine the flour, baking powder, baking soda and salt; cut in butter until mixture resembles coarse crumbs. Stir in enough buttermilk just to moisten dough.
2. Turn onto a lightly floured surface; knead 3-4 times. Pat or roll to ¾-in. thickness. Cut with a floured 2½-in. biscuit cutter. Place on a baking sheet coated with cooking spray.
3. Brush with milk. Bake at 450° for 12-15 minutes or until golden brown.

CINNAMON COFFEE CAKE

You'll love the excellent texture of this old-fashioned streusel-topped coffee cake. Always a crowd-pleaser, its lovely vanilla flavor enriched by sour cream may remind you of brunch at Grandma's!
—Eleanor Harris, Cape Coral, FL

Prep: 20 min. • **Bake:** 1 hour + cooling
Makes: 20 servings

- 1 cup butter, softened
- 2¾ cups sugar, divided
- 4 large eggs
- 2 teaspoons vanilla extract
- 3 cups all-purpose flour
- 1 teaspoon baking soda
- 1 teaspoon salt
- 2 cups (16 ounces) sour cream
- 2 tablespoons ground cinnamon
- ½ cup chopped walnuts

1. In a large bowl, cream butter and 2 cups sugar until light fluffy. Add eggs, one at a time, beating well after each addition. Beat in vanilla. Combine flour, baking soda and salt; add alternately with sour cream, beating just enough after each addition to keep batter smooth.
2. Spoon a third of batter into a greased 10-in. tube pan. Combine cinnamon, nuts and remaining sugar; sprinkle a third over batter in pan. Repeat layers two more times. Bake at 350° for 60-65 minutes or until a toothpick inserted in the center comes out clean. Cool for 15 minutes before removing from pan to a wire rack to cool completely.

ASPARAGUS, BACON & SHALLOT TART

My tart is an adaptation of my mom's quiche recipe. She lives thousands of miles away in the UK, so whenever I make it, it stirs up happy memories of home.
—Paula Nolan, Granite Bay, CA

Prep: 40 min. + chilling
Bake: 25 min. + standing
Makes: 12 servings

	Pastry for single-crust pie
1	pound fresh asparagus
6	thick-sliced center-cut bacon strips, coarsely chopped
1	tablespoon extra virgin olive oil
1	medium red onion, thinly sliced
1	shallot, thinly sliced
1	tablespoon red wine vinegar
⅓	cup oil-packed sun-dried tomatoes, coarsely chopped
1	tablespoon chopped fresh parsley
1	teaspoon grated lemon peel
¼	teaspoon salt
¼	teaspoon pepper
3	large eggs, lightly beaten
1¼	cups half-and-half cream
1½	cups shredded sharp cheddar cheese
¼	cup shredded Gruyere cheese

1. Preheat oven to 400°. On a lightly floured surface, roll pie pastry to a ⅛-in.-thick circle; transfer to an 11-in. tart pan and press into edges. Refrigerate 30 minutes. Prick the pastry with a fork 5 times; line with a double thickness of foil. Fill with dried beans (or pie weights). Bake 12-15 minutes. Remove foil and beans (or weights); bake crust until light golden brown, 5 minutes more. Cool on a wire rack. Reduce oven setting to 375°.
2. Trim tough ends from the asparagus. Reserve 8 spears; cut remaining asparagus into ½-in. pieces.

3. In a large skillet, cook bacon over medium heat until crisp, 6-8 minutes; remove and drain. Add olive oil to skillet, then red onion, shallot and chopped asparagus; cook and stir until softened, 6-8 minutes. Stir in the vinegar; cook 3 minutes. Reduce heat to low. Return bacon to pan; stir in tomatoes, parsley, lemon peel, salt and pepper. Spoon into pastry shell.
4. Whisk eggs and cream; stir in cheddar cheese until blended. Pour over top. Arrange reserved asparagus spears in a spoke pattern with tips facing outward. Sprinkle with Gruyere cheese. Bake until a knife inserted in center comes out clean, 25-30 minutes. Let stand 10 minutes before cutting.
Pastry for single-crust pie: Combine 1¼ cups all-purpose flour and ¼ teaspoon salt; cut in ½ cup cold butter until crumbly. Gradually add 3-5 tablespoons ice water, tossing with a fork until dough holds together when pressed. Wrap in plastic wrap and refrigerate 1 hour.

How to Prep Asparagus
To clean, rinse asparagus stalks well in cold water. The tender stalk should easily break from the tough white portion when gently bent. If it doesn't, cut off and discard the tough white portion.

Barbecued
Picnic Chicken
page 93

Main Dishes

You're invited to a shindig and the host asked you to bring an entree! Don't sweat over finding the perfect dish. Look here for the best in oven-baked casseroles, slow-cooked sensations, cookout classics, pasta favorites and even meatless options. You've got this!

ITALIAN SAUSAGE & SPINACH PIE

The basic recipe for this savory pie came from my mother, but I added a few ingredients. The flavors blend well, and it even tastes good cold. It makes a hearty supper, especially when you serve it with a side of pasta.
—Teresa Johnson, Peru, IL

Prep: 25 min. • **Bake:** 50 min. + standing
Makes: 8 servings

- 1 pound bulk Italian sausage
- 1 medium onion, chopped
- 6 large eggs
- 2 packages (10 ounces each) frozen chopped spinach, thawed and squeezed dry
- 4 cups shredded mozzarella cheese
- 1 cup ricotta cheese
- ½ teaspoon garlic powder
- ¼ teaspoon pepper
  Pastry for double-crust pie (9 inches)
- 1 tablespoon water

1. In a large skillet, brown sausage and onion over medium heat 6-8 minutes or until sausage is no longer pink, breaking sausage into crumbles; drain.
2. Separate 1 egg; reserve yolk for brushing pastry. In a large bowl, whisk remaining eggs and egg white. Stir in sausage mixture, spinach, mozzarella cheese, ricotta cheese, garlic powder and pepper.
3. Preheat oven to 375°. On a lightly floured surface, roll one half of pastry dough to a ⅛-in.-thick circle; transfer to a 9-in. deep-dish pie plate. Trim pastry even with rim. Add sausage mixture. Roll remaining pastry dough to a ⅛-in.-thick circle. Place over filling. Trim, seal and flute edge.
4. In a small bowl, whisk water and the reserved egg yolk; brush over pastry. Cut slits in top.
5. Bake 50 minutes or until golden brown. Let stand 10 minutes before serving.
Pastry for double-crust pie (9 inches): Combine 2½ cups all-purpose flour and ½ tsp. salt; cut in 1 cup cold butter until crumbly. Gradually add ⅓ to ⅔ cup ice water, tossing with a fork until dough holds together when pressed. Divide dough in half and shape into disks; wrap in plastic wrap and refrigerate 1 hour.

NO-FUSS CHICKEN

This chicken lives up to its name! It has a wonderful tangy taste, and no one will know you used convenient ingredients like a bottle of salad dressing and onion soup mix.
—Marilyn Dick, Centralia, MO

Prep: 5 min. • **Bake:** 40 min.
Makes: 16 servings

- 1 bottle (16 ounces) Russian or Catalina salad dressing
- ⅔ cup apricot preserves
- 2 envelopes onion soup mix
- 16 boneless skinless chicken breast halves
  Hot cooked rice

Preheat oven to 350°. In a bowl, combine dressing, preserves and soup mix. Place chicken in two ungreased 13x9-in. baking dishes; top with dressing mixture. Cover and bake 20 minutes; baste. Bake, uncovered, 20 minutes longer or until chicken juices run clear. Serve over rice.

CHICKEN ALFREDO LASAGNA

My family was growing tired of traditional red sauce lasagna, so I created this fun twist using a creamy homemade Alfredo sauce. Store-bought rotisserie chicken keeps prep simple and fast.

—Caitlin MacNeilly, Uncasville, CT

Prep: 35 min. • **Bake:** 45 min. + standing
Makes: 12 servings

- 4 ounces thinly sliced pancetta, cut into strips
- 3 ounces thinly sliced prosciutto or deli ham, cut into strips
- 3 cups shredded rotisserie chicken
- 5 tablespoons unsalted butter, cubed
- ¼ cup all-purpose flour

- 4 cups whole milk
- 2 cups shredded Asiago cheese, divided
- 2 tablespoons minced fresh parsley, divided
- ¼ teaspoon coarsely ground pepper Pinch ground nutmeg
- 9 no-cook lasagna noodles
- 1½ cups shredded part-skim mozzarella cheese
- 1½ cups shredded Parmesan cheese

1. In a large skillet, cook pancetta and prosciutto over medium heat until browned. Drain on paper towels. Transfer to a large bowl; add chicken and toss to combine.

2. For sauce, in a large saucepan, melt butter over medium heat. Stir in flour until smooth; gradually whisk in milk. Bring to a boil, stirring constantly; cook and stir 1-2 minutes or until thickened. Remove from heat; stir in ½ cup Asiago cheese, 1 tablespoon parsley, pepper and nutmeg.

3. Preheat oven to 375°. Spread ½ cup sauce into a greased 13x9-in. baking dish. Layer with a third of each of the following: noodles, sauce, meat mixture, Asiago, mozzarella and Parmesan cheeses. Repeat layers twice.

4. Bake, covered, 30 minutes. Uncover; bake 15 minutes longer or until bubbly. Sprinkle with remaining parsley. Let stand 10 minutes before serving.

SWEET & TANGY PULLED PORK

The slow cooker makes these sandwiches a convenient option for busy weeknights. The apricot preserves lend a sweet flavor to the pork.

—Megan Klimkewicz, Kaiser, MO

Prep: 15 min. • **Cook:** 8 hours
Makes: 12 servings

- 1 jar (18 ounces) apricot preserves
- 1 large onion, chopped
- 2 tablespoons reduced-sodium soy sauce
- 2 tablespoons Dijon mustard
- 1 boneless pork shoulder butt roast (3 to 4 pounds) Hamburger buns, split, optional

1. Mix first four ingredients. Place roast in a 4- or 5-qt. slow cooker; top with preserves mixture. Cook, covered, on low until meat is tender, 8-10 hours.

2. Remove pork from slow cooker. Skim fat from cooking juices. Shred pork with two forks; return to slow cooker and heat through. If desired, serve on buns.

POTLUCK FRIED CHICKEN

This Sunday dinner staple is first fried and then baked to a crispy golden brown. Well-seasoned with oregano and sage, it's sure to satisfy diners at church potlucks or late-summer picnics.
—Donna Kuhaupt, Slinger, WI

Prep: 40 min. • **Bake:** 25 min.
Makes: 12 servings

- 1½ cups all-purpose flour
- ½ cup cornmeal
- ¼ cup cornstarch
- 3 teaspoons salt
- 2 teaspoons paprika
- 1 teaspoon dried oregano
- 1 teaspoon rubbed sage
- 1 teaspoon pepper
- 2 large eggs
- ¼ cup water
- 2 broiler/fryer chickens
  (3 to 4 pounds each), cut up
  Oil for frying

1. In a large resealable plastic bag, combine the flour, cornmeal, cornstarch, salt, paprika, oregano, sage and pepper. In a shallow bowl, beat eggs and water. Dip chicken in egg mixture; place in the bag, a few pieces at a time, and shake to coat.
2. In an electric skillet, heat 1 in. of oil to 375°. Fry chicken, a few pieces at a time, for 3-5 minutes on each side or until golden and crispy.
3. Place in two ungreased 15x10x1-in. baking pans. Bake, uncovered, at 350° for 25-30 minutes or until juices run clear.

SAUSAGE BREAD SANDWICHES

I make these sandwiches in my spare time and freeze them so they're ready when I need them. They're a favorite for tailgating at Kansas State football games.
—Donna Roberts, Manhattan, KS

Prep: 30 min. • **Bake:** 20 min.
Makes: 4 sandwich loaves
(3 pieces each)

- 1 package (16 ounces) hot roll mix
- 2 pounds reduced-fat bulk pork sausage
- 2 tablespoons dried parsley flakes
- 2 teaspoons garlic powder
- 1 teaspoon onion powder
- ½ teaspoon dried oregano
- 2 cups shredded part-skim mozzarella cheese
- ½ cup grated Parmesan cheese
- 1 large egg
- 1 tablespoon water

1. Preheat oven to 350°. Prepare roll mix dough according to package directions.
2. Meanwhile, in a large skillet, cook sausage over medium heat 8-10 minutes or until no longer pink, breaking into crumbles; drain. Stir in seasonings.
3. Divide dough into four portions. On a lightly floured surface, roll each into a 14x8-in. rectangle. Top each with 1¼ cups sausage mixture to within 1 inch of edges; sprinkle with ½ cup mozzarella cheese and 2 tablespoons Parmesan cheese. Roll up jelly-roll style, starting with a long side; pinch seams and ends to seal.
4. Transfer to greased baking sheets, seam side down. In a small bowl, whisk egg with water; brush over loaves. Bake for 20-25 minutes or until golden brown and heated through. Cool 5 minutes before slicing loaves.

Freeze option: Cool cooked sandwiches 1 hour on wire racks. Cut each sandwich into thirds; wrap each securely in foil. Freeze until serving. To reheat sandwiches in the oven, place wrapped frozen sandwiches on a baking sheet. Heat in a preheated 375° oven for 20-25 minutes or until heated through.

SEAFOOD TORTILLA LASAGNA

My husband and I love lasagna, seafood and Mexican fare. One night, I combined all three of our faves into this deliciously different entree. It's a tantalizing change of pace from traditional Italian-style lasagna casseroles.

—Sharon Sawicki, Carol Stream, IL

Prep: 40 min. • **Bake:** 30 min. + standing
Makes: 12 servings

- 1 jar (20 ounces) picante sauce
- 1½ pounds uncooked medium shrimp, peeled and deveined
- ⅛ teaspoon cayenne pepper
- 1 tablespoon olive oil
- 4 to 6 garlic cloves, minced
- ⅓ cup butter, cubed
- ⅓ cup all-purpose flour
- 1 can (14½ ounces) chicken broth
- ½ cup heavy whipping cream
- 15 corn tortillas (6 inches), warmed
- 1 package (16 ounces) imitation crabmeat, flaked
- 3 cups (12 ounces) shredded Colby-Monterey Jack cheese Sour cream and minced fresh cilantro, optional

1. Place picante sauce in a blender; cover and process until smooth. Set aside. In a large skillet cook shrimp and cayenne in oil for about 3 minutes or until shrimp turn pink. Add garlic; cook 1 minute longer. Remove and set aside.
2. In the same skillet, melt butter. Stir in flour until smooth. Gradually add broth. Bring to a boil; cook and stir for 2 minutes or until thickened. Reduce heat. Stir in cream and picante sauce; heat through.
3. Spread ½ cup of sauce in a greased 13x9-in. baking dish. Layer with six tortillas, half of the shrimp, crab and sauce and 1¼ cups cheese. Repeat layers. Tear or cut remaining tortillas; arrange over cheese. Sprinkle with remaining cheese.
4. Bake, uncovered, at 375° for 30-35 minutes or until bubbly. Let stand for 15 minutes before cutting. If desired, garnish with sour cream and cilantro.

FINNISH MEAT PIE

I make this traditional meat pie year-round, but my family particularly enjoys it during hunting season when we're all craving warm comfort food. This is one of those "keeper" recipes I'll pass on to our seven children.

—Laurel Skoog, Frazee, MN

Prep: 25 min. + chilling • **Bake:** 1¼ hours
Makes: 8 servings

- 1 cup shortening
- 1 cup boiling water
- 3 cups all-purpose flour
- 1 teaspoon salt

FILLING
- 4 cups shredded peeled potatoes
- 1½ pounds lean ground beef (90% lean)
- 2 cups shredded carrots
- 1 medium onion, chopped
- ½ cup shredded peeled rutabaga
- 1½ teaspoons salt
- ¼ teaspoon pepper

EGG WASH
- 1 large egg
- 1 tablespoon 2% milk

1. Place shortening in a large bowl. Add boiling water; stir until shortening is melted. In a small bowl, mix flour and salt. Add to shortening mixture; stir until a soft ball forms. Cover and refrigerate until cooled, about 1 hour.
2. Preheat oven to 350°. Divide dough in half. On a lightly floured surface, roll one half of dough into a 17x13-in. rectangle. Transfer to an ungreased 13x9-in. baking dish. Press onto bottom and up sides of dish. Trim pastry to ½ in. beyond rim.
3. In a large bowl, combine the filling ingredients. Spoon into pastry. Roll out remaining dough into a 13x9-in. rectangle. Place over filling. Fold bottom pastry over top pastry; press with a fork to seal. In a small bowl, whisk egg and milk; brush over pastry. Cut slits in top. Bake 1¼ hours or until golden brown.

BUTTERNUT & PORTOBELLO LASAGNA

Lasagna gets fresh flavor and color when you make it with roasted butternut squash, portobello mushrooms, basil and spinach.

—Edward and Danielle Walker
Traverse City, MI

Prep: 1 hour • **Bake:** 45 min. + standing
Makes: 12 servings

- 1 package (10 ounces) frozen cubed butternut squash, thawed
- 2 teaspoons olive oil

- 1 teaspoon brown sugar
- ¼ teaspoon salt
- ⅛ teaspoon pepper

MUSHROOMS
- 4 large portobello mushrooms, coarsely chopped
- 2 teaspoons balsamic vinegar
- 2 teaspoons olive oil
- ¼ teaspoon salt
- ⅛ teaspoon pepper

SAUCE
- 2 cans (28 ounces each) whole tomatoes, undrained
- 2 teaspoons olive oil
- 2 garlic cloves, minced

- 1 teaspoon crushed red pepper flakes
- ½ cup fresh basil leaves, thinly sliced
- ¼ teaspoon salt
- ⅛ teaspoon pepper

LASAGNA
- 9 no-cook lasagna noodles
- 4 ounces fresh baby spinach (about 5 cups)
- 3 cups part-skim ricotta cheese
- 1½ cups shredded part-skim mozzarella cheese

1. Preheat oven to 350°. In a large bowl, combine the first five ingredients. In another bowl, combine ingredients for mushrooms. Transfer vegetables to separate foil-lined 15x10x1-in. baking pans. Roast 14-16 minutes or until tender, stirring occasionally.

2. Meanwhile, for sauce, drain tomatoes, reserving juices; coarsely chop tomatoes. In a large saucepan, heat oil over medium heat. Add garlic and pepper flakes; cook 1 minute longer. Stir in the chopped tomatoes, reserved tomato juices, basil, salt and pepper; bring to a boil. Reduce heat; simmer, uncovered, 35-45 minutes or until thickened, stirring occasionally.

3. Spread 1 cup sauce into a greased 13x9-in. baking dish. Layer with three noodles, 1 cup sauce, spinach and mushrooms. Continue layering with three noodles, 1 cup sauce, ricotta cheese and roasted squash. Top with the remaining noodles and sauce. Sprinkle lasagna with mozzarella cheese.

4. Bake lasagna, covered, 30 minutes. Bake, uncovered, 15-20 minutes longer or until bubbly. Let stand 15 minutes before serving.

SPICY PORK TENDERLOIN

A few years ago, a friend gave me this recipe for marvelously flavorful pork. It sparks up a barbecue and is popular wherever I serve it. I guarantee you'll get many requests for the recipe!
—Diana Steger, Prospect, KY

Prep: 5 min. + chilling • **Grill:** 25 min.
Makes: 8 servings

- 1 to 3 tablespoon chili powder
- 1 teaspoon salt
- ¼ teaspoon ground ginger
- ¼ teaspoon ground thyme
- ¼ teaspoon pepper
- 2 pork tenderloins (about 1 pound each)

1. Combine the first five ingredients; rub over tenderloins. Cover and refrigerate for 2-4 hours.
2. Grill, covered, over medium-hot indirect heat for 25-40 minutes or until thermometer reads 160°.

GROUND BEEF & PEPPERONI STROMBOLI

I've made this delicious stromboli many times. It's perfect when friends and family get together to watch football and basketball games. It always satisfies big appetites.
—Shelley Banzhaf, Maywood, NE

Prep: 25 min. + rising
Bake: 30 min.
Makes: 2 stromboli (8 servings each)

- 2 loaves (1 pound each) frozen bread dough, thawed
- 2 large eggs, lightly beaten
- ⅓ cup olive oil
- ½ teaspoon garlic powder
- ½ teaspoon salt
- ½ teaspoon pepper
- ½ teaspoon ground mustard
- ½ teaspoon dried oregano
- 1 pound ground beef, cooked and drained
- 1 package (3½ ounces) sliced pepperoni
- 2 cups shredded part-skim mozzarella cheese
- 1 cup shredded cheddar cheese
- 1 small onion, chopped

1. Place each loaf of bread dough in a large greased bowl, turning once to grease top. Cover and let rise in a warm place until doubled, about 45 minutes.
2. Preheat oven to 375°. Punch dough down. Roll each loaf into a 15x12-in. rectangle.
3. In a small bowl, combine eggs, oil and seasonings. Brush over dough to within ½ in. of edges; set remaining egg mixture aside. Layer beef, pepperoni, cheeses and onion on dough to within ½ in. of edges. Roll up, jelly-roll style, beginning with a long side. Tuck ends underneath; seal edges well.
4. Place seam side down on greased baking sheets. Brush with remaining egg mixture. Bake until lightly browned, 30-35 minutes, brushing with egg mixture midway through baking. Let loaves stand 5-10 minutes before cutting.

HERBED TURKEY TETRAZZINI

There are many varieties of this old-fashioned casserole. I use thyme and lemon zest to give my version its fresh flavor. It's a nice way to spice up those holiday leftovers.
—Brigitte Garringer, Copper Canyon, TX

Prep: 30 min. • **Bake:** 25 min.
Makes: 12 servings

6 cups uncooked egg noodles
2 tablespoons olive oil
⅓ cup sliced green onions
1 pound sliced fresh mushrooms
3 tablespoons minced fresh parsley
1 tablespoon minced fresh thyme
   or 1 teaspoon dried thyme
2 bay leaves
1 garlic clove, minced
2 teaspoons grated lemon zest
¼ cup butter, cubed
¼ cup all-purpose flour
2 cups chicken broth
1 cup milk
1 large egg yolk, lightly beaten
4 cups cubed cooked turkey
   Salt and pepper to taste
⅓ cup dry bread crumbs
⅓ cup grated Parmesan cheese
½ cup sliced almonds, toasted

1. Cook noodles according to package directions. Meanwhile, in a Dutch oven, heat oil over medium heat. Add green onions; cook and stir 3 minutes. Add the mushrooms, parsley, thyme and bay leaves. Cook until mushrooms are lightly browned. Add garlic; cook 1 minute longer. Discard bay leaves.
2. Transfer mushroom mixture to a small bowl; stir in lemon zest and set aside. Drain noodles.
3. Preheat oven to 350°. In the Dutch oven, melt butter over medium heat. Stir in flour until smooth. Whisk in broth. Bring to a boil; stir until thickened, about 2 minutes. Combine milk and egg yolk; add to the sauce. Cook, stirring, for 2 minutes longer.
4. Stir in mushroom mixture and turkey; heat through. Fold in noodles. Season with salt and pepper.
5. Spoon into a greased 13x9-in. baking dish. Toss bread crumbs and cheese; sprinkle over top. Bake, uncovered, until lightly browned, 25-30 minutes. Sprinkle with almonds.

EASY CHILI VERDE

I love chili verde and order it whenever I see it on the menu at restaurants. A few years ago, I figured out how to make an easy version at home. There are never leftovers when I make it for my family.
—Julie Rowland, Salt Lake City, UT

Prep: 10 min. • **Cook:** 5 hours
Makes: 12 servings (3 quarts)

1 boneless pork shoulder roast
   (4 to 5 pounds), cut
   into 1-inch pieces
3 cans (10 ounces each)
   green enchilada sauce
1 cup salsa verde
1 can (4 ounces) chopped
   green chilies
½ teaspoon salt
   Hot cooked rice
   Sour cream, optional

In a 5-qt. slow cooker, combine pork, enchilada sauce, salsa verde, green chilies and salt. Cook, covered, on low 5-6 hours or until pork is tender. Serve with rice. If desired, top with sour cream.

BLT MEATBALL SLIDERS

Take meatball sliders to a whole new level with the addition of bacon, ground pork and zesty ranch mayo. These are great for game-day parties and tailgating.
—Damali Campbell, New York, NY

Prep: 25 min. • **Bake:** 30 min.
Makes: 1½ dozen

- 1 pound uncooked bacon strips
- 1 cup 2% milk
- 1 large egg
- 1 cup dry bread crumbs
- 1 small onion, finely chopped
- 1 tablespoon fennel seed, crushed
- 1 teaspoon salt
- 1 teaspoon pepper
- ½ teaspoon crushed red pepper flakes
- ¾ pound ground pork
- ½ pound lean ground beef (90% lean)
- ⅔ cup mayonnaise
- 1½ teaspoons ranch dip mix
- 18 dinner rolls, split
- 3 cups spring mix salad greens
- 3 plum tomatoes, sliced

1. Place bacon in a food processor; cover and process until finely chopped. In a large bowl, combine the milk, egg, bread crumbs, onion and seasonings. Crumble the bacon, pork and beef over mixture and mix well. Shape into 2-in. meatballs.
2. Place in an ungreased 15x10x1-in. baking pan. Bake at 425° for 30-35 minutes or until a thermometer reads 160°.
3. Combine mayonnaise and dip mix; spread over rolls. Layer each roll bottom with salad greens, a tomato slice and a meatball; replace tops.

CHICKEN RIGGIES

Rigatoni cooked with cream and cream cheese spells comfort when combined with chicken marinated in sherry and garlic.
—Jackie Scanlan, Dayton, OH

Prep: 30 min. + marinating
Cook: 15 min.
Makes: 12 servings (1¾ cups each)

- ½ cup dry sherry
- 2 tablespoons olive oil
- 3 garlic cloves, minced
- 1 teaspoon dried oregano
- 2 pounds boneless skinless chicken breasts, cubed

SAUCE

- 2 tablespoons butter
- 1 each medium sweet red and green pepper, chopped
- 4 pickled hot cherry peppers, chopped
- 1 medium onion, chopped
- 2 garlic cloves, minced
- 1 cup dry sherry
- 2 cans (one 29 ounces, one 15 ounces) tomato puree
- ¼ teaspoon salt
- ⅛ teaspoon pepper
- 2 packages (16 ounces each) uncooked rigatoni
- 1½ cups heavy whipping cream
- 6 ounces cream cheese, cut up
- 1½ cups grated Romano cheese

1. In a large resealable plastic bag, combine sherry, oil, garlic and oregano. Add chicken; seal bag and turn to coat. Refrigerate 1 hour.
2. Drain chicken, discarding marinade. Heat a Dutch oven over medium-high heat. Add chicken in batches; cook and stir until no longer pink. Remove from pan.
3. In same pan, heat butter over medium-high heat. Add peppers, onion and garlic; cook and stir until tender. Add sherry; bring to a boil. Stir in tomato puree, salt and pepper; return to a boil. Reduce heat; simmer 8-10 minutes or until slightly thickened, stirring occasionally. Add chicken; heat through.
4. Meanwhile, in a stockpot, cook rigatoni according to package directions. In a small saucepan, combine cream and cream cheese over medium heat; cook and stir until blended. Add to chicken mixture; stir in Romano cheese.
5. Drain rigatoni; return to stockpot. Add sauce to pasta; toss to combine.

BAVARIAN POT ROAST

Since all of my grandparents were German, it's no wonder that so many Bavarian recipes have been handed down to me. Because the Midwest has such a large German population, I feel this recipe represents the area well.
—Susan Robertson, Hamilton, OH

Prep: 15 min. • **Cook:** 2¾ hours
Makes: 10 servings

- 1 boneless beef chuck pot roast (about 3 pounds)
- 2 tablespoons canola oil
- 1¼ cups water
- ¾ cup beer or beef broth
- 1 can (8 ounces) tomato sauce
- ½ cup chopped onion
- 2 tablespoons sugar
- 1 tablespoon vinegar
- 2 teaspoons salt
- 1 teaspoon ground cinnamon
- 1 bay leaf
- ½ teaspoon pepper
- ½ teaspoon ground ginger
  Cornstarch and water, optional

1. In a Dutch oven, brown roast in hot oil. Combine water, beer, tomato sauce, onion, sugar, vinegar, salt, cinnamon, bay leaf, pepper and ginger. Pour over meat and bring to a boil. Reduce heat; cover and simmer until meat is tender, about 2½-3 hours.
2. Remove meat. Discard bay leaf. If desired, thicken juices with cornstarch and water.
Freeze option: Place sliced pot roast in freezer containers; top with cooking juices. Cool and freeze. To use, partially thaw in refrigerator overnight. Microwave, covered, on high in a microwave-safe dish until heated through, gently stirring and adding a little broth to pot roast if necessary.

POTLUCK CORDON BLEU CASSEROLE

Whenever I'm invited to a potluck, I'm asked to bring this tempting casserole. The turkey, ham and cheddar cheese are delectable combined with the crunchy bread crumb topping. Try it the next time you have holiday leftovers to use up.
—Joyce Paul, Moose Jaw, SK

Prep: 25 min. • **Bake:** 30 min.
Makes: 10 servings

- 4 cups cubed cooked turkey
- 3 cups cubed fully cooked ham
- 1 cup shredded cheddar cheese
- 1 cup chopped onion
- ¼ cup butter, cubed
- ⅓ cup all-purpose flour
- 2 cups half-and-half cream
- 1 teaspoon dill weed
- ⅛ teaspoon ground mustard
- ⅛ teaspoon ground nutmeg

TOPPING
- 1 cup dry bread crumbs
- 2 tablespoons butter, melted
- ¼ teaspoon dill weed
- ¼ cup shredded cheddar cheese
- ¼ cup chopped walnuts

1. In a large bowl, combine the turkey, ham and cheese; set aside. In a large saucepan, saute onion in butter until tender. Add flour; stir until blended. Gradually add cream, stirring constantly. Bring mixture to a boil; cook and stir for 1-2 minutes or until thickened. Stir in the dill, mustard and nutmeg. Remove from the heat and pour over meat mixture.
2. Spoon into a greased 13x9-in. baking dish. In a small bowl, combine the bread crumbs, butter and dill. Stir in cheese and walnuts. Sprinkle over casserole.
3. Bake, uncovered, at 350° for 30 minutes or until heated through.

CHURCH SUPPER SPAGHETTI

My famous spaghetti is perfect for church dinners, potlucks or whenever you have a large crowd with a big appetite! We live on a farm and employ several workers, so this recipe comes in handy often.

—Verlyn Wilson, Wilkinson, IN

Prep: 50 min. • **Bake:** 20 min.
Makes: 12 servings

- 1 pound ground beef
- 1 large onion, chopped
- 1 medium green pepper, chopped
- 1 can (14½ ounces) diced tomatoes, undrained
- 1 cup water
- 2 tablespoons chili powder
- 1 package (10 ounces) frozen corn, thawed
- 1 package (10 ounces) frozen peas, thawed
- 1 can (4 ounces) mushroom stems and pieces, drained
  Salt and pepper to taste
- 12 ounces spaghetti, cooked and drained
- 2 cups shredded cheddar cheese, divided

1. In a large skillet, cook beef, onion and green pepper over medium heat until meat is no longer pink. Add tomatoes, water and chili powder. Cover and simmer for 30 minutes. Add the corn, peas, mushrooms, salt and pepper. Stir in spaghetti.

2. Layer half of the mixture in a greased 4-qt. baking dish. Sprinkle with 1 cup cheese; repeat layers.

3. Bake casserole, uncovered, at 350° for 20 minutes or until heated through.

BARBECUED PICNIC CHICKEN

I serve this savory barbecued chicken at family picnics. The poultry stays so tender and juicy cooked on a covered grill. Everyone loves the zesty, slightly sweet homemade sauce—and it's so easy to make!

—Priscilla Weaver, Hagerstown, MD

Prep: 15 min. • **Grill:** 45 min.
Makes: 8 servings

- 2 garlic cloves, minced
- 2 teaspoons butter
- 1 cup ketchup
- ¼ cup packed brown sugar
- ¼ cup chili sauce
- 2 tablespoons Worcestershire sauce
- 1 tablespoon celery seed
- 1 tablespoon prepared mustard
- ½ teaspoon salt
- 2 dashes hot pepper sauce
- 2 broiler/fryer chickens (3½ to 4 pounds each), cut up

1. In a large saucepan, saute garlic in butter until tender. Add the next eight ingredients. Bring to a boil, stirring constantly. Remove sauce from the heat; set aside.

2. On a lightly greased grill rack, grill chicken, covered, over medium heat for 30 minutes, turning occasionally. Baste with sauce. Grill 15 minutes longer or until a thermometer reaches 170°, basting and turning several times.

TEST KITCHEN TIP
This sauce is best when made a day or two in advance, giving the flavors time to come together. If you don't have chili sauce on hand, you can use ¼ cup extra ketchup or ¼ cup cocktail sauce. Try this cool-guy move if you don't have a basting brush: Tie a few sprigs of rosemary or another hearty herb together with twine, then baste with it.

BEEF BRISKET ON BUNS

This beef turns out tender and delicious every time!
—Debra Waggoner
Grand Island, NE

Prep: 25 min. + standing • **Bake:** 5 hours
Makes: 16 servings

- ½ teaspoon ground ginger
- ½ teaspoon ground mustard
- 1 fresh beef brisket (4 to 5 pounds)
- 2 cups water
- 1 cup ketchup
- ½ cup Worcestershire sauce
- 2 tablespoons brown sugar
- 2 teaspoons liquid smoke, optional
- 1 teaspoon chili powder
- 16 to 20 sandwich buns, split, optional

1. Combine the ginger and mustard; rub over brisket. Place on a rack in a shallow roasting pan. Bake, uncovered, at 325° for 2 hours.
2. Let stand for 20 minutes. Thinly slice meat across the grain. Place in a foil-lined 13x9-in. baking dish. In a bowl, combine the water, ketchup, Worcestershire sauce, brown sugar, liquid smoke if desired and chili powder; pour over meat. Cover tightly with foil; bake 3 hours longer or until tender. If desired, serve on buns.
Note: This is a fresh beef brisket, not corned beef.

BARBECUED CHICKEN

When our neighborhood has a cookout, I take this chicken and watch it quickly disappear. My family loves this recipe because of the zesty seasoning blend and barbecue sauce.
—Linda Scott, Hahira, GA

Prep: 10 min. • **Grill:** 40 min.
Makes: 8 servings

- 2 broiler/fryer chickens (3 to 4 pounds each), cut up
- **SPICE RUB**
- 2 tablespoons onion powder
- 4 teaspoons salt or salt substitute
- 1 tablespoon paprika
- 2 teaspoons garlic powder
- 1½ teaspoons chili powder
- 1½ teaspoons pepper
- ¼ teaspoon ground turmeric
  Pinch cayenne pepper
- **SAUCE**
- 2 cups ketchup
- 3 tablespoons brown sugar
- 2 tablespoons dried minced onion
- 2 tablespoons thawed orange juice concentrate
- ½ teaspoon liquid smoke, optional

1. Pat chicken pieces dry. In a small bowl, mix spice rub ingredients; reserve 1 tablespoon spice rub for sauce. Rub remaining spice rub on all sides of chicken.
2. Grill chicken, uncovered, over medium heat for 20 minutes, skin side down. Meanwhile, combine all sauce ingredients; stir in reserved spice rub. Turn chicken; grill 20-30 minutes longer or until juices run clear, basting frequently with sauce.

1 large carrot, grated
2 garlic cloves, minced
1 can (14½ ounces) diced
  tomatoes, drained
1 bottle (12 ounces)
  Buffalo wing sauce
½ cup water
1½ teaspoons Italian seasoning
½ teaspoon salt
¼ teaspoon pepper
9 lasagna noodles
1 carton (15 ounces) ricotta cheese
1¾ cups crumbled blue
  cheese, divided
½ cup minced Italian flat leaf parsley
1 large egg, lightly beaten
3 cups shredded part-skim
  mozzarella cheese
2 cups shredded white
  cheddar cheese

BEEF BARBECUE

We like to keep our freezer stocked with plenty of beef roasts. When we're not in the mood for pot roast, I fix satisfying sandwiches instead. The meat cooks in a tasty sauce while I'm at work. Then I just shred the meat and serve it on rolls with the sauce.
—Karen Walker, Sterling, VA

Prep: 5 min. • **Cook:** 6 hours 20 min.
Makes: 12 servings

1 boneless beef chuck
  roast (3 pounds)
1 cup barbecue sauce
½ cup apricot preserves
⅓ cup chopped green or
  sweet red pepper
1 small onion, chopped
1 tablespoon Dijon mustard
2 teaspoons brown sugar
12 sandwich rolls, split

1. Cut the roast into quarters; place in a greased 5-qt. slow cooker. In a bowl, combine barbecue sauce, preserves, green pepper, onion, mustard and brown sugar; pour over roast. Cover and cook on low for 6-8 hours or until meat is tender.
2. Remove roast. When meat is cool enough to handle, shred with two forks; return to slow cooker and stir gently. Cook, covered, 20-30 minutes longer. Skim fat from sauce. Serve beef and sauce on rolls.

BUFFALO CHICKEN LASAGNA

This recipe was inspired by my daughter's favorite food—Buffalo wings! It tastes as if it came from a restaurant.
—Melissa Millwood, Lyman, SC

Prep: 1 hour 40 min.
Bake: 40 min. + standing
Makes: 12 servings

1 tablespoon canola oil
1½ pounds ground chicken
1 small onion, chopped
1 celery rib, finely chopped

1. In a Dutch oven, heat oil over medium heat. Add chicken, onion, celery and carrot; cook and stir until meat is no longer pink and vegetables are tender. Add garlic; cook 2 minutes longer. Stir in tomatoes, wing sauce, water, Italian seasoning, salt and pepper; bring to a boil. Reduce heat; cover and simmer 1 hour.
2. Meanwhile, cook noodles according to package directions; drain. In a small bowl, mix the ricotta cheese, ¾ cup blue cheese, parsley and egg. Preheat oven to 350°.
3. Spread 1½ cups sauce into a greased 13x9-in. baking dish. Layer with three noodles, 1½ cups sauce, ⅔ cup ricotta mixture, 1 cup mozzarella cheese, ⅔ cup cheddar cheese and ⅓ cup blue cheese. Repeat layers twice.
4. Bake, covered, 20 minutes. Uncover; bake until bubbly and cheese is melted, 20-25 minutes. Let stand 10 minutes before serving.

SHREDDED PORK BURRITOS

Pork roast is slow-cooked with sweet and savory ingredients, including a can of cola, to create tender shredded pork burritos. A tomatillo sauce, made easy with a dressing mix, tops the pork for an out-of-this-world entree.
—Katherine Nelson, Centerville, UT

....

Prep: 25 min. • **Cook:** 9 hours
Makes: 16 servings (2⅓ cups sauce)

- 1   bone-in pork shoulder roast (5 pounds)
- 2   tablespoons plus ½ cup packed brown sugar, divided
- 4   teaspoons paprika, divided
- 2   teaspoons crushed red pepper flakes
- 2   teaspoons ground cumin
- 1   teaspoon salt
- 1   can (12 ounces) cola
- 1   cup chicken broth
- 1   large sweet onion, thinly sliced
- 2   garlic cloves, minced

TOMATILLO SAUCE
- 1   cup mayonnaise
- ½   cup 2% milk
- 2   tomatillos, husks removed
- ¾   cup fresh cilantro leaves
- 1   jalapeno pepper, seeded and cut into chunks
- 1   envelope ranch salad dressing mix
- 1   tablespoon lime juice
- 1   garlic clove, peeled
- ⅛   teaspoon cayenne pepper
- 16 flour tortillas (8 inches), room temperature

1. Cut the pork roast in half. Combine 2 tablespoons brown sugar, 2 teaspoons paprika, pepper flakes, cumin and salt; rub over meat. Place in a 4-qt. slow cooker. Add the cola, broth, onion and garlic. Cover and cook on low for 8-10 hours or until meat is tender.

2. Set meat aside until cool enough to handle. Remove meat from bones; discard bones. Shred meat with two forks. Skim fat from cooking juices and return meat to slow cooker. Stir in remaining brown sugar and paprika. Cover and cook on low for 1 hour or until heated through.

3. Meanwhile, in a blender, combine the mayonnaise, milk, tomatillos, cilantro, jalapeno, dressing mix, lime juice, garlic and cayenne. Cover and process until blended. Pour mixture into a small bowl. Chill until serving.

4. Using a slotted spoon, spoon ½ cup filling off center on each tortilla. Drizzle with some of the tomatillo sauce. Fold sides and ends over filling and roll up. Serve with remaining sauce.

Note: Wear disposable gloves when cutting hot peppers; the oils can burn skin. Avoid touching your face.

NEW ORLEANS-STYLE SPICY SHRIMP

We have family members who attended college in New Orleans. This shrimp captures their favorite flavors from The Big Easy, with the right touch of spices and heat.
—Susan Seymour, Valatie, NY

Prep: 15 min. • **Bake:** 20 min.
Makes: 12 servings

- 3 medium lemons, sliced
- ⅔ cup butter, cubed
- ½ cup ketchup
- ¼ cup Worcestershire sauce
- 2 tablespoons seafood seasoning
- 2 tablespoons chili garlic sauce
- 2 tablespoons Louisiana-style hot sauce
- 1 tablespoon Italian salad dressing mix
- 4 pounds uncooked shell-on shrimp (31-40 per pound)
- 2 bay leaves
   French bread

1. Preheat oven to 350°. In a microwave-safe bowl, combine the first eight ingredients. Microwave, covered, on high 2-3 minutes or until butter is melted; stir until blended.
2. Divide shrimp and bay leaves between two ungreased 13x9-in. baking dishes. Add half of the lemon mixture to each dish; toss to combine.
3. Bake, uncovered, 20-25 minutes or until shrimp turn pink; stir halfway through baking time. Remove bay leaves. Serve with bread.

TERIYAKI PINEAPPLE DRUMSTICKS

We have a large family and love to throw big backyard barbecues. My husband is usually on grill duty, so I look for main dish recipes that I can help make inside. These roasted drumsticks keep everyone happy and enjoying the party!
—Erica Allen, Tuckerton, NJ

Prep: 35 min. • **Bake:** 1½ hours
Makes: 12 servings

- 1 tablespoon garlic salt
- 1 tablespoon minced chives
- 1½ teaspoons paprika
- 1½ teaspoons pepper
- ½ teaspoon salt
- 24 chicken drumsticks
- ½ cup canola oil
- 1 can (8 ounces) crushed pineapple
- ½ cup water
- ¼ cup packed brown sugar
- ¼ cup Worcestershire sauce
- ¼ cup yellow mustard
- 4 teaspoons cornstarch
- 2 tablespoons cold water

1. Preheat oven to 350°. Mix the first five ingredients; sprinkle over chicken. In a large skillet, heat oil over medium-high heat. Brown drumsticks in batches. Transfer to a roasting pan.
2. Meanwhile, combine pineapple, ½ cup water, brown sugar, Worcestershire sauce and mustard; pour over chicken. Cover; bake until tender, about 1½-2 hours, uncovering during the last 20-30 minutes of baking to let skin crisp.
3. Remove drumsticks to a platter; keep warm. Transfer cooking juices to a small saucepan; skim fat. Bring juices to a boil. In a bowl, mix cornstarch and cold water until smooth; stir into cooking juices. Return to a boil; cook and stir 1-2 minutes or until thickened. Serve with drumsticks.

TEXAS-STYLE LASAGNA

My spicy, Southwestern-style lasagna is a crowd-pleaser. It goes great with side servings of picante sauce, guacamole and tortilla chips.
—Effie Gish, Fort Worth, TX

....

Prep: 40 min.
Bake: 30 min. + standing
Makes: 12 servings

1½ **pounds ground beef**
1 **teaspoon seasoned salt**
1 **package (1¼ ounces) taco seasoning**
1 **can (14½ ounces) diced tomatoes, undrained**
1 **can (15 ounces) tomato sauce**
1 **can (4 ounces) chopped green chilies**
2 **cups (16 ounces) 4% cottage cheese**
2 **large eggs, lightly beaten**
12 **corn tortillas (6 inches), torn**
3½ **to 4 cups shredded Monterey Jack cheese**
Optional toppings: crushed tortilla chips, salsa and cubed avocado

1. In a large skillet, cook beef over medium heat until no longer pink; drain. Add the seasoned salt, taco seasoning mix, tomatoes, tomato sauce and chilies. Reduce heat; simmer, uncovered, for 15-20 minutes. In a small bowl, combine cottage cheese and eggs.
2. In a greased 13x9-in. baking dish, layer half of each of the following: meat sauce, tortillas, cottage cheese mixture and Monterey Jack cheese. Repeat layers.
3. Bake lasagna, uncovered, at 350° for 30 minutes or until bubbly. Let stand 10 minutes before serving. If desired, garnish with toppings.

Freeze option: Before baking, cover and freeze lasagna up to 3 months. Thaw in the refrigerator overnight. Remove from refrigerator 30 minutes before baking. Bake as directed, increasing time as necessary for a thermometer to read 160°.

BRATWURST SUPPER

This meal-in-one grills to perfection in heavy-duty foil packets. Loaded with chunks of bratwurst, red potatoes, mushrooms and carrots, it's easy to season with onion soup mix and a little soy sauce.
—Janice Meyer, Medford, WI

....

Prep: 10 min. • **Grill:** 45 min.
Makes: 12 servings

3 **pounds uncooked bratwurst links**
3 **pounds small red potatoes, cut into wedges**
1 **pound baby carrots**
1 **large red onion, sliced and separated into rings**
2 **jars (4½ ounces each) whole mushrooms, drained**
¼ **cup butter, cubed**
1 **envelope onion soup mix**
2 **tablespoons soy sauce**
½ **teaspoon pepper**

1. For each of two foil packets, arrange a double thickness of heavy-duty foil (about 17x15 in.) on a flat surface.
2. Cut brats into thirds. Divide the brats, potatoes, carrots, onion and mushrooms evenly between the two double-layer foil pieces. Dot with butter. Sprinkle with soup mix, soy sauce and pepper. Bring edges of foil together; crimp to seal, forming two large packets. Seal tightly; turn to coat.
3. Grill, covered, over medium heat for 23-28 minutes on each side or until vegetables are tender and sausage is no longer pink.

CHICKEN TATER BAKE

You'll please everyone in the family with this inviting dish. It tastes like a chicken potpie with a crispy Tater Tot crust.
—Fran Allen, St. Louis, MO

Prep: 20 min. • **Bake:** 40 min.
Makes: 2 casseroles (6 servings each)

> 2 cans (10¾ ounces each) condensed cream of chicken soup, undiluted
> ½ cup 2% milk
> ¼ cup butter, cubed
> 3 cups cubed cooked chicken
> 1 package (16 ounces) frozen peas and carrots, thawed
> 1½ cups (6 ounces) shredded cheddar cheese, divided
> 1 package (32 ounces) frozen Tater Tots

1. In a large saucepan, combine the soup, milk and butter. Cook and stir over medium heat until heated through. Remove from the heat; stir in the chicken, peas and carrots, and 1 cup cheese.
2. Transfer to two greased 8-in. square baking dishes. Top with Tater Tots; sprinkle with remaining cheese.
3. Cover and freeze one casserole for up to 3 months. Cover and bake the remaining casserole at 350° for 35 minutes. Uncover; bake 5-10 minutes longer or until heated through.
To use frozen casserole: Remove from the freezer 30 minutes before baking (do not thaw). Cover and bake at 350° for 1½ -1¾ hours or until heated through.
Beef Tater Bake: Do not make chicken filling. Cook 2 pounds ground beef with 1 cup each chopped onion and celery; drain. Add 2 cans condensed cream of celery soup, 1 teaspoon salt and ½ teaspoon pepper. Place filling in baking dishes; proceed as directed.

BROCCOLI-CHICKEN CUPS

I first sampled these when my cousin made them for a bridal shower. All the ladies raved over the fantastic flavor of their individual casseroles.
—Shirley Gerber, Roanoke, IL

Prep: 15 min. • **Bake:** 20 min.
Makes: 10-12 servings

- 2 tubes (10 ounces each) refrigerated biscuits
- 2 cups (8 ounces) shredded cheddar cheese, divided
- 1⅓ cups Rice Krispies
- 1 cup cubed cooked chicken
- 1 can (10¾ ounces) condensed cream of mushroom soup, undiluted
- 3 cups frozen chopped broccoli, cooked and drained

1. Place biscuits in greased muffin cups, pressing dough onto the bottom and up the sides. Add 1 tablespoon cheese and cereal to each cup.

2. In a large bowl, combine the chicken, soup and broccoli; spoon into each muffin cup. Bake at 375° for 20-25 minutes or until bubbly. Sprinkle with remaining shredded cheese.

SLOW-COOKED PULLED PORK WITH MOJITO SAUCE

Infused with Cuban flavor, this twist on slow-cooked pulled pork is knock-your-socks-off good, whether you press it into a classic Cuban sandwich or serve it on its own with rice and beans on the side.
—Kristina Wiley, Jupiter, FL

Prep: 25 min. + marinating
Cook: 8 hours
Makes: 12 servings (1½ cups sauce)

- 2 large onions, quartered
- 12 garlic cloves
- 1 bottle (18 ounces) Cuban-style mojo sauce and marinade
- ½ cup lime juice
- ½ teaspoon salt
- ¼ teaspoon pepper

- 1 bone-in pork shoulder butt roast (5 to 5¼ pounds)

MOJITO SAUCE
- ¾ cup canola oil
- 1 medium onion, finely chopped
- 6 garlic cloves, finely chopped
- ⅓ cup lime juice
- ½ teaspoon salt
- ¼ teaspoon pepper
  Additional chopped onion and lime wedges, optional

1. Place onions and garlic in a food processor; process until finely chopped. Add mojo marinade, lime juice, salt and pepper; process until blended. Pour half of the marinade into a large resealable plastic bag. Cut roast into quarters; add to bag. Seal bag and turn to coat. Refrigerate 8 hours or overnight. Transfer remaining marinade to a small bowl; refrigerate, covered, while marinating meat.

2. Drain pork, discarding marinade in bag. Place pork in a 5-qt. slow cooker coated with cooking spray. Top with reserved marinade. Cook, covered, on low for 8-10 hours or until meat is tender.

3. For sauce, in a small saucepan, heat oil over medium heat 2½-3 minutes or until a thermometer reads 200°. Carefully add onion; cook 2 minutes, stirring occasionally. Stir in garlic; remove from heat. Stir in lime juice, salt and pepper.

4. Remove pork from slow cooker; cool slightly. Skim fat from cooking juices. Remove meat from bone; discard bone. Shred pork with two forks. Return cooking juices and pork to slow cooker; heat through.

5. Transfer pork to a platter; serve with warm mojito sauce, stirring just before serving. If desired, sprinkle pork with chopped onion and serve with lime wedges.

CAJUN CHICKEN PASTA BAKE

My family loves noodles, so I got creative and came up with my own pasta bake. It's quick, easy and, best of all, delicious! This recipe yields two casseroles, so save one in the freezer to enjoy on a busy night.
—Kim Weishuhn, Pensacola, FL

Prep: 30 min. • **Bake:** 20 min.
Makes: 2 casseroles (6 servings each)

- 2 packages (12 ounces each) bow tie pasta
- 2 pounds boneless skinless chicken breasts, cut into 1-inch strips
- 2 tablespoons olive oil, divided
- 2 bunches green onions, chopped
- 2 medium green peppers, chopped
- 2 medium sweet red peppers, chopped
- 1 can (14½ ounces) reduced-sodium chicken broth
- 2 cans (10¾ ounces each) condensed cream of chicken soup, undiluted
- 1 can (10¾ ounces) condensed cream of mushroom soup, undiluted
- ¾ cup 2% milk
- 2½ teaspoons Cajun seasoning
- 1½ teaspoons garlic powder
- 2 cups (8 ounces) shredded Colby-Monterey Jack cheese

1. Preheat oven to 350°. Cook pasta according to directions for al dente.
2. Meanwhile, in a Dutch oven, saute chicken in 1 tablespoon oil until juices run clear. Remove with a slotted spoon and set aside. In same pan, saute onions and peppers in remaining oil until tender. Add broth, soups, milk, Cajun seasoning and garlic powder. Bring to a boil; remove from heat.

3. Drain pasta. Add pasta and chicken to soup mixture; toss to coat. Divide between two greased 13x9-in. baking dishes. Sprinkle with cheese. Cover and bake 20-25 minutes or until bubbly.
Freeze option: Cool unbaked casseroles; cover and freeze. To use, partially thaw in refrigerator overnight. Remove from refrigerator 30 minutes before baking. Preheat oven to 350°. Bake casseroles, as directed, increasing time to 55-60 minutes or until heated through and a thermometer in center reads 165°.

KODIAK CASSEROLE

I came across this Alaskan recipe back in the 1950s. It must have been a keeper because I still make it today! It packs a little kick and has an interesting and tasty mix of ingredients, making it the perfect dish for a potluck.
—Kathy Crow, Cordova, AK

Prep: 15 min. • **Bake:** 1 hour
Makes: 16-20 servings

- 2 pounds ground beef
- 4 cups diced onions
- 2 garlic cloves, minced
- 3 medium green peppers, diced
- 4 cups diced celery
- 1 jar (5¾ ounces) pimiento-stuffed olives, undrained
- 1 can (4 ounces) mushroom stems and pieces, undrained
- 1 can (10¾ ounces) condensed tomato soup, undiluted
- 1 jar (8 ounces) picante sauce
- 1 bottle (18 ounces) barbecue sauce
- 2 tablespoons Worcestershire sauce
- 3 to 4 cups medium egg noodles, cooked and drained
- 1 cup shredded cheddar cheese

1. In a Dutch oven, cook beef and onions over medium heat until meat is no longer pink. Add garlic; cook 1 minute longer. Drain. Stir in the remaining ingredients except cheese.
2. Cover and bake at 350° for 1 hour or until bubbly. Sprinkle with cheese just before serving.

SLOW COOKER KALUA PORK & CABBAGE

My slow cooker pork has four ingredients and takes less than 10 minutes to prep. The result tastes just like the Kalua pork made in Hawaii that's slow roasted all day in an underground oven.
—Rholinelle DeTorres, San Jose, CA

Prep: 10 min. • **Cook:** 9 hours
Makes: 12 servings

7   **bacon strips, divided**
1   **boneless pork shoulder butt roast (3 to 4 pounds), well trimmed**
1   **tablespoon coarse sea salt**
1   **medium head cabbage (about 2 pounds), coarsely chopped**

1. Line bottom of a 6-qt. slow cooker with four bacon strips. Sprinkle all sides of roast with salt; place in slow cooker. Arrange the remaining bacon over top of roast.

2. Cook, covered, on low 8-10 hours or until pork is tender. Add cabbage, spreading cabbage around roast. Cook, covered, 1-1¼ hours longer or until cabbage is tender.

3. Remove pork to a serving bowl; shred pork with two forks. Using a slotted spoon, add cabbage to pork and toss to combine. If desired, skim fat from some of the cooking juices; stir juices into pork mixture or serve on the side.

CORN DOG CASSEROLE

Reminiscent of traditional corn dogs, this fun hot dish always hits the spot. It tastes especially good right from the oven.
—Marcy Suzanne Olipane, Belleville, IL

Prep: 25 min. • **Bake:** 30 min.
Makes: 12 servings

- 2 cups thinly sliced celery
- 2 tablespoons butter
- 1½ cups sliced green onions
- 1½ pounds hot dogs
- 2 large eggs
- 1½ cups 2% milk
- 2 teaspoons rubbed sage
- ¼ teaspoon pepper
- 2 packages (8½ ounces each) cornbread/muffin mix
- 2 cups (8 ounces) shredded sharp cheddar cheese, divided

1. In a small skillet, saute celery in butter 5 minutes. Add onions; saute 5 minutes longer or until vegetables are tender. Place in a large bowl; set aside.
2. Preheat oven to 400°. Cut hot dogs lengthwise into quarters, then cut into thirds. In the same skillet, saute hot dogs 5 minutes or until lightly browned; add to vegetables. Set aside 1 cup.
3. In a large bowl, whisk eggs, milk, sage and pepper. Add remaining hot dog mixture. Stir in cornbread mixes. Add 1½ cups cheese. Spread into a shallow 3-qt. baking dish. Top with reserved hot dog mixture and remaining cheese.
4. Bake, uncovered, 30 minutes or until golden brown.

EPIPHANY HAM

I wanted to cook a ham but didn't have the ingredients for my usual glaze recipe, so I made a few easy substitutions. You can, too! Instead of black cherry, try another flavored soda, or use sweet and sour sauce in place of duck sauce.
—Edith Griffith, Havre de Grace, MD

Prep: 10 min. • **Bake:** 3 hours
Makes: 12 servings

- 1 fully cooked bone-in ham (8 to 10 pounds; not spiral cut)
- 1 can (12 ounces) black cherry soda
- 2 teaspoons Chinese five-spice powder
- ⅔ cup duck sauce

1. Preheat oven to 350°. Place ham on a rack in a baking pan or dish; pour soda over ham. Sprinkle with five-spice powder. Cover ham with aluminum foil; bake for 30 minutes.
2. Remove foil and discard. Baste with duck sauce; return to oven and bake, uncovered, until a thermometer reads 140°, about 2½ hours, basting again halfway through baking.

LISA'S ALL-DAY SUGAR & SALT PORK ROAST

My family loves this tender, juicy roast on sandwiches. I include it on the menu often. The salty crust on the pork meat makes it extra delicious.

—Lisa Allen, Joppa, AL

Prep: 15 min. + marinating
Cook: 6¼ hours
Makes: 12 servings

- 1 cup plus 1 tablespoon sea salt, divided
- 1 cup granulated sugar
- 1 bone-in pork shoulder butt roast (6 to 8 pounds)
- ¼ cup barbecue seasoning
- ½ teaspoon pepper
- ½ cup packed brown sugar
- 12 hamburger buns or kaiser rolls, split

1. Combine 1 cup sea salt and granulated sugar; rub onto all sides of pork roast. Place roast in a shallow dish; refrigerate, covered, overnight.
2. Preheat oven to 300°. Using a kitchen knife, scrape salt and sugar coating from roast; discard any accumulated juices. Transfer pork to a large shallow roasting pan. Rub with barbecue seasoning; sprinkle with pepper. Roast until tender, 6-8 hours.
3. Increase oven temperature to 500°. Combine brown sugar and 1 tablespoon sea salt; sprinkle over cooked pork. Return pork to oven until a crisp crust forms, 10-15 minutes. Remove; when cool enough to handle, shred meat with two forks. Serve warm on fresh buns or rolls.

MAKE AHEAD

ZIPPY CHICKEN ENCHILADAS

Leftover chicken gets an awesome makeover in this rich and creamy casserole. This colorful dish is loaded with flavor. It's a nice change of pace from beef enchiladas.

—Julie Moutray, Wichita, KS

Prep: 15 min. • **Bake:** 35 min.
Makes: 10 servings

- 1 can (16 ounces) refried beans
- 10 flour tortillas (8 inches), warmed
- 1 can (10¾ ounces) condensed cream of chicken soup, undiluted
- 1 cup (8 ounces) sour cream
- 3 to 4 cups cubed cooked chicken
- 3 cups (12 ounces) shredded cheddar cheese, divided
- 1 can (15 ounces) enchilada sauce
- ¼ cup sliced green onions
- ¼ cup sliced ripe olives
  Shredded lettuce, optional

1. Spread about 2 tablespoons of beans on each tortilla. Combine soup and sour cream; stir in chicken. Spoon ⅓ to ½ cup down the center of each tortilla; top with 1 tablespoon cheese.
2. Roll up and place seam side down in a greased 13x9-in. baking dish. Pour enchilada sauce over top; sprinkle with the onions, olives and remaining cheese.
3. Bake enchiladas, uncovered, at 350° for 35 minutes or until heated through. If desired, sprinkle shredded lettuce around enchiladas just before serving.
Freeze option: Cover and freeze unbaked casserole. To use, partially thaw in refrigerator overnight. Remove from refrigerator 30 minutes before baking. Preheat oven to 350°. Bake casserole as directed, increasing time as necessary to heat through and for a thermometer inserted in center to read 165°.

GREEK PASTA & BEEF

This casserole gives everyday macaroni and cheese an international flavor. A co-worker who's a pro at Greek cooking shared the recipe.
—Dorothy Bateman, Carver, MA

....

Prep: 30 min. • **Bake:** 45 min.
Makes: 12 servings

- 1 package (16 ounces) elbow macaroni
- 1 pound ground beef
- 1 large onion, chopped
- 1 garlic clove, minced
- 1 can (8 ounces) tomato sauce
- ½ cup water
- 1 teaspoon salt
- ½ teaspoon ground cinnamon
- ¼ teaspoon ground nutmeg
- ¼ teaspoon pepper
- 1 large egg, lightly beaten
- ½ cup grated Parmesan cheese

SAUCE
- ¼ cup butter
- ¼ cup all-purpose flour
- ¼ teaspoon ground cinnamon
- 3 cups 2% milk
- 2 large eggs, lightly beaten
- ⅓ cup grated Parmesan cheese

1. Cook macaroni according to package directions. In a large skillet, cook beef and onion over medium heat until meat is no longer pink. Add garlic; cook 1 minute longer. Drain. Stir in the tomato sauce, water and seasonings. Cover and simmer for 10 minutes, stirring occasionally.

2. Drain macaroni and place in a large bowl. Stir in egg and cheese; set aside.

3. For sauce, in a large saucepan, melt butter; stir in flour and cinnamon until smooth. Gradually add milk. Bring to a boil over medium heat; cook and stir for 2 minutes or until slightly thickened. Remove from the heat. Stir a small amount of hot mixture into eggs; return all to pan, stirring constantly. Stir in Parmesan cheese.

4. In a greased 3-qt. baking dish, spread half of the macaroni mixture. Top with beef mixture and remaining macaroni mixture. Pour sauce over the top. Bake, uncovered, at 350° for 45-50 minutes or until a thermometer reads 160°. Let stand for 5 minutes before serving.

MAKE AHEAD
CHICKEN SWISS BUNDLES

 These yummy sandwich bundles, made with convenient frozen dinner rolls, are a favorite at our house. They're great hot from the oven but they also freeze well if you want to save them for later. I serve them with tomato soup.
—Trisha Kruse, Eagle, ID

....

Prep: 30 min. • **Bake:** 20 min.
Makes: 12 servings

- 1 small onion, finely chopped
- ½ cup sliced fresh mushrooms
- 1½ teaspoons butter
- 1 garlic clove, minced
- 1 cup cubed cooked chicken breast
- ½ cup chopped roasted sweet red peppers
- 1 tablespoon honey mustard
- ¼ teaspoon salt
- ¼ teaspoon lemon-pepper seasoning
- ¼ teaspoon Italian seasoning
- 2 cups (8 ounces) shredded Swiss cheese
- 12 frozen bread dough dinner rolls, thawed
- 2 tablespoons butter, melted

1. In a large skillet, saute the onion and mushrooms in butter until tender. Add the garlic; cook 1 minute longer. Add the chicken, peppers, mustard and seasonings; heat through. Remove from the heat; stir in cheese.

2. Flatten each roll into a 5-in. circle. Place ¼ cup chicken mixture in the center of six circles. Brush edges with water; top with remaining circles. Press edges with a fork to seal.

3. Place bundles on greased baking sheets; brush with melted butter. Bake at 350° for 18-22 minutes or until golden brown. Cut bundles in half to serve.

Freeze option: Cover and freeze unbaked bundles on a waxed paper-lined baking sheet until firm. Transfer to a resealable plastic freezer bag; return to freezer. To use, bake bundles as directed, increasing time as necessary to heat through.

BACON CHEESEBURGER BUNS

Try these stuffed pastries for a fun way to serve bacon cheeseburgers without the fuss of assembling sandwiches. Serve ketchup or barbecue sauce on the side for dipping.

—Marjorie Miller, Haven, KS

Prep: 1 hour + rising
Bake: 10 min.
Makes: 2 dozen

  2   packages (¼ ounce each)
      active dry yeast
  ⅔   cup warm water (110° to 115°)
  ⅔   cup warm milk (110° to 115°)
  ¼   cup sugar
  ¼   cup shortening
  2   large eggs
  2   teaspoons salt
  4½ to 5 cups all-purpose flour
FILLING
  1   pound sliced bacon, diced
  2   pounds ground beef
  1   small onion, chopped
  1½ teaspoons salt
  ½   teaspoon pepper
  1   pound process cheese
      (Velveeta), cubed
  3   to 4 tablespoons butter, melted
      Ketchup or barbecue sauce,
      optional

1. In a large bowl, dissolve yeast in warm water. Add the milk, sugar, shortening, eggs, salt and 3½ cups flour; beat until smooth. Stir in enough remaining flour to form a soft dough.
2. Turn onto a floured surface; knead until smooth and elastic, about 6-8 minutes. Place in a greased bowl, turning once to grease top. Cover and let rise in a warm place until doubled, about 1 hour.
3. Meanwhile, in a large skillet, cook bacon over medium heat until crisp. Using a slotted spoon, remove to paper towels. In a Dutch oven, cook the beef, onion, salt and pepper over medium heat until meat is no longer pink; drain. Add the bacon and cheese; cook and stir until cheese is melted. Remove from the heat.
4. Punch dough down. Turn onto a lightly floured surface; divide into fourths. Roll each portion into an 12x8-in. rectangle; cut each into six squares. Place ¼ cup meat mixture in the center of each square. Bring corners together in the center and pinch to seal.
5. Place 2 in. apart on greased baking sheets. Bake at 400° for 9-11 minutes or until lightly browned. Brush with butter. Serve warm, with ketchup if desired.

CHICKEN & RICE CASSEROLE

Everyone loves this casserole's tasty combination of hearty and crunchy ingredients mixed in a creamy sauce. It's a time-tested classic.

—Myrtle Matthews, Marietta, GA

Prep: 15 min. • **Bake:** 1 hour
Makes: 12 servings

  4   cups cooked white rice or a
      combination of wild and white rice
  4   cups diced cooked chicken
  ½   cup slivered almonds
  1   small onion, chopped
  1   can (8 ounces) sliced water
      chestnuts, drained
  1   package (10 ounces)
      frozen peas, thawed
  ¾   cup chopped celery
  1   can (10¾ ounces) condensed
      cream of celery soup, undiluted
  1   can (10¾ ounces) condensed
      cream of chicken soup, undiluted
  1   cup mayonnaise
  2   teaspoons lemon juice
  1   teaspoon salt
  2   cups crushed potato chips
      Paprika

1. Preheat oven to 350°. In a greased 13x9-in. baking dish, combine first seven ingredients. In a large bowl, combine soups, mayonnaise, lemon juice and salt. Pour over the chicken mixture and toss to coat.
2. Sprinkle with potato chips and paprika. Bake 1 hour or until heated through.

MATT'S JERK CHICKEN

Get ready for a trip to the islands! You may think jerk chicken is complicated, but all it takes is time. Put on some reggae tunes, grab an icy drink and prepare to be transported. If you have a smoker, smoke the chicken first and finish it on the grill.

—Jenn Hall, Collingswood, NJ

Prep: 25 min. + marinating
Grill: 50 minutes
Makes: 16 servings

- 1 large onion, chopped
- 3 green onions, chopped
- ¾ cup white vinegar
- ½ cup orange juice
- ¼ cup dark rum
- ¼ cup olive oil
- ¼ cup soy sauce
- 2 tablespoons lime juice
- 1 habanero or Scotch bonnet pepper, seeded and minced
- 2 tablespoons garlic powder
- 1 tablespoon sugar
- 1 tablespoon ground allspice
- 1 tablespoon dried thyme
- 1½ teaspoons cayenne pepper
- 1½ teaspoons rubbed sage
- 1½ teaspoons pepper
- ¾ teaspoon ground nutmeg
- ¾ teaspoon ground cinnamon
- 8 pounds bone-in chicken breast halves and thighs
- ½ cup whole allspice berries
- 1 cup applewood chips
- ½ cup ketchup

1. Process first 18 ingredients, covered, in a blender until smooth. Divide chicken into two large resealable plastic bags; pour half of onion mixture in each. Seal bags; turn to coat. Refrigerate overnight.

2. Soak allspice berries in water for 30 minutes. Drain the chicken, reserving 1½ cups marinade. Preheat grill and prepare for indirect heat. On a piece of heavy-duty foil (12 in. square), place soaked allspice berries; fold foil around berries to form a packet, crimping edges to seal. Using a small skewer, poke holes in packet. Repeat process for the applewood chips. Place packets over heat on grate of gas grill or in coals of charcoal grill.

3. Place chicken on greased grill rack, skin side down. Grill, covered, over indirect medium heat until a thermometer reads 165° when inserted into breasts and 170°-175° when inserted into thighs, about 50-60 minutes.

4. Meanwhile, in a small saucepan over high heat, bring the reserved marinade to a full rolling boil for at least 1 minute. Add ketchup; cook and stir until heated through. Remove from heat.

5. To serve Jamaican-style, remove meat from bones and chop with a cleaver. Toss chicken with sauce.

Freeze option: Arrange grilled chicken pieces in a greased 13x9-in. baking dish; add sauce. Cool; cover and freeze. To use, partially thaw in refrigerator overnight. Remove from refrigerator 30 minutes before baking. Preheat oven to 350°. Reheat chicken, covered, until a thermometer reads 165°, about 40-50 minutes.

❋
TEST KITCHEN TIP
Be warned—this dish is spicy! If you're sensitive to peppers, substitute jalapeno for the habanero or Scotch bonnet pepper. Don't skip the allspice berries on the grill. It's about as close as you can get to the flavor of the pimiento wood found in Jamaica. Don't scrape off the marinade before grilling. While it does prevent the chicken from getting really browned, it adds a lot of flavor.

LAYERED PICNIC LOAVES

This big sandwich is inspired by one I fell in love with at a New York deli. It's easy to make ahead of time and cart to any party. Kids and adults alike say it's super.
—Marion Lowery, Medford, OR

Prep: 15 min. + chilling
Makes: 2 loaves (12 servings each)

- 2 unsliced loaves (1 pound each) Italian bread
- ¼ cup olive oil
- 3 garlic cloves, minced
- 2 teaspoons Italian seasoning, divided
- ½ pound deli roast beef
- 12 slices part-skim mozzarella cheese (1 ounce each)
- 16 fresh basil leaves
- 3 medium tomatoes, thinly sliced
- ¼ pound thinly sliced salami
- 1 jar (6½ ounces) marinated artichoke hearts, drained and sliced
- 1 package (10 ounces) ready-to-serve salad greens
- 8 ounces thinly sliced deli chicken
- 1 medium onion, thinly sliced
- ¼ teaspoon salt
- ⅛ teaspoon pepper

1. Cut loaves in half horizontally; hollow out tops and bottoms, leaving ½-in. shells (discard removed bread or save for another use).
2. Combine oil and garlic; brush inside bread shells. Sprinkle with 1 teaspoon Italian seasoning. Layer bottom of each loaf with a fourth of the roast beef, mozzarella, basil, tomatoes, salami, artichokes, salad greens, chicken and onion. Repeat layers. Season with salt, pepper and remaining Italian seasoning.
3. If desired, drizzle with remaining oil mixture. Replace bread tops; wrap tightly in plastic wrap. Refrigerate at least 1 hour before slicing.

LEMON-BASIL TURKEY BREAST

Transform turkey into a season-spanning dish that's great for company with this fresh and citrusy version. It roasts up moist, tender and golden brown.
—Sharon Delaney-Chronis
South Milwaukee, WI

Prep: 20 min. • **Bake:** 2 hours
Makes: 12 servings

- 6 medium carrots
- 3 celery ribs
- 2 medium onions
- 2 cups reduced-sodium chicken broth
- 1 cup water
- 1 cup minced fresh basil
- 2 tablespoons grated lemon zest
- 4 garlic cloves, minced
- ½ teaspoon salt
- ½ teaspoon pepper
- 1 bone-in turkey breast (5 to 6 pounds)
- 2 medium lemons, sliced

1. Cut carrots and celery into 2-in. lengths; cut onions into wedges. Place in a roasting pan; add broth and water.
2. In a small bowl, combine the basil, lemon zest, garlic, salt and pepper. With fingers, carefully loosen skin from the turkey breast; rub mixture under the skin. Secure skin to underside of breast with toothpicks. Place the turkey breast over the carrot mixture. Place lemon slices over the skin.
3. Bake turkey, uncovered, at 325° for 2-2½ hours or until a thermometer reads 170°, basting every 30 minutes. Cover loosely with foil if turkey browns too quickly. Cover and let stand for 15 minutes before slicing. Serve with vegetables.

CURRIED CHICKEN TURNOVERS

Whenever I have leftover chicken, these turnovers are on the menu. The tasty secret is in the curry.
—Laverne Kohut, Manning, AB

Prep: 30 min. • **Bake:** 15 min.
Makes: 8 servings

- 1 cup finely chopped cooked chicken
- 1 medium apple, peeled and finely chopped
- ½ cup mayonnaise
- ¼ cup chopped cashews or peanuts
- 1 green onion, finely chopped
- 1 to 2 teaspoons curry powder
- ¼ teaspoon salt
- ¼ teaspoon pepper
- Pastry for double-crust pie
- 1 large egg, lightly beaten

1. Preheat oven to 425°. In a small bowl, combine the first eight ingredients. Divide dough into eight portions.
2. On a lightly floured surface, roll each portion into a 5-in. circle. Place about ¼ cup filling on one side. Moisten edges of pastry with water. Fold dough over filling; press edges with a fork to seal.
3. Place on greased baking sheets. Brush with egg. Cut ½-in. slits in top of each. Bake 15-20 minutes or until golden brown.
Pastry for double-crust pie (9 inches): Combine 2½ cups all-purpose flour and ½ tsp. salt; cut in 1 cup cold butter until crumbly. Gradually add ⅓ to ⅔ cup ice water, tossing with a fork until dough holds together when pressed. Wrap in plastic wrap and refrigerate 1 hour.

MAKE AHEAD
POLISH CASSEROLE

When I first made this dish, my 2-year-old son liked it so much that he asked for it for every meal! Since then, it's been a welcome addition to the dinner rotation. You can use almost any pasta that will hold the sauce.
—Crystal Jo Bruns, Iliff, CO

Prep: 25 min. • **Bake:** 45 min.
Makes: 2 casseroles (6 servings each)

- 4 cups uncooked penne pasta
- 1½ pounds smoked Polish sausage or kielbasa, cut into ½-inch slices
- 2 cans (10¾ ounces each) condensed cream of mushroom soup, undiluted
- 1 jar (16 ounces) sauerkraut, rinsed and well drained
- 3 cups (12 ounces) shredded Swiss cheese, divided
- 1⅓ cups 2% milk
- 4 green onions, chopped
- 2 tablespoons Dijon mustard
- 4 garlic cloves, minced

1. Preheat oven to 350°. Cook pasta according to package directions; drain and transfer to a large bowl. Stir in sausage, soup, sauerkraut, 2 cups cheese, milk, onions, mustard and garlic.
2. Spoon into two greased 8-in. square baking dishes; sprinkle with remaining cheese. Bake, uncovered, 45-50 minutes or until golden brown and bubbly.
Freeze option: Cover and freeze unbaked casserole up to 3 months. Thaw in the refrigerator overnight. Remove from refrigerator 30 minutes before baking. Preheat oven to 350°. Bake, uncovered, 50-55 minutes or until golden brown and bubbly.

Island Mango Slaw
page 130

Sides & Salads

When it comes to bring-a-dish parties, side dishes and salads are no-brainers. Use these simple but impressive ideas to make sure your contribution stands out. You'll even find buttery breads perfect for rounding out any buffet.

VEGETABLE & CHEESE FOCACCIA

My family eats this flavorful bread as fast as I can make it. Sometimes I may add different herbs, red onion or crumbled bacon. It's one of my best recipes!
—Mary Cass, Baltimore, MD

Prep: 20 min. + rising • **Bake:** 30 min.
Makes: 15 servings

  1   cup water (70° to 80°)
4½ teaspoons olive oil
4½ teaspoons sugar
  2   teaspoons dried oregano
1¼ teaspoons salt
3¼ cups bread flour
1½ teaspoons active dry yeast
TOPPING
  1   tablespoon olive oil
  1   tablespoon dried basil
  2   medium tomatoes, thinly sliced
  1   medium onion, thinly sliced
  1   cup frozen chopped
      broccoli, thawed
  ¼ teaspoon salt
  ¼ teaspoon pepper
  ¾ cup grated Parmesan cheese
  1   cup shredded part-skim
      mozzarella cheese

1. In bread machine pan, place the first seven ingredients in order suggested by manufacturer. Select dough setting; check dough after 5 minutes of mixing; add 1-2 tablespoons of water or flour if needed.

2. When cycle is completed, turn dough onto a lightly floured surface. Punch dough down. Roll into a 13x9-in. rectangle; transfer to a 13x9-in. baking dish coated with cooking spray.

3. For topping, brush dough with olive oil; sprinkle with basil. Layer with the tomatoes, onion and broccoli; sprinkle with salt, pepper and Parmesan cheese.

Cover and let rise in a warm place until doubled, about 30 minutes.

4. Bake at 350° for 20 minutes. Sprinkle with mozzarella cheese; bake 10-15 minutes longer or until golden brown and cheese is melted.

CREAMY CRANBERRY SALAD

One of my piano students taught me the perfect lesson in salad for the holidays. The keys are cranberries, pineapple, marshmallows and nuts.
—Alexandra Lypecky, Dearborn, MI

Prep: 15 min. + chilling
Makes: 16 servings (½ cup each)

  3   cups fresh or thawed frozen
      cranberries, chopped
  1   can (20 ounces) unsweetened
      crushed pineapple, drained
  2   cups miniature marshmallows
  1   medium apple, chopped
  ⅔ cup sugar
  ⅛ teaspoon salt
  2   cups heavy whipping cream
  ¼ cup chopped walnuts

1. In a large bowl, mix first six ingredients. Refrigerate, covered, overnight.

2. To serve, beat cream until stiff peaks form. Fold whipped cream and walnuts into cranberry mixture.

TEST KITCHEN TIP
Make it easy on yourself! Simply pulse cranberries in a food processor to chop them. To really bring the walnuts to life, toast them for a few minutes in a dry skillet. Stir occasionally and watch closely so they don't burn; remove from the heat when fragrant.

ORANGE GELATIN PRETZEL SALAD

Savory pretzels pair nicely with the sweet fruit in this refreshing layered salad. It's a family favorite, and it also makes a pretty potluck dish.

—Peggy Boyd, Northport, AL

Prep: 20 min. + chilling
Bake: 10 min. + cooling
Makes: 12 servings

- ¾ cup butter, melted
- 1 tablespoon plus ¾ cup sugar, divided
- 2 cups finely crushed pretzels
- 2 cups boiling water
- 2 packages (3 ounces each) orange gelatin
- 2 cans (8 ounces each) crushed pineapple, drained
- 1 can (11 ounces) mandarin oranges, drained
- 1 package (8 ounces) cream cheese, softened
- 2 cups whipped topping
  Additional whipped topping and mandarin oranges, optional

1. Preheat oven to 350°. Mix melted butter and 1 tablespoon sugar; stir in pretzels. Press onto bottom of an ungreased 13x9-in. baking dish. Bake 10 minutes. Cool completely on a wire rack.
2. In a large bowl, add boiling water to gelatin; stir 2 minutes to completely dissolve. Stir in fruit. Refrigerate until partially set, about 30 minutes.
3. Meanwhile, in a bowl, beat the cream cheese and remaining sugar until smooth. Fold in the whipped topping. Spread over the pretzel crust.
4. Gently spoon gelatin mixture over top. Refrigerate, covered, until firm, 2-4 hours. To serve, cut into squares. If desired, top with additional whipped topping and mandarin oranges.
Note: For single servings, prepare layers as directed. In each of twelve 9-oz. cups or ½-pint canning jars, layer about 2 tablespoons pretzel mixture, 2 tablespoons cream cheese mixture and ⅓ cup gelatin mixture. Refrigerate and top as directed.

ARROZ CON GANDULES (RICE WITH PIGEON PEAS)

Feed a crowd with this authentic Puerto Rican rice dish, which was handed down to me from my mom. It's a staple with the familia at all our gatherings.

—Evelyn Robles, Oak Creek, WI

Prep: 15 min. • **Cook:** 30 min.
Makes: 18 servings (¾ cup each)

- ½ cup sofrito
- 2 tablespoons canola oil
- 4 cups uncooked long grain rice
- 1 envelope Goya sazon with coriander and annatto
- 7 cups water
- 1 can (15 ounces) pigeon peas, drained
- 2 cans (5 ounces each) Vienna sausage, drained and chopped
- ½ cup tomato sauce
- 1¼ teaspoons salt
- 1 envelope Goya ham-flavored concentrate
- ½ teaspoon chicken bouillon granules
- ¼ teaspoon pepper

In a Dutch oven, combine sofrito and oil; cook over medium-low heat for 5 minutes, stirring occasionally. Add rice and sazon; cook and stir for 3-4 minutes or until the rice is lightly toasted. Add the remaining ingredients. Bring to a boil. Reduce heat; cover and simmer for 15-20 minutes or until rice is tender. Fluff with a fork.
Note: Sofrito is a cooking base frequently used in Puerto Rican recipes. Goya Sazon is a seasoning blend. Look for them in the international foods section.

GREAT GRAIN SALAD

I can't think of a better dish to round out a party buffet. My grain salad features all my favorite nuts, seeds and fruits. Try adding grilled chicken to make it a healthy one-dish meal.
—Rachel Dueker, Gervais, OR

Prep: 15 min. • **Cook:** 1 hour + chilling
Makes: 12 servings (¾ cup each)

- 3 cups water
- ½ cup medium pearl barley
- ½ cup uncooked wild rice
- ⅔ cup uncooked basmati rice
- ½ cup slivered almonds
- ½ cup sunflower kernels
- ½ cup salted pumpkin seeds or pepitas
- ½ cup each golden raisins, chopped dried apricots and dried cranberries
- ⅓ cup minced fresh parsley
- 4 teaspoons grated orange peel

VINAIGRETTE

- ⅔ cup walnut oil
- ⅔ cup raspberry vinegar
- 2 teaspoons orange juice
- 2 teaspoons pepper
- 1 teaspoon salt

1. In a large saucepan, bring water to a boil. Add barley and wild rice. Reduce heat; cover and simmer for 55-65 minutes or until tender. Meanwhile, cook basmati rice according to package directions. Cool barley and rices to room temperature.
2. In a large bowl, combine the almonds, sunflower kernels, pumpkin seeds, dried fruit, parsley and orange peel; add barley and rices.
3. In a small bowl, whisk the vinaigrette ingredients. Pour over salad and gently toss to coat. Cover and refrigerate for at least 2 hours.

SLOW-COOKED POTLUCK MACARONI & CHEESE

This no-fuss dish turns out rich, cheesy and extra creamy. Keep it in the slow cooker to make travel a snap!
—Jennifer Babcock, Chicopee, MA

Prep: 25 min. • **Cook:** 2 hours
Makes: 16 servings (¾ cup each)

- 3 cups uncooked elbow macaroni
- 1 package (16 ounces) process cheese (Velveeta), cubed
- 2 cups shredded Mexican cheese blend
- 2 cups shredded white cheddar cheese
- 1¾ cups whole milk
- 1 can (12 ounces) evaporated milk
- ¾ cup butter, melted
- 3 large eggs, lightly beaten

1. Cook macaroni according to package directions for al dente; drain. Transfer to a greased 5-qt. slow cooker. Stir in the remaining ingredients.
2. Cook mixture, covered, on low until a thermometer reads at least 160°, 2 to 2½ hours, stirring once.

PRETZEL-TOPPED SWEET POTATOES

Everyone I've shared this recipe with agrees that it's the tastiest way to serve sweet potatoes. I like to make it for special dinners...and even for brunch as a colorful go-with dish. The mingled sweet, tart and salty flavors are an unusual treat.
—Sue Mallory, Lancaster, PA

Prep: 20 min. • **Bake:** 25 min.
Makes: 12 servings

- 2 cups chopped pretzel rods (about 13)
- 1 cup chopped pecans
- 1 cup fresh or frozen cranberries
- 1 cup packed brown sugar
- 1 cup butter, melted, divided
- 1 can (2½ pounds) sweet potatoes, drained
- 1 can (5 ounces) evaporated milk
- ½ cup sugar
- 1 teaspoon vanilla extract

1. In a large bowl, combine the pretzels, pecans, cranberries, brown sugar and ½ cup butter; set aside.
2. In a large bowl, beat the sweet potatoes until smooth. Gradually add the milk, sugar, vanilla and remaining butter; beat until well blended.
3. Spoon into a greased shallow 2-qt. baking dish; sprinkle with pretzel mixture. Bake, uncovered, at 350° for 25-30 minutes or until the edges are bubbly.

MOIST POULTRY DRESSING

Tasty mushrooms and onions complement the big herb flavor in this crowd-pleasing side dish. It stays so moist because it's made in the slow cooker.
—Ruth Ann Stelfox, Raymond, AB

Prep: 20 min. • **Cook:** 4 hours
Makes: 16 servings

- 2 jars (4½ ounces each) sliced mushrooms, drained
- 4 celery ribs, chopped
- 2 medium onions, chopped
- ¼ cup minced fresh parsley
- ¾ cup butter, cubed
- 1½ pounds day-old bread, crusts removed and cubed (about 13 cups)
- 1½ teaspoons salt
- 1½ teaspoons rubbed sage
- 1 teaspoon poultry seasoning
- 1 teaspoon dried thyme
- ½ teaspoon pepper
- 2 large eggs
- 1 can (14½ ounces) chicken broth or 14½ ounces vegetable broth

1. In a large skillet, saute the mushrooms, celery, onions and parsley in butter until the vegetables are tender. In a large bowl, toss the bread cubes with salt, sage, poultry seasoning, thyme and pepper. Add the mushroom mixture. Combine eggs and broth; add to the bread mixture and toss.
2. Transfer to 5-qt. slow cooker. Cover and cook dressing on low for 4-5 hours or until a thermometer reads 160°.

Freeze option: Cover and freeze unbaked casserole. To use, partially thaw in refrigerator overnight. Remove from refrigerator 30 minutes before baking. Preheat oven to 350°. Cover casserole with foil; bake as directed, increasing covered time to 1¼-1½ hours or until heated through and a thermometer inserted in center reads 165°. Uncover; bake 15-20 minutes longer or until lightly browned. Just before serving, stir to combine and, if desired, sprinkle with additional parsley.

QUICK AND COLORFUL CORN-BEAN SALAD

This quick recipe couldn't be easier. Liquid from the corn relish makes an instant dressing! It's a perfect salad to bring to summer outings.
—TerryAnn Moore, Vineland, NJ

Start to Finish: 15 min.
Makes: 12 servings (½ cup each)

- 1 can (15 ounces) black beans, rinsed and drained
- 1 jar (13 ounces) corn relish
- ½ cup canned kidney beans
- ½ cup quartered cherry tomatoes
- ½ cup chopped celery
- ¼ cup chopped sweet orange pepper
- ¼ cup sliced pimiento-stuffed olives
- 2 teaspoons minced fresh parsley

In a large bowl, combine all ingredients. Cover and refrigerate until serving.

MAKE AHEAD
FAVORITE CHEESY POTATOES

What's a party without cheesy potatoes! My kids, husband and nephews love this version. I make a big batch in disposable pans and serve them at many of our get-togethers. The holidays aren't the same without them.
—Brenda Smith, Curran, MI

Prep: 30 min. • **Bake:** 45 min.
Makes: 12 servings (⅔ cup each)

- 3½ pounds potatoes (about 7 medium), peeled and cut into ¾-inch cubes
- 1 can (10½ ounces) condensed cream of potato soup, undiluted
- 1 cup French onion dip
- ¾ cup 2% milk
- ⅔ cup sour cream
- 1 teaspoon minced fresh parsley
- ¼ teaspoon salt
- ¼ teaspoon pepper
- 1 package (16 ounces) process cheese (Velveeta), cubed
    Additional minced fresh parsley

1. Preheat oven to 350°. Place potatoes in a Dutch oven; add water to cover. Bring to a boil. Reduce heat; cook, uncovered, 8-12 minutes or until tender. Drain. Cool the potatoes slightly.
2. In a large bowl, mix soup, onion dip, milk, sour cream, parsley, salt and pepper; gently fold in the potatoes and cheese. Transfer to a greased 13x9-in. baking dish.
3. Bake, covered, 30 minutes. Uncover; bake 15-20 minutes longer or until heated through and cheese is melted. Just before serving, stir to combine and sprinkle with additional parsley. (Potatoes will thicken upon standing.)

COLESLAW WITH POPPY SEED DRESSING

I love this slaw because I can keep it in the fridge for a couple of days and it just gets better. It packs lots of crunch and flavor for very little effort. If you prefer raisins or dried cranberries, toss some in.
—Trisha Kruse, Eagle, ID

Prep: 20 min. + chilling
Makes: 12 servings (¾ cup each)

½ medium head cabbage, shredded (about 4½ cups)
6 large carrots, shredded (about 4½ cups)
8 green onions, chopped (about 1 cup)
1 cup fat-free poppy seed salad dressing
⅓ cup sunflower kernels

In a large bowl, combine cabbage, carrots and green onions. Drizzle with dressing; toss to coat. Refrigerate, covered, at least 1 hour. Just before serving, top with the sunflower kernels.

4. Finely grate enough peel from oranges to measure 2 teaspoons; place in a large bowl. Cut a thin slice from the top and bottom of each orange; stand orange upright on a cutting board. With a knife, cut off peel and outer membrane from orange. Working over the same large bowl with orange peel to catch juices, cut along the membrane of each segment to remove fruit. Cut orange sections in half; stir into orange juice and peel. Add the cranberries, almonds, parsley, rice, quinoa and onion mixture.

5. In a small bowl, whisk oil, thyme, vinegar, salt and pepper until blended. Pour over rice mixture; toss to coat.

CHEESY SLOW-COOKED CORN

Even those who usually don't reach for corn at the table often ask for seconds once they try this side dish. Guests love the flavor, but I like how easy it is to make with ingredients I have on hand.
—Mary Ann Truitt, Wichita, KS

Prep: 5 min. • **Cook:** 3 hours
Makes: 12 servings

- 9½ cups (48 ounces) frozen corn
- 11 ounces cream cheese, softened
- ¼ cup butter, cubed
- 3 tablespoons water
- 3 tablespoons milk
- 2 tablespoons sugar
- 6 slices process American cheese, cut into small pieces

In a 4- or 5-qt. slow cooker, combine all ingredients. Cook, covered, on low, until heated through and cheese is melted, 3-4 hours, stirring once.

WILD RICE, QUINOA & CRANBERRY SALAD

For a fragrant side dish, we combined dried cranberries and oranges with some wild rice and quinoa. Add cooked turkey or chicken and turn it into a quick meal the next day.
—Jerilyn Korver, Bellflower, CA

Prep: 20 min. • **Cook:** 1 hour
Makes: 12 servings (¾ cup each)

- 2 cups uncooked wild rice
- 2 cartons (32 ounces each) reduced-sodium chicken broth, divided
- 1½ cups quinoa, rinsed
- 1 medium onion, chopped
- 4 garlic cloves, minced
- 2 medium navel oranges
- 1 cup dried cranberries
- 1 cup sliced almonds
- 2 tablespoons minced fresh parsley or 2 teaspoons dried parsley flakes
- 3 tablespoons olive oil
- 2 teaspoons minced fresh thyme or ½ teaspoon dried thyme
- 2 teaspoons rice vinegar
- 1 teaspoon salt
- ½ teaspoon pepper

1. Rinse wild rice thoroughly; drain. In a large saucepan, combine rice and 5 cups broth; bring to a boil. Reduce heat; simmer, covered, 60-70 minutes or until rice is fluffy and tender. Drain if necessary.
2. Meanwhile, in a small saucepan, bring remaining broth to a boil. Add quinoa. Reduce heat; simmer, covered, 15-20 minutes or until liquid is absorbed. Remove from heat; fluff with a fork.
3. Place a large nonstick skillet coated with cooking spray over medium-high heat. Add onion; cook and stir 6-8 minutes or until onion is tender. Add garlic; cook 1 minute longer.

WINTER PANZANELLA WITH APPLE DRESSING

Panzanella is my favorite salad, so I created this winter version featuring butternut squash, apple and cranberries.

—Julie Merriman, Seattle, WA

....

Prep: 30 min. • **Bake:** 30 min.
Makes: 14 servings (1 cup each)

1 medium butternut squash, peeled, seeded and cut into cubes
2 tablespoons olive oil, divided
   Dash each salt and pepper
1 loaf sourdough bread (1 pound), cut into cubes
2 tablespoons each minced fresh basil, cilantro and mint, divided
1 cup fresh arugula
1 medium apple, thinly sliced
1 small red onion, thinly sliced
½ cup dried cranberries
½ cup pitted Greek olives, sliced
2 tablespoons lime juice
1½ teaspoons grated lime peel

APPLE DRESSING
¼ cup chopped peeled apple
2 tablespoons honey, divided
1 tablespoon plus ½ cup olive oil, divided
¼ cup white balsamic vinegar
1 tablespoon apple brandy or apple cider
1 tablespoon Dijon mustard
¼ teaspoon salt
¼ teaspoon pepper

1. Place squash cubes in a 15x10x1-in. baking pan. Toss with 1 tablespoon olive oil and sprinkle with salt and pepper. Bake, uncovered, at 400° for 20-25 minutes or until tender and lightly browned, stirring occasionally. Remove from oven and cool.

2. In a large bowl, toss bread cubes with 1 tablespoon olive oil and 1 tablespoon each basil, cilantro and mint. Transfer cubes to a baking sheet. Bake at 400° for 10 minutes or until lightly browned, stirring occasionally. Set aside.

3. Place the cooled squash, arugula, apple slices, onion, cranberries, olives, lime juice and peel, croutons and remaining herbs in a large bowl.

4. In a skillet, cook apple in 1 tablespoon each honey and oil over medium heat until apple is softened and caramelized, stirring often. Transfer to a blender.

5. Add the vinegar, brandy, mustard, salt, pepper and remaining honey. Cover and process until pureed. While processing, gradually add remaining oil in a steady stream. Drizzle over salad; toss to coat.

CHERRY & FONTINA STUFFED PORTOBELLOS

I developed this hearty dish for my mushroom-lovin' kids. They're grown now with families of their own, but they still lobby for these when I need to bring a dish to pass to family parties.
—Wendy Rusch, Cameron, WI

Prep: 30 min. • **Bake:** 15 min.
Makes: 12 servings

- 6 large portobello mushrooms
- ½ cup butter, cubed
- 1 medium onion, chopped
- 1 cup pecan halves, toasted
- 1 package (5 ounces) dried tart cherries, coarsely chopped
- ½ teaspoon poultry seasoning
- ½ teaspoon dried thyme
- 7 ounces (about 4½ cups) seasoned stuffing cubes
- 1½ to 2 cups chicken broth
- 1½ cups (6 ounces) shredded fontina cheese, divided

1. Preheat oven to 375°. Wipe mushroom caps clean with a damp paper towel; remove stems and gills and discard. Place caps on a foil-lined 15x10-in. baking pan.
2. In a large skillet, melt the butter over medium heat until it begins to brown and smell nutty. Add onion; saute until translucent, stirring occasionally. Stir in pecans, cherries and seasonings; cook and stir 3 minutes. Remove from heat.
3. Combine onion mixture and stuffing cubes, tossing to coat evenly. Add 1½ cups broth to onion-stuffing mixture, stirring until well mixed. Add remaining broth as needed. Stir in 1 cup cheese.
4. Fill mushroom caps with stuffing until mounded, about 1 cup each. Sprinkle with remaining cheese. Bake until mushrooms

are heated through and cheese is melted, 15-20 minutes.

Note: To toast nuts, bake in a shallow pan in a 350° oven for 5-10 minutes or cook in a skillet over low heat until lightly browned, stirring nuts occasionally.

FENNEL-POTATO AU GRATIN

The tender potato slices in this cozy casserole have a mild fennel flavor with a hint of nutmeg. Add a creamy sauce and a sprinkling of Parmesan, and you have a homey side dish friends and family will ask for time and again.
—Karen Haen, Sturgeon Bay, WI

Prep: 40 min. • **Bake:** 1¼ hours
Makes: 12 servings

- 9 cups sliced peeled potatoes
- 2 medium fennel bulbs, sliced
- 1 tablespoon butter
- 2 tablespoons all-purpose flour
- 1¼ cups chicken broth
- 1 cup heavy whipping cream
- 1 teaspoon salt
- ½ teaspoon pepper
- ¼ teaspoon ground nutmeg
- ¾ cup shredded Parmesan cheese

1. In a greased 3-qt. baking dish, combine the potatoes and fennel; set aside.
2. In a small saucepan, melt butter. Stir in flour until smooth; gradually add the broth, cream, salt, pepper and nutmeg. Bring to a boil; cook and stir for 2 minutes or until thickened. Pour over the potato mixture; gently toss to coat.
3. Cover and bake at 350° for 1 hour or until potatoes are tender. Uncover; sprinkle with cheese. Bake 15 minutes longer or until cheese is melted.

1 pound fresh mushrooms, sliced
⅓ cup chicken broth
1 tablespoon all-purpose flour
½ cup evaporated milk
4 packages (10 ounces each) frozen chopped spinach, thawed and squeezed dry
2 cans (14½ ounces each) diced tomatoes, drained
2 cans (14 ounces each) water-packed artichoke hearts, rinsed, drained and thinly sliced
1 cup (8 ounces) sour cream
½ cup mayonnaise
3 tablespoons lemon juice
½ teaspoon garlic powder
¼ teaspoon salt
¼ teaspoon pepper
Paprika, optional

1. In a large skillet, cook mushrooms and broth over medium heat until tender, about 3 minutes. Remove mushrooms with a slotted spoon and set aside.
2. Whisk flour and milk until smooth; add to skillet. Bring to a boil; cook and stir for 2 minutes. Remove from the heat; stir in spinach, tomatoes and mushrooms.
3. Place half of the artichokes in an ungreased 13x9-in. baking dish. Top with half of the spinach mixture. Repeat layers. Combine sour cream, mayonnaise, lemon juice, garlic powder, salt and pepper; dollop mixture over casserole. Sprinkle with paprika if desired.
4. Bake, uncovered, at 350° for 25-30 minutes or until bubbly.

POMEGRANATE PERSIMMON SALAD

To bring some sunshine to the table, I toss up a bright salad of persimmons and pomegranate seeds, dressed with a quick vinaigrette.
—Linda Tambunan, Dublin, CA

Start to Finish: 15 min.
Makes: 12 servings

½ cup olive oil
½ cup maple syrup
¼ cup rice vinegar
2 tablespoons Dijon mustard
¼ teaspoon salt
¼ teaspoon pepper
SALAD
3 ripe Fuyu persimmons or 3 plums, sliced
2 packages (10 ounces each) baby kale salad blend
1 cup pomegranate seeds

1. Place first six ingredients in a jar with a lid; shake well. Refrigerate until serving.
2. To serve, shake vinaigrette and toss ½ cup with persimmons. Toss remaining vinaigrette with salad blend. Top with persimmons and pomegranate seeds.

ARTICHOKE SPINACH CASSEROLE

Although he isn't a fan of spinach, my husband loves this dish. The combination of ingredients may sound unusual, but the flavors meld well. It's an excellent side for a formal dinner with friends.
—Judy Johnson, Missoula, MT

Prep: 25 min. • **Bake:** 25 min.
Makes: 14 servings

½ jalapeno pepper, seeded
   and coarsely chopped
¼ teaspoon pepper

In a serving bowl, combine first eight ingredients. Process dressing ingredients in a blender until smooth. Toss dressing with slaw at least 30 minutes before serving. Refrigerate.

GREEN BEANS WITH PEPPERS

We created this festive side that's simple to make for a large dinner with friends.
—*Taste of Home* Test Kitchen

Start to Finish: 20 min.
Makes: 12 servings (¾ cup each)

2 pounds fresh green
   beans, trimmed
2 tablespoons olive oil
2 medium sweet red peppers,
   finely chopped (about 2 cups)
1 small onion, finely chopped
3 tablespoons chopped fresh basil
   or 1 tablespoon dried basil
¾ teaspoon salt
¼ teaspoon pepper

1. In a large saucepan, place steamer basket over 1 in. of water. Place beans in batches in basket. Bring water to a boil. Reduce heat to maintain a simmer; steam, covered, 6-8 minutes or until crisp-tender.
2. In a nonstick skillet, heat oil the over medium-high heat. Add red peppers and onion; cook and stir until tender. Add beans, basil, salt and pepper; toss to coat.

ISLAND MANGO SLAW

The cooling effect of mango and Greek yogurt meets jalapeno spice in this snappy take on a slaw. You may want to buy your mango a day or two ahead to ensure it's at peak ripeness.
—Jenn Hall, Collingswood, NJ

Prep: 25 min. + chilling
Makes: 12 servings

½ medium head Savoy cabbage,
   thinly sliced into 3-inch
   strips (about 8 cups)
½ small head red cabbage,
   thinly sliced into 3-inch
   strips (about 6 cups)
2 medium carrots, cut into
   thin 2-inch strips
1 small sweet yellow pepper,
   cut into thin 2-inch strips
1 small sweet red pepper, cut
   into thin 2-inch strips
1 small red onion, halved
   and thinly sliced
½ medium mango, peeled, cut
   into thin 2-inch strips
½ jalapeno pepper, seeded
   and finely chopped
DRESSING
½ cup plain Greek yogurt
¼ cup thawed orange
   juice concentrate
4 teaspoons lime juice
½ teaspoon olive oil
½ medium mango, peeled
   and coarsely chopped
2 teaspoons minced
   fresh gingerroot
1 teaspoon kosher salt

BAKED TWO-CHEESE & BACON GRITS

To a southerner, grits are a true staple. Combine them with bacon and cheese, and even northerners will be asking for a second helping.
—Melissa Rogers, Tuscaloosa, AL

Prep: 25 min. • **Bake:** 40 min. + standing
Makes: 12 servings

- 6 thick-sliced bacon strips, chopped
- 3 cups water
- 3 cups chicken stock
- 1 teaspoon garlic powder
- ½ teaspoon pepper
- 2 cups quick-cooking grits
- 12 ounces process cheese (Velveeta), cubed (about 2⅓ cups)
- ½ cup butter, cubed
- ½ cup 2% milk
- 4 large eggs, lightly beaten
- 2 cups shredded white cheddar cheese

1. Preheat oven to 350°. In a large saucepan, cook bacon over medium heat until crisp, stirring occasionally. Remove pan from heat. Remove bacon with a slotted spoon; drain on paper towels.

2. Add water, stock, garlic powder and pepper to bacon drippings; bring to a boil. Slowly stir in the grits. Reduce heat to medium-low; cook, covered, 5-7 minutes or until thickened, stirring occasionally. Remove from heat.

3. Add process cheese and butter; stir until melted. Stir in milk. Slowly stir in the eggs until blended. Transfer to a greased 13x9-in. baking dish. Sprinkle with bacon and shredded cheese. Bake, uncovered, 40-45 minutes or until edges are golden brown and cheese is melted. Let stand 10 minutes before serving.

Freeze option: Cool unbaked casserole; cover and freeze. To use, partially thaw in refrigerator overnight. Remove casserole from refrigerator 30 minutes before baking. Preheat oven to 350°. Bake grits as directed, increasing time to 50-60 minutes or until heated through and a thermometer inserted in center reads 165°.

WATERCRESS & ORANGE SALAD

Keep this recipe on hand for when you need to make a special salad in a hurry. The citrus vinaigrette adds a refreshing taste to the greens and oranges.
—Alpha Wilson, Roswell, NM

Start to Finish: 20 min.
Makes: 12 servings

- 3 bunches watercress, trimmed (about 10 cups)
- 4 medium oranges, peeled and sectioned
- ¼ cup olive oil
- 3 tablespoons orange juice
- 2 teaspoons grated orange peel
- ½ teaspoon lemon juice
- ¼ teaspoon sugar
- ⅛ teaspoon salt
  Dash pepper

In a large bowl, combine watercress and oranges. In a small bowl, whisk the remaining ingredients. Drizzle over salad; toss to coat.

VEGETABLE NOODLE CASSEROLE

If you're looking for a filling side dish, look no further. My recipe combines nutritious vegetables and hearty noodles in a delectable cream sauce. Whenever I serve it, the pan is scraped clean.
—Jeanette Hios, Brooklyn, NY

Prep: 15 min. • **Bake:** 45 min.
Makes: 14 servings

- 1 can (10¾ ounces) condensed cream of chicken soup, undiluted
- 1 can (10¾ ounces) condensed cream of broccoli soup, undiluted
- 1½ cups 2% milk
- 1 cup grated Parmesan cheese, divided
- 3 garlic cloves, minced
- 2 tablespoons dried parsley flakes
- ½ teaspoon pepper
- ¼ teaspoon salt
- 1 package (16 ounces) wide egg noodles, cooked and drained
- 1 package (16 ounces) frozen California-blend vegetables, thawed
- 2 cup frozen corn, thawed

1. Preheat oven to 350°. In a large bowl, combine soups, milk, ¾ cup cheese, garlic, parsley, pepper and salt. Stir in the noodles, vegetable blend and corn.
2. Pour into a greased 13x9-in. baking dish. Sprinkle with remaining cheese. Cover and bake 45-50 minutes or until heated through.

SWISS CHEESE BREAD

This bread will receive rave reviews, whether you serve it as an appetizer or with a meal. For real convenience, you can make it ahead of time and freeze it!
—Karla Boice, Mahtomedi, MN

Start to Finish: 30 min.
Makes: 24 servings

- 1 loaf (18-20 inches) French bread
- 8 ounces (2 sticks) butter, softened
- 2 cups shredded Swiss cheese
- ¾ teaspoon celery seed
- ¾ teaspoon garlic powder
- 3 tablespoons dried parsley flakes

1. Cut the bread in half. Make diagonal cuts, 1 in. thick, through bread but not through bottom. Combine all remaining ingredients. Spread half of the butter mixture between the bread slices. Spread the remaining mixture over the top and sides of bread.
2. Place bread on double thickness of foil; cover loosely with additional foil. Bake at 425° for 20-30 minutes. For the last 5 minutes, remove foil covering bread to allow it to brown.

CORN STUFFING BALLS

My mom had many winning recipes, and this was one of our family's favorites. I can still picture these serving-size balls encircling the large meat platter piled high with one of her delicious entrees.
—Audrey Groe, Lake Mills, IA

Prep: 20 min. • **Bake:** 30 min.
Makes: 12 servings

- 6 cups herb-seasoned stuffing croutons
- 1 cup chopped celery
- ½ cup chopped onion
- ¾ cup butter, divided
- 1 can (14¾ ounces) cream-style corn
- 1 cup water
- 1½ teaspoons poultry seasoning
- ¾ teaspoon salt
- ¼ teaspoon pepper
- 3 large eggs yolks, beaten

Place croutons in a large bowl and set aside. In a skillet, saute celery and onion in ½ cup butter. Add the corn, water, poultry seasoning, salt and pepper; bring to a boil. Remove from the heat; cool for 5 minutes. Pour over croutons. Add egg yolks and mix gently. Shape ½ cupfuls into balls; flatten slightly. Place in a greased 15x10x1-in. baking pan. Melt remaining butter; drizzle over stuffing balls. Bake, uncovered, at 375° for 30 minutes or until stuffing is lightly browned.

BUTTERNUT SQUASH ROLLS

With their cheery yellow color and delicious aroma, these appealing rolls will brighten any buffet table. I've found this recipe is a great way to utilize squash from the garden.
—Bernice Morris, Marshfield, MO

Prep: 30 min. + rising • **Bake:** 20 min.
Makes: 2 dozen

- 1 package (¼ ounce) active dry yeast
- 1 cup warm whole milk (110° to 115°)
- ¼ cup warm water (110° to 115°)
- 3 tablespoons butter, softened
- 2 teaspoons salt
- ½ cup sugar
- 1 cup mashed cooked butternut squash
- 5 to 5½ cups all-purpose flour, divided

1. In a large bowl, dissolve yeast in milk and water. Add the butter, salt, sugar, squash and 3 cups flour; beat until smooth. Add enough remaining flour to form a soft dough.
2. Turn onto a floured surface; knead until smooth and elastic, 6-8 minutes. Place in a greased bowl, turning once to grease top. Cover and let rise in a warm place until doubled, about 1 hour.
3. Punch dough down. Form into 24 rolls; place in two greased 10-in. cast-iron skillets or 9-in. round baking pans. Cover the rolls and let rise until doubled, about 30 minutes.
4. Bake at 375° for 20-25 minutes or until golden brown.

CUMIN-ROASTED CARROTS

Carrots make a super side—big on flavor and a breeze to cook. Plus, I can actually get my husband to eat these spiced veggies.
—Taylor Kiser, Brandon, FL

Prep: 20 min. • **Cook:** 35 min.
Makes: 12 servings

- 2 **tablespoons coriander seeds**
- 2 **tablespoons cumin seeds**
- 3 **pounds carrots, peeled and cut into 4x½-inch sticks**
- 3 **tablespoons coconut oil or butter, melted**
- 8 **garlic cloves, minced**
- 1 **teaspoon salt**
- ½ **teaspoon pepper**
  Minced fresh cilantro, optional

1. Preheat oven to 400°. In a dry small skillet, toast coriander and cumin seeds over medium heat 45-60 seconds or until aromatic, stirring frequently. Cool slightly. Grind in a spice grinder, or with a mortar and pestle, until finely crushed.
2. Place carrots in a large bowl. Add melted coconut oil, garlic, salt, pepper and crushed spices, and toss to coat. Divide carrots between two 15x10x1-in. baking pans coated with cooking spray, spreading evenly.
3. Roast 35-40 minutes or until crisp-tender and lightly browned, stirring and rotating pans halfway. Before serving, sprinkle with cilantro if desired.

Note: Two tablespoons each ground coriander and ground cumin may be substituted for whole spices. Before using, toast ground spices in a dry skillet until aromatic, stirring frequently.

MAKE AHEAD
DELUXE HASH BROWN CASSEROLE

My son-in-law gave me the recipe for this casserole with hash browns, which my kids say is addictive. It's also an amazing make-ahead dish for potlucks and such.
—Amy Oswalt, Burr, NE

Prep: 10 min. • **Bake:** 50 min.
Makes: 12 servings

- 1½ **cups sour cream onion dip**
- 1 **can (10¾ ounces) condensed cream of chicken soup, undiluted**
- 1 **envelope ranch salad dressing mix**
- 1 **teaspoon onion powder**
- 1 **teaspoon garlic powder**
- ½ **teaspoon pepper**
- 1 **package (30 ounces) frozen shredded hash brown potatoes, thawed**
- 2 **cups shredded cheddar cheese**
- ½ **cup crumbled cooked bacon**

Preheat oven to 375°. In a large bowl, mix the first six ingredients; stir in potatoes, cheese and bacon. Transfer to a greased 13x9-in. baking dish. Bake 50-60 minutes or until golden brown.

Freeze option: Cover and freeze unbaked casserole. To use, partially thaw in refrigerator overnight. Remove from refrigerator 30 minutes before baking. Preheat oven to 375°. Bake casserole as directed, increasing time to 1¼-1½ hours or until the top is golden brown and a thermometer inserted in center of casserole reads 165°.

LAYERED SALAD FOR A CROWD

I once took this salad to a luncheon honoring our school district's food service manager, and she asked for the recipe! I make the dressing the day before so the flavors blend.
—Linda Ashley, Leesburg, GA

Start to Finish: 20 min.
Makes: 20 servings

1 cup mayonnaise
¼ cup whole milk
2 teaspoons dill weed
½ teaspoon seasoning blend
1 bunch romaine, torn
2 medium carrots, grated
1 cup chopped red onion
1 medium cucumber, sliced
1 package (10 ounces) frozen peas, thawed
1½ cups shredded cheddar cheese
8 bacon strips, cooked and crumbled

1. For dressing, in a small bowl, whisk the first four ingredients.
2. In a 4-qt. clear glass serving bowl, layer the romaine, carrots, onion and cucumber (do not toss). Pour dressing over the top; sprinkle with peas, cheese and bacon. Cover and refrigerate until serving.
Note: This recipe was tested with Nature's Seasons seasoning blend by Morton. Look for it in the spice aisle.

INTERNATIONAL POTATO CAKE

Over the years, I've made this potato cake with lamb, ham and hard salami. It's a perfect side for a group lunch or a bring-a-dish dinner party.
—Judy Batson, Tampa, FL

Prep: 40 min. • **Bake:** 35 min. + cooling
Makes: 12 servings

¼ cup seasoned bread crumbs
3 pounds potatoes (about 9 medium), peeled and cubed
½ cup heavy whipping cream
¼ cup butter, cubed
3 large eggs, beaten
1 teaspoon Greek seasoning
¼ teaspoon garlic salt
¼ teaspoon lemon-pepper seasoning
¼ pound thinly sliced fontina cheese
¼ pound thinly sliced hard salami, coarsely chopped

TOPPING
⅓ cup grated Parmesan cheese
1 tablespoon seasoned bread crumbs
1 tablespoon butter, melted

1. Sprinkle seasoned bread crumbs onto the bottom of a greased 9-in. springform pan; set aside.
2. Place potatoes in a large saucepan and cover with water. Bring to a boil. Reduce heat; cover and simmer 10-15 minutes or until tender. Drain; transfer to a large bowl. Mash potatoes with cream, butter, eggs and seasonings.
3. Preheat oven to 350°. Spoon half the potatoes into prepared pan. Layer with cheese and salami; top with remaining potatoes. Combine topping ingredients; spoon over potatoes.
4. Cover and bake 30 minutes. Uncover; bake 5-10 minutes longer or until topping is golden brown and a thermometer reads 160°. Cool on a wire rack 10 minutes. Carefully run a knife around edge of pan to loosen; remove sides of pan. Serve warm.

DELUXE GERMAN POTATO SALAD

I make this salad for all occasions because it goes well with any kind of meat. I often take the warm salad to bring-a-dish events, and there are rarely leftovers!
—Betty Perkins, Hot Springs, AR

....

Start to Finish: 30 min.
Makes: 16 servings

- ½ pound sliced bacon, diced
- 1 cup thinly sliced celery
- 1 cup chopped onion
- 1 cup sugar
- 2 tablespoons all-purpose flour
- 1 teaspoon salt
- ¾ teaspoon ground mustard
- 1 cup cider vinegar
- ½ cup water
- 5 pounds unpeeled small red potatoes, cooked and sliced
- 2 medium carrots, shredded
- 2 tablespoons minced fresh parsley
  Additional salt, optional

1. In a large skillet, cook the bacon over medium heat until it is crisp. Remove bacon to paper towels. Drain the skillet, reserving ¼ cup drippings. Saute celery and onion in drippings until tender.

2. In a large bowl, combine the sugar, flour, salt, mustard, vinegar and water until smooth. Add to the skillet. Bring to a boil. Cook and stir for 1-2 minutes until sauce is thickened.

3. In a large serving bowl, combine the potatoes, carrots and parsley. Drizzle with warm sauce and stir gently to coat. Season with additional salt if desired. Crumble the bacon; sprinkle on salad. Serve warm. Refrigerate leftovers.

GARLIC HERB BUBBLE LOAF

I adapted an old sour cream bread recipe for this deliciously different pull-apart loaf that smells heavenly while baking. It has a light crust, tender interior and lots of herb and butter flavor. We think it's simply wonderful!
—Katie Crill, Priest River, ID

....

Prep: 25 min. + rising • **Bake:** 35 min.
Makes: 1 loaf (18 servings)

- ½ cup water (70° to 80°)
- ½ cup sour cream
- 2 tablespoons butter, softened
- 3 tablespoons sugar
- 1½ teaspoons salt
- 3 cups bread flour
- 2¼ teaspoons active dry yeast

GARLIC HERB BUTTER
- ¼ cup butter, melted
- 4 garlic cloves, minced
- ¼ teaspoon each dried oregano, thyme and rosemary, crushed

1. In bread machine pan, place the first seven ingredients in order suggested by manufacturer. Select dough setting; check dough after 5 minutes of mixing; add 1 to 2 tablespoons of water or flour if needed.

2. When cycle is completed, turn dough onto a lightly floured surface. Cover and let rest for 15 minutes. Divide dough into 36 pieces. Shape each piece into a ball. In a shallow bowl, combine butter, garlic and herbs. Dip each ball in mixture; place in an ungreased 9x5-in. loaf pan. Cover and let rise in a warm place until doubled, about 45 minutes.

3. Bake at 375° for 35-40 minutes or until golden brown (cover loosely with foil if bread browns too quickly). Remove from pan to a wire rack. Serve warm.

Note: We recommend you do not use a bread machine's time-delay feature for this recipe.

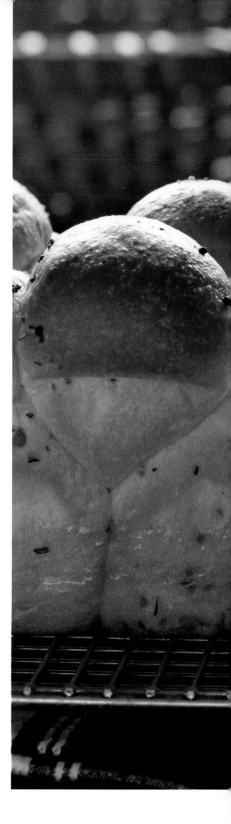

CITRUS SWEET POTATOES

A mild orange glaze lets the flavor of sweet potatoes shine through in this nut-topped side dish. When I was dating my husband, my mother would make this whenever he'd come over for Sunday dinner. We've been married more than 40 years and he thinks I still make it as well as Mom did.

—Pauline Kelley, St. Peters, MO

Prep: 1 hour • **Bake:** 30 min.
Makes: 12 servings

6 medium sweet potatoes, peeled
⅓ cup packed brown sugar
1 tablespoon cornstarch
1 cup orange juice concentrate
2 teaspoons grated lemon peel
½ cup chopped pecans, optional

1. Place the sweet potatoes in a large saucepan; cover with water. Bring to a boil. Reduce heat; cover and simmer for 40-45 minutes or until tender. Drain and cool. Cut into ½-in. slices. Place in a greased 13 x9-in. baking dish.
2. In a small saucepan, combine brown sugar and cornstarch. Whisk in orange juice concentrate and lemon peel. Bring to a boil; cook and stir for 1-2 minutes or until thickened. Pour over sweet potatoes. Sprinkle with pecans if desired.
3. Bake, uncovered, at 325° for 30-35 minutes or until sweet potatoes are heated through and sauce is bubbly.

GREEN BEAN–CHERRY TOMATO SALAD

My grandmother made a cold green bean salad with potatoes for every family barbecue. Now I bring my own version of the recipe to parties. With added color and taste from the cherry tomatoes, the classic dish is even better.

—Angela Lemoine, Howell, NJ

Prep: 25 min. • **Cook:** 10 min.
Makes: 12 servings

1½ pounds fresh green beans, trimmed
1 pint cherry tomatoes, halved
1 small red onion, halved and thinly sliced
3 tablespoons red wine vinegar
1½ teaspoons sugar
¾ teaspoon dried oregano
¾ teaspoon salt
¼ teaspoon garlic powder
¼ teaspoon pepper
¼ cup olive oil

1. In a 6-qt. stockpot, bring 6 cups water to a boil. Add beans in batches; cook, uncovered, 2-3 minutes or just until crisp-tender. Remove the beans and immediately drop into ice water. Drain and pat dry.
2. Transfer beans to a large bowl. Add tomatoes and onion; toss to combine. In a small bowl, whisk vinegar, sugar, oregano, salt, garlic powder and pepper. Gradually whisk in oil until blended. Pour over bean mixture; toss to coat.

CHEESY CORN SPOON BREAD

Homey and comforting, this moist side dish, almost like a souffle, is a favorite at potlucks and large dinners. The jalapeno pepper adds just the right bite. Second helpings of this tasty casserole are common—leftovers aren't.
—Katherine Franklin, Carbondale, IL

Prep: 15 min. • **Bake:** 35 min.
Makes: 15 servings

- ¼ cup butter, cubed
- 1 medium onion, chopped
- 2 large eggs
- 2 cups (16 ounces) sour cream
- 1 can (15¼ ounces) whole kernel corn, drained
- 1 can (14¾ ounces) cream-style corn
- ¼ teaspoon salt
- ¼ teaspoon pepper
- 1 package (8½ ounces) corn bread/muffin mix
- 2 medium jalapeno peppers, divided
- 2 cups shredded cheddar cheese, divided

1. Preheat oven to 375°. In a large skillet, heat butter over medium-high heat. Add onion; saute until tender. Set aside.
2. Beat eggs; add sour cream, both cans of corn, salt and pepper. Stir in corn bread mix just until blended. Mince 1 jalapeno pepper; fold into corn mixture with sauteed onion and 1½ cups of cheese.
3. Transfer to a greased shallow 3-qt. baking dish. Sprinkle with remaining cheese. Bake, uncovered, until a toothpick inserted in center comes out clean, 35-40 minutes; cool slightly. Slice remaining jalapeno; sprinkle over dish.
Note: Wear disposable gloves when cutting hot peppers; the oils can burn skin. Avoid touching your face.

CAULIFLOWER AU GRATIN

A lighter version of a classic white sauce coats the cauliflower in this perfect potluck buffet dish. Thick and creamy with a golden brown top layer, it's a super side dish that tastes just as comforting as it looks.
—*Taste of Home* Test Kitchen

Prep: 30 min. • **Bake:** 30 min.
Makes: 12 servings

- 3 packages (16 ounces each) frozen cauliflower, thawed
- 1 large onion, chopped
- ⅓ cup butter, cubed
- ⅓ cup all-purpose flour
- ½ teaspoon salt
- ¼ teaspoon ground mustard
- ¼ teaspoon pepper
- 2 cups fat-free milk
- ½ cup grated Parmesan cheese

TOPPING
- ½ cup soft whole wheat bread crumbs
- 2 tablespoons butter, melted
- ¼ teaspoon paprika

1. Place 1 in. of water in a Dutch oven; add cauliflower. Bring to a boil. Reduce heat; cover and cook for 4-6 minutes or until crisp-tender. Drain and pat dry.
2. Meanwhile, in a large saucepan, saute onion in butter until tender. Stir in the flour, salt, mustard and pepper until blended; gradually add milk. Bring to a boil; cook and stir for 1-2 minutes or until thickened. Remove from the heat. Add cheese; stir until melted.
3. Place cauliflower in a 13x9-in. baking dish coated with cooking spray. Pour sauce over top.
4. For topping, combine the bread crumbs, butter and paprika. Sprinkle over sauce. Bake, uncovered, at 350° for 30-35 minutes or until bubbly.

FESTIVE FALL TORTELLINI TOSS

I love mushrooms, squash, apples and walnuts, so I combined them with pasta to make this delicious side. You can easily double the recipe, and it tastes great served up warm or at room temperature.
—Roxanne Chan, Albany, CA

Prep: 25 min. • **Cook:** 10 min.
Makes: 12 servings (⅔ cup each)

- 1 package (9 ounces) refrigerated cheese tortellini
- 2 tablespoons olive oil
- ½ pound sliced baby portobello mushrooms
- 1¾ cups cubed peeled butternut squash (about ¼-inch cubes)
- ½ teaspoon poultry seasoning
- 1 medium tart apple, chopped
- 3 tablespoons thawed apple juice concentrate
- 3 tablespoons cider vinegar
- 1 green onion, thinly sliced
- ⅓ cup chopped walnuts, toasted
- ⅓ cup cubed smoked Gouda cheese (about ¼-inch cubes)
- 2 tablespoons minced fresh parsley

1. Cook tortellini according to package directions. In a large skillet, heat oil over medium-high heat. Add mushrooms, squash and poultry seasoning; cook and stir 6-8 minutes or until the mushrooms are tender.
2. Add the chopped apple, apple juice concentrate, vinegar and onion; cook 2-3 minutes longer or until squash is tender.
3. Drain the tortellini; rinse with cold water and place in a large bowl. Add the squash mixture, walnuts, cheese and parsley; toss gently to coat.

PULL-APART BACON BREAD

I stumbled across this recipe while looking for something different to take to a brunch. Boy, am I glad I did! Everyone who asked for the recipe was surprised it only called for five ingredients. It's the perfect treat to bake for an informal get-together.
—Traci Collins, Cheyenne, WY

Prep: 20 min. + rising • **Bake:** 55 min.
Makes: 1 loaf

- 12 bacon strips, diced
- 1 loaf (1 pound) frozen bread dough, thawed
- 2 tablespoons olive oil, divided
- 1 cup shredded part-skim mozzarella cheese
- 1 envelope (1 ounce) ranch salad dressing mix

1. In a large skillet, cook bacon over medium heat for 5 minutes or until partially cooked; drain on paper towels. Roll out dough to ½-in. thickness; brush with 1 tablespoon of oil. Cut into 1-in. pieces; place in a large bowl. Add the bacon, cheese, dressing mix and remaining oil; toss to coat.

2. Arrange pieces in a 9x5-in. oval on a parchment paper-lined baking sheet, layering as needed. Cover and let rise in a warm place for 30 minutes or until doubled.

3. Bake at 350° for 40 minutes. Cover with foil; bake bread 15 minutes longer or until golden brown.

ROASTED BALSAMIC SWEET POTATOES

By the end of summer, I'm done with the usual potato salad. This warm, spicy side kicks off cozy season.
—Karen Vande Slunt, Watertown, WI

Prep: 30 min. • **Cook:** 30 min.
Makes: 12 servings

- 6 medium sweet potatoes, cubed
- 1 teaspoon olive oil
- ½ teaspoon salt
- ½ teaspoon pepper
- 1 pound bacon strips, chopped
- 4 celery ribs, chopped
- 1 medium onion, thinly sliced
- 3 garlic cloves, minced
- 1 cup beef stock
- ⅔ cup balsamic vinegar
- 4 teaspoons paprika
- ¾ teaspoon ground cumin, optional
- 6 green onions, chopped
  Minced fresh parsley, optional

1. Preheat oven to 375°. Place sweet potatoes in a 15x10-in. pan; drizzle with olive oil and sprinkle with salt and pepper. Turn to coat. Bake until tender, about 30-35 minutes.

2. Meanwhile, in a large skillet, cook bacon over medium-low heat until crisp; drain. Discard all but 4 teaspoons drippings.

3. Cook celery and onion in drippings over medium heat until tender, 6-8 minutes. Stir in garlic; cook 1 minute. Add beef stock and balsamic vinegar; simmer until liquid is reduced by half, 5-8 minutes. Add the paprika and, if desired, cumin; cook 1 minute longer.

4. Pour balsamic mixture over the sweet potatoes; add bacon. Toss to coat. Top with green onions and, if desired, minced fresh parsley; serve immediately.

3. In a 3-qt. trifle bowl or glass bowl, layer a third of the corn bread and half of each of the following: romaine, tomatoes, pepper, onion, bacon, cheese and mayonnaise mixture. Repeat layers. Top with remaining corn bread and, if desired, additional chopped tomato and bacon. Refrigerate, covered, 2-4 hours before serving.

WINTER SQUASH CASSEROLE

Years ago, our vegetable garden kept us well-supplied all year long. Dad stored huge piles of potatoes and squash in the coldest part of the basement. In winter the squash was so hard, Mother sometimes used an ax to cut it into small pieces for cooking! Her hard work was worth it, because we really enjoyed this wonderful casserole.
—Glendora Hauger, Siren, WI

Prep: 15 min. • **Bake:** 45 min.
Makes: 12 servings

- 6 cups mashed cooked winter squash
- ½ cup butter, melted
- 6 large eggs, lightly beaten
- 1 cup sugar
- ½ teaspoon salt

TOPPING
- ¾ cup packed brown sugar
- ⅓ cup butter, softened
- ⅓ cup all-purpose flour
- ½ cup slivered almonds

1. In a large bowl, combine the first five ingredients. Pour into a ungreased 13x9-in. baking dish.
2. Combine topping ingredients and crumble over the top. Bake casserole, uncovered, at 350° for 45 minutes or until a thermometer reads 160°.

COLORFUL CORN BREAD SALAD

When my garden comes in, I harvest the veggies for potluck dishes. I live in the South, and we think bacon and corn bread make everything better, even salad, as you can see (and taste).
—Rebecca Clark, Warrior, AL

Prep: 45 min. + chilling
Makes: 14 servings (¾ cup each)

- 1 package (8½ ounces) corn bread/muffin mix
- 1 cup mayonnaise
- ½ cup sour cream
- 1 envelope ranch salad dressing mix
- 1 to 2 tablespoons adobo sauce from canned chipotle peppers
- 4 to 6 cups torn romaine
- 4 medium tomatoes, chopped
- 1 medium green pepper, chopped
- 1 medium onion, chopped
- 1 pound bacon strips, cooked and crumbled
- 4 cups shredded cheddar cheese
  Additional tomato and crumbled bacon, optional

1. Preheat oven to 400°. Prepare corn bread batter according to package directions. Pour into a greased 8-in. square baking pan. Bake 15-20 minutes or until a toothpick inserted in center comes out clean. Cool completely in pan on a wire rack.
2. Coarsely crumble corn bread into a large bowl. In a small bowl, mix the mayonnaise, sour cream, salad dressing mix and adobo sauce.

MUSHROOM STUFFING

I first tried this stuffing a few years ago, and it fast became our family's favorite. Mixing corn bread with mushrooms and bacon yields spectacular results.
—Kathy Traetow, Waverly, IA

Prep: 30 min. • **Bake:** 40 min.
Makes: 13 cups

4	bacon strips, diced
4	celery ribs, chopped
1	medium onion, chopped
1	pound fresh mushrooms, chopped
1	teaspoon rubbed sage
½	teaspoon salt
¼	teaspoon pepper
1	package (16 ounces) corn bread stuffing
½	cup chopped celery leaves
2	tablespoons minced fresh parsley
4	large eggs, lightly beaten
2½	cups chicken broth
1	tablespoon butter

1. In a large skillet, cook bacon until crisp; remove with a slotted spoon to paper towel. Drain, reserving 2 tablespoons of the drippings.
2. Saute celery and onion in drippings until tender. Add mushrooms, sage, salt and pepper; cook and stir for 5 minutes. Remove from the heat; stir in the stuffing, celery leaves, parsley and bacon. Combine eggs and broth. Stir into stuffing mixture.
3. Spread in a greased 13x9-in. baking dish (dish will be full). Dot with butter. Cover and bake at 350° for 30 minutes and stuffing temperature reaches 165°. Uncover and bake 10 minutes longer or until lightly browned.

GARLIC PEPPER CORN

I've enjoyed corn on the cob served with this seasoning since I was a child. It makes the familiar veggie seem extra special.
—Anna Minegar, Zolfo Springs, FL

Start to Finish: 25 min.
Makes: 8 servings

1	tablespoon dried parsley flakes
1	tablespoon garlic pepper blend
½	teaspoon paprika
¼	teaspoon salt
8	medium ears sweet corn, husked
¼	cup butter, melted

1. In a small bowl, combine the parsley, garlic pepper, paprika and salt; set aside.
2. Place corn in a Dutch oven; cover with water. Bring to a boil; cover and cook for 3 minutes or until tender. Drain.
3. Brush corn with butter; sprinkle with seasoning mixture.

Springtime Beignets
page 167

Big Batch Dishes

Attending a particularly large bash? These recipes serve anywhere from 20 to 100 guests! From appetizers to desserts, these are the ultimate crowd-pleasers... with an emphasis on the word "crowd"!

SOUR CREAM ROLLS WITH WALNUT FILLING

When I was a little girl, my grandmother taught me how to make these rolls. I remember feeling so special when we served them. If you have never worked with yeast, this is the recipe for you.
—Nadine Mesch, Mount Healthy, OH

Prep: 1 hour + rising • **Bake:** 20 min.
Makes: 8 loaves (6 servings each)

- 4 cups ground walnuts (about 14 ounces)
- 1 cup sugar
- ¾ cup butter, melted
- ½ cup 2% milk
- ⅓ cup honey

DOUGH
- 2 packages (¼ ounce each) active dry yeast
- 1 teaspoon plus ⅓ cup sugar, divided
- ½ cup warm 2% milk (110° to 115°)
- 1 cup butter, melted
- 1 cup (8 ounces) sour cream
- 4 large eggs, divided use
- 1 teaspoon salt
- 5¼ to 5¾ cups all-purpose flour

1. In a large bowl, mix the first five ingredients until blended. In a small bowl, dissolve yeast and 1 teaspoon sugar in warm milk; let stand 15 minutes. In a large bowl, combine melted butter, sour cream, three eggs, salt, remaining sugar, the yeast mixture and 2 cups flour; beat on medium speed 3 minutes. Stir in enough remaining flour to form a soft dough (the dough will be sticky).

2. Turn dough onto a floured surface; knead until smooth and elastic, about 6-8 minutes. Place in a greased bowl, turning once to grease the top. Cover with plastic wrap and let rise in a warm place until doubled, about 1 hour.

3. Punch down dough. Turn onto a lightly floured surface; divide and shape into eight portions. Roll each into a 12x8-in. rectangle (dough will be very thin).

4. Spread each rectangle with ½ cup walnut mixture to within ¾ in. of the edges. Carefully roll up jelly-roll style, starting with a long side; pinch seam and ends to seal.

5. Place rolls 2 in. apart on parchment paper-lined baking sheets, seam side down. Prick tops with a fork. Cover with kitchen towels; let rise in a warm place until almost doubled, about 1 hour. Preheat oven to 350°.

6. Lightly beat remaining egg; brush over rolls. Bake 20-25 minutes or until golden brown, switching position of pans halfway through baking (filling may leak during baking). Remove loaves to wire racks to cool. To serve, cut into slices.

THYME-SEA SALT CRACKERS

These homemade crackers are decidedly light and crispy. They are irresistible on their own as a snack or pair well with a sharp white cheddar.
—Jessica Wirth, Charlotte, NC

Prep: 25 min. • **Bake:** 10 min./batch
Makes: about 7 dozen

- 2½ cups all-purpose flour
- ½ cup white whole wheat flour
- 1 teaspoon salt
- ¾ cup water
- ¼ cup plus 1 tablespoon olive oil, divided
- 1 to 2 tablespoons minced fresh thyme
- ¾ teaspoon sea or kosher salt

1. Preheat oven to 375°. In a large bowl, whisk flours and salt. Gradually add water and ¼ cup oil, tossing with a fork until dough holds together when pressed.

2. Divide dough into three portions. On a lightly floured surface, roll each portion of dough to ⅛-in. thickness. Cut with a floured 1½-in. round cookie cutter. Place 1 in. apart on ungreased baking sheets. Prick each cracker with a fork; brush lightly with remaining oil. Mix thyme and sea salt; sprinkle over crackers.

3. Bake 9-11 minutes or until bottoms are lightly browned.

BOW TIE PASTA SALAD

This was originally a vegetable dish, but I added pasta to stretch it for large church potlucks and family gatherings. You can also add sliced mushrooms and diced tomatoes before serving.
—Barbara Burks, Huntsville, AL

Prep: 30 min. + chilling • **Cook:** 10 min.
Makes: 24 servings (¾ cup each)

- 1 medium cucumber
- 1 medium yellow summer squash
- 1 medium zucchini
- 1 medium sweet red pepper
- 1 medium green pepper
- 4 cups fresh broccoli florets
- 3 cups fresh cauliflowerets
- 1 small red onion, finely chopped
- 2 packages Italian salad dressing mix
- 4½ cups uncooked bow tie pasta
- ¼ cup olive oil
- ¼ cup red wine vinegar
- ¾ teaspoon salt
- ½ teaspoon pepper

1. Wash the first five ingredients but do not dry; chop and transfer to a large bowl. Add remaining vegetables. Sprinkle with dry dressing mix; toss to coat. Refrigerate, covered, 4-6 hours or overnight.
2. Cook pasta according to package directions. Drain; rinse with cold water. Add to vegetable mixture. In a small bowl, whisk remaining ingredients. Add to salad; toss to coat.

ROASTED TURKEY WITH MAPLE CRANBERRY GLAZE

Prepare turkey with a taste of Canada in mind! Here, the sweet maple flavor comes through even in the breast meat. You may start to notice a caramelized color after about two hours. That's when I cover the bird loosely with foil while it finishes cooking. The meat stays tender and juicy.
—Suzanne Anctil, Aldergrove, BC

Prep: 10 min. • **Bake:** 3 hours + standing
Makes: 24 (5-ounce) servings

- 1 turkey (12 to 14 pounds)
- 1 cup maple syrup
- ¾ cup whole-berry cranberry sauce
- ¼ cup finely chopped walnuts

1. Preheat oven to 325°. Place turkey on a rack in a shallow roasting pan, breast side up. Tuck wings under turkey; tie drumsticks together. In a small bowl, combine the maple syrup, cranberry sauce and walnuts. Pour over the turkey.
2. Bake, uncovered, for 3-3½ hours or until a thermometer inserted in thickest part of thigh reads 170°-175°, basting occasionally with pan drippings. Cover loosely with foil if turkey browns too quickly. Cover and let stand for 20 minutes before carving.

CARDAMOM BRAID BREAD

I came across this recipe in 1983 and have been making it for holidays ever since.
—Rita Bergman, Olympia, WA

Prep: 30 min. + rising
Bake: 20 min. + cooling
Makes: 2 loaves (20 slices each)

- 6 cups all-purpose flour
- 2 packages (¼ ounce each) active dry yeast
- 1½ teaspoons ground cardamom
- 1 teaspoon salt
- 1½ cups plus 2 tablespoons milk, divided
- ½ cup butter, cubed
- ½ cup honey
- 2 large eggs
- 2 tablespoons sugar

1. In a large bowl, combine 2 cups flour, yeast, cardamom and salt. In a small saucepan, heat 1½ cups milk, butter and honey to 120°-130°. Add to the dry ingredients; beat just until moistened. Add eggs; beat until smooth. Stir in enough remaining flour to form a firm dough (dough will be sticky).
2. Turn onto a floured surface; knead until smooth and elastic, about 6-8 minutes. Place in a greased bowl, turning once to grease top. Cover and let rise in a warm place until doubled, about 45 minutes.
3. Punch dough down. Turn onto a lightly floured surface; divide in half. Divide each portion into thirds. Shape each into a 14-in. rope. Place three ropes on a greased baking sheet and braid; pinch ends to seal and tuck under. Repeat with remaining dough. Cover and let rise until doubled, about 30 minutes.
4. Brush with remaining milk and sprinkle with sugar. Bake at 375° for 20-25 minutes or until golden brown. Remove from pans to wire racks to cool.

HOMEMADE ANTIPASTO SALAD

This colorful salad is a tasty crowd-pleaser. Guests always love the homemade dressing, which is a nice change from bottled Italian.
—Linda Harrington, Windham, NH

Prep: 50 minutes + chilling • **Cook:** 10 min.
Makes: 50 servings

- 2 packages (1 pound each) spiral pasta
- 4 to 5 large tomatoes, chopped
- 3 large onions, chopped
- 2 large green peppers, chopped
- 2 cans (15 to 16 ounces each) garbanzo beans or chickpeas, rinsed and drained
- 1 pound thinly sliced Genoa salami, julienned
- 1 pound sliced pepperoni, julienned
- ½ pound provolone cheese, cubed
- 1 cup pitted ripe olives, halved

DRESSING
- 1 cup red wine vinegar
- ½ cup sugar
- 2 tablespoons dried oregano
- 2 teaspoons salt
- 1 teaspoon pepper
- 1½ cups olive oil

1. Cook pasta according to package directions. Drain; rinse with cold water. In several large bowls, combine pasta with next eight ingredients.
2. For dressing, pulse vinegar, sugar, oregano, salt and pepper in a blender. While processing, gradually add oil in a steady stream. Pour over salad; toss to coat. Refrigerate, covered, 4 hours or overnight.

ICING
1 cup confectioners' sugar
2 tablespoons milk
⅛ teaspoon vanilla extract

1. In a small bowl, dissolve yeast in warm water. In a large bowl, combine the flour, sugar and salt; cut in shortening until crumbly. Add the yeast mixture, milk and eggs; beat until smooth (dough will be soft). Do not knead. Cover and refrigerate overnight.

2. For filling, in a small bowl, beat the cream cheese, sugar and flour until smooth. Add egg, poppy seeds and extracts; mix until blended.

3. Punch dough down. Turn onto a well-floured surface; divide into thirds. Return two portions to the refrigerator. Roll remaining portion into a 14x8-in. rectangle; place on a parchment-lined baking sheet. Spread a third of the filling down center of rectangle.

4. On each long side, cut ¾-in.-wide strips, about 2¼ in. into the center. Starting at one end, fold alternating strips at an angle across filling. Pinch ends to seal. Repeat with remaining dough and filling. Cover and let rise in a warm place until doubled, about 45 minutes. Preheat oven to 350°.

5. Bake for 20-25 minutes or until golden brown. Cool on pans on wire racks. Combine icing ingredients; drizzle over coffee cakes.

★ ★ ★ ★ ★ ★ **READER REVIEW**

"Delicious! I made only half of the recipe for the dough, but made the whole recipe of the filling. I will definitely be making this again!"

ADAMSCOOK TASTEOFHOME.COM

DANISH COFFEE CAKES

I think that as long as I'm in the kitchen baking I might as well make enough to share. This traditional recipe gives me three cheese-filled coffee cakes drizzled with a sweet vanilla icing.

—Sheri Kratcha, Avoca, WI

Prep: 45 min. + chilling
Bake: 20 min. + cooling
Makes: 3 coffee cakes (10 slices each)

1 package (¼ ounce) active dry yeast
¼ cup warm water (110° to 115°)
4 cups all-purpose flour
¼ cup sugar
1 teaspoon salt
1 cup shortening
1 cup warm 2% milk (110° to 115°)
2 large eggs, lightly beaten

FILLING
1 package (8 ounces) cream cheese, softened
¾ cup sugar
2 tablespoons all-purpose flour
1 large egg, lightly beaten
1 teaspoon poppy seeds
1 teaspoon vanilla extract
½ teaspoon lemon extract

QUADRUPLE CHOCOLATE CHUNK COOKIES

When your cookies feature Oreos, candy bars and all of the other goodies that go into a sweet treat, you are pretty much guaranteed to be a hero with everyone at the party.
—Jeff King, Duluth, MN

Prep: 25 min. • **Bake:** 10 min./batch
Makes: 8 dozen

- 1 **cup butter, softened**
- 1 **cup sugar**
- 1 **cup packed brown sugar**
- 2 **large eggs**
- 2 **teaspoons vanilla extract**
- 2½ **cups all-purpose flour**
- ¾ **cup Dutch-processed cocoa**
- 1 **teaspoon baking soda**
- ¼ **teaspoon salt**
- 1 **cup white baking chips, chopped**
- 1 **cup semisweet chocolate chips, chopped**
- 1 **cup chopped Oreo cookies (about 10 cookies)**
- 1 **Hershey's Cookies 'n' Creme candy bar (1.55 ounces), chopped**

1. Preheat oven to 375°. In a large bowl, cream butter, sugar and brown sugar until light and fluffy. Beat in eggs and vanilla. In another bowl, whisk flour, cocoa, baking soda and salt; gradually beat into creamed mixture. Stir in remaining ingredients.
2. Drop by tablespoonfuls 2 in. apart onto greased baking sheets. Bake 6-8 minutes or until set. Cool on pans 1 minute.
3. Remove from pans to wire racks to cool completely. Store in an airtight container.

MAKE AHEAD

BROCCOLI-CHEDDAR TASSIES

Our family adores broccoli casserole. I wanted to try it as an appetizer, so I used a pecan tassie recipe for the crust. The result? We're talking scrumptious!
—Gail Gaiser, Ewing, NJ

Prep: 45 min. + chilling
Bake: 20 min./batch
Makes: about 4 dozen

- 1 **cup butter, softened**
- 6 **ounces cream cheese, softened**
- 2 **cups all-purpose flour**

FILLING
- 1 **package (16 ounces) frozen chopped broccoli**
- 1 **large egg, lightly beaten**
- 1 **can (10¾ ounces) condensed cream of celery soup, undiluted**
- ¼ **cup 2% milk**
- ¼ **cup mayonnaise**
- ½ **cup shredded sharp cheddar cheese**

TOPPING
- ¼ **cup dry bread crumbs**
- 1 **tablespoon butter, melted**

1. In a small bowl, cream butter and cream cheese until smooth. Gradually beat flour into the creamed mixture. Divide dough in half. Shape each into a disk; wrap in plastic. Refrigerate 1 hour or until firm enough to handle.
2. Preheat oven to 350°. Shape dough into 1-in. balls; place in greased mini-muffin cups. Using floured fingers, press evenly onto bottoms and up sides of cups.
3. Cook broccoli according to package directions; drain. In a large bowl, combine the egg, condensed soup, milk and mayonnaise; stir in cheese and cooked broccoli. Spoon about 1 tablespoon filling into each cup. For topping, mix bread crumbs and melted butter; sprinkle over the filling.
4. Bake until the edges are golden brown, 18-22 minutes. Cool in pans for 2 minutes before removing to wire racks. Serve tassies warm.
Freeze option: Freeze cooled pastries on waxed paper-lined baking sheets until firm. Transfer to resealable plastic freezer bags. To use, reheat pastries on ungreased baking sheets in a preheated 350° oven 14-16 minutes or until lightly browned and heated through.

SOUTHWESTERN BEAN DIP

Just by using different types of beans, you can make this dip as spicy as you like it. My family could eat this as a complete meal. It's that good!
—Jeanne Shear, Sabetha, KS

Prep: 20 min. • **Bake:** 30 min.
Makes: about 9 cups

- 2 pounds ground beef
- 1 tablespoon dried minced onion
- 1 can (8 ounces) tomato sauce
- 1 can (16 ounces) kidney beans, rinsed and drained
- 1 can (16 ounces) chili beans, undrained
- 4 cups shredded cheddar cheese
  Sliced jalapeno pepper
  Tortilla chips

1. Preheat oven to 350°. In a large skillet, cook beef over medium heat until no longer pink; drain. Transfer to a bowl; add the onion. Mash with a fork until crumbly; set aside.
2. In a blender, process tomato sauce and beans until chunky. Add to beef mixture and mix well. Spoon half into a greased 13x9-in. baking dish; top with half of the cheese. Repeat layers.
3. Bake, uncovered, for 30 minutes or until cheese is melted. Top with sliced jalapeno. Serve warm with chips.

BANANA BEIGNET BITES

When I was a little girl, my grandmother took me aside one day and taught me how to make her famous banana beignets. Although we made them during the holidays, they're pretty fantastic any time of the year.

—Amy Downing, South Riding, VA

Start to Finish: 30 min.
Makes: about 3 dozen

- ¾ cup sugar
- ¼ cup packed brown sugar
- 1½ teaspoons ground cinnamon

BEIGNETS

- 2 cups cake flour
- ¾ cup sugar
- 2½ teaspoons baking powder
- ½ teaspoon ground cinnamon
- 1 teaspoon salt
- 1 large egg
- 1 cup mashed ripe bananas (about 2 medium)
- ½ cup whole milk
- 2 tablespoons canola oil
  Oil for deep-fat frying

1. In a small bowl, mix sugars and cinnamon until blended. In a large bowl, whisk the first five beignet ingredients. In another bowl, whisk egg, bananas, milk and 2 tablespoons oil until blended. Add to flour mixture; stir just until moistened.
2. In an electric skillet or deep fryer, heat oil to 375°. Drop tablespoonfuls of batter, a few at a time, into hot oil. Fry about 45-60 seconds on each side or until golden brown. Drain on paper towels. Roll warm beignets in sugar mixture.

MELON & GRAPE SALAD

Fruit salad is a cheery way to round out a potluck. This one, with an easy and refreshing citrus dressing, always makes a nice addition to any buffet.
—Mary Etta Buran
Olmsted Township, OH

....

Prep: 20 min. + chilling
Makes: 50-54 servings
(about 1 cup each)

- 1 **medium-large watermelon, cut into cubes or balls**
- 3 **honeydew melons, cut into cubes or balls**
- 3 **cantaloupe melons, cut into cubes or balls**
- 1½ **pounds seedless green grapes**
- 1½ **pounds seedless red grapes**
- 3 **cups sugar**
- ⅓ **cup lemon juice**
- ⅓ **cup lime juice**
- ⅓ **cup orange juice**

Combine melons and grapes. Combine sugar and juices; pour over fruit and toss to coat. Cover and chill for 1 hour. Serve with a slotted spoon.

MAKE AHEAD
GREEK SALAD RAVIOLI

Turn the fresh flavors of a Greek salad into a warm dish for cold winter nights. Ideal as an appetizer or small pasta course for a potluck, these ravioli are also wonderful as a family meal. I like to make a large batch, freeze them, then simply drop them into simmering water for dinner in about five minutes!
—Carla Mendres, Winnipeg, MB

....

Prep: 45 min. • **Cook:** 5 min./batch
Makes: 4 dozen

- 10 **ounces (about 12 cups) fresh baby spinach**
- ½ **cup finely chopped roasted sweet red peppers**
- ½ **cup pitted and finely chopped ripe olives**
- ½ **cup crumbled feta cheese**
- 3 **tablespoons snipped fresh dill**
- 2 **to 3 teaspoons dried oregano**
- 2 **tablespoons butter**
- 3 **tablespoons all-purpose flour**
- 2 **cups whole milk**
- 96 **pot sticker or gyoza wrappers Snipped fresh dill and sauce of choice, optional**

1. In a large skillet over medium heat, cook and stir spinach in batches until wilted, 3-4 minutes. Drain on paper towels. Combine with next five ingredients.
2. In a small saucepan, melt butter over medium heat. Stir in flour until smooth; gradually whisk in milk. Bring to a boil, stirring constantly, until sauce thickens and coats a spoon, 2-3 minutes. Stir into spinach mixture.
3. Place 1 tablespoon spinach mixture in center of a pot sticker wrapper. (Cover remaining wrappers with a damp paper towel until ready to use.) Moisten wrapper edges with water, and place another wrapper on top. Press edges to seal. Repeat with remaining wrappers.
4. Fill a Dutch oven two-thirds full with water; bring to a boil. Reduce heat; drop ravioli in batches into simmering water until cooked through, 3-4 minutes. If desired, sprinkle with additional dill, and serve with sauce of choice.
Freeze option: Cover and freeze uncooked ravioli on waxed paper-lined baking sheets until firm. Transfer to resealable plastic freezer bags; return to freezer. To use, cook as directed, increasing time to 6 minutes.
Note: Wonton wrappers may be substituted for pot sticker or gyoza wrappers. Stack two or three wonton wrappers on a work surface; cut into circles with a 3½-in. biscuit or round cookie cutter. Fill and wrap as directed.

PUMPKIN COOKIES WITH PENUCHE FROSTING

For our parties, we have pumpkin cookies with penuche—a caramel-flavored frosting of brown sugar, butter and milk. We sometimes use home-canned pumpkin.
—Priscilla Anderson, Salt Lake City, UT

Prep: 25 min.
Bake: 10 min./batch + cooling
Makes: about 7 dozen

- 1   cup butter, softened
- ½   cup sugar
- ½   cup packed brown sugar
- 1   large egg
- 1   cup canned pumpkin
- 2   teaspoons vanilla extract
- 2   cups all-purpose flour
- 1   teaspoon baking powder
- 1   teaspoon baking soda
- 1   teaspoon ground cinnamon
- ½   teaspoon salt
- ¾   cup chopped pecans

FROSTING

- ¼   cup packed brown sugar
- 3   tablespoons butter
- ¼   cup 2% milk
- 2½ to 3 cups confectioners' sugar

1. Preheat oven to 350°. In a large bowl, cream butter and sugars until light and fluffy. Beat in egg, pumpkin and vanilla. In another bowl, whisk flour, baking powder, baking soda, cinnamon and salt; gradually beat into creamed mixture. Stir in pecans.
2. Drop dough by rounded teaspoonfuls 2 in. apart onto ungreased baking sheets. Bake 9-11 minutes or until edges are light brown. Remove from pans to wire racks to cool completely.
3. For frosting, in a small saucepan, bring brown sugar and butter to a boil. Cook and stir over medium heat 1 minute. Remove from heat; cool 10 minutes. Transfer to a large bowl; beat in milk. Gradually beat in enough confectioners' sugar to achieve spreading consistency. Frost cookies.

3 Easy Ways to Soften Butter

SLICE Cut the butter stick in half lengthwise. Stack the halves and slice lengthwise again. Stack all four butter strips and slice crosswise to make cubes. The butter cubes will soften in about 15 minutes.

ROLL Place the butter between two sheets of waxed paper. Use a rolling pin to roll or pound the butter out flat.

GRATE Partially unwrap the butter and shred it using the largest holes of a box grater. You can even use the wrapped half as a handle!

SWEET & SPICY ASIAN MEATBALLS

For my niece's annual Halloween party, I make glazed meatballs and deliver them in a slow cooker so they're hot, spicy-sweet and ready to eat.
—Gail Borczyk, Boca Raton, FL

Prep: 1 hour • **Cook:** 3 hours
Makes: about 5 dozen

- 1   large egg, lightly beaten
- ½   medium onion, finely chopped
- ⅓   cup sliced water chestnuts, minced
- 3   tablespoons minced fresh cilantro
- 1   jalapeno pepper, seeded and finely chopped
- 3   tablespoons reduced-sodium soy sauce
- 4   garlic cloves, minced
- 1   tablespoon minced fresh gingerroot
- ⅔   cup panko (Japanese) bread crumbs
- 2   pounds ground pork

SAUCE
- 2   cups sweet-and-sour sauce
- ¼   cup barbecue sauce
- ¼   cup duck sauce
- 2   tablespoons chicken broth
- 1   tablespoon minced fresh cilantro
- 1   tablespoon reduced-sodium soy sauce
- 2   garlic cloves, minced
- 1½ teaspoons minced fresh gingerroot
      Thinly sliced green onions, optional

1. Preheat oven to 375°. In a large bowl, combine the first eight ingredients; stir in bread crumbs. Add pork; mix lightly but thoroughly. Shape into 1¼-in. balls. Place the meatballs on a greased rack in a 15x10x1-in. baking pan. Bake for 18-22 minutes or until lightly browned.
2. Transfer meatballs to a 4-qt. slow cooker. In small bowl, mix the first eight sauce ingredients. Pour over meatballs. Cook, covered, on low 3-4 hours or until meatballs are cooked through. If desired, sprinkle with green onions.

Freeze option: Freeze cooled meatball mixture in freezer containers. To use, partially thaw in refrigerator overnight. Heat through in a covered saucepan, gently stirring and adding a little broth or water if necessary. Sprinkle with green onions if desired.
Note: Wear disposable gloves when cutting hot peppers; the oils can burn skin. Avoid touching your face.

SUPER CHUNKY COOKIES

Chocolate lovers will go crazy over these cookies that feature loads of chocolate! When friends ask me to make "those cookies," I know exactly what recipe they are talking about.

—Rebecca Jendry, Spring Branch, TX

Prep: 15 min. • **Bake:** 10 min./batch
Makes: 6½ dozen

- ½ cup butter-flavored shortening
- ½ cup butter, softened
- 1 cup packed brown sugar
- ¾ cup sugar
- 2 large eggs
- 2 teaspoons vanilla extract
- 2½ cups all-purpose flour
- 1 teaspoon baking soda
- ⅛ teaspoon salt
- 1 cup miniature semisweet chocolate chips
- 1 cup milk chocolate chips
- 1 cup vanilla or white chips
- 4 ounces bittersweet chocolate, coarsely chopped
- ¾ cup English toffee bits or almond brickle chips
- ½ cup chopped pecans

1. In a large bowl, cream the shortening, butter and sugars until light and fluffy. Add eggs, one at a time, beating well after each addition. Beat in vanilla. Combine the flour, baking soda and salt; gradually add to the creamed mixture and mix well. Stir in the remaining ingredients.

2. Drop by tablespoonfuls 3 in. apart onto ungreased baking sheets. Bake at 350° for 10-12 minutes or until lightly browned. Cool for 2-3 minutes before removing to wire racks to cool completely.

MAKE AHEAD

SPANAKOPITA BITES

Enjoy the taste of classic spanakopita without all the hassle. This version is cut into squares instead of being folded into triangle-shaped pockets.
—Barbara Smith, Chipley, FL

Prep: 20 min. + freezing • **Bake:** 35 min.
Makes: 10½ dozen

- 1   large egg, lightly beaten
- 1   package (10 ounces) frozen chopped spinach, thawed and squeezed dry
- 2   cups (8 ounces) crumbled feta cheese
- 1   cup (8 ounces) 4% small-curd cottage cheese
- ¾   cup butter, melted
- 16 sheets phyllo dough (14x9-inch size)

1. Preheat oven to 350°. In a large bowl, mix egg, spinach and cheeses. Brush a 15x10x1-in. baking pan with some of the butter.

2. Place one sheet of phyllo dough in prepared pan; brush with butter. Layer with seven additional phyllo sheets, brushing each layer. (Keep remaining phyllo dough covered with plastic wrap and a damp towel to prevent it from drying out.)

3. Spread top with spinach mixture. Top with remaining phyllo dough, brushing each sheet with butter.

4. Freeze, covered, 30 minutes. Using a sharp knife, cut into 1-in. squares. Bake 35-45 minutes or until golden brown. Refrigerate leftovers.

To make ahead: Cover and freeze until ready to use. Cut and bake as directed.

MINI SAUSAGE QUICHES

These bite-size quiches are loaded with sausage and cheese, plus their crescent roll base makes preparation a breeze. Serve the cute "muffinettes" at any large brunch or potluck gathering.
—Jan Mead, Milford, CT

Prep: 25 min. • **Bake:** 20 min.
Makes: 4 dozen

- ½   pound bulk hot Italian sausage
- 2   tablespoons dried minced onion
- 2   tablespoons minced chives
- 1   tube (8 ounces) refrigerated crescent rolls
- 4   large eggs, lightly beaten
- 2   cups (8 ounces) shredded Swiss cheese
- 1   cup (8 ounces) 4% cottage cheese
- ⅓   cup grated Parmesan cheese Paprika

1. In a large skillet, brown sausage and onion over medium heat for 4-5 minutes or until meat is no longer pink; drain. Stir in chives.

2. On a lightly floured surface, unroll crescent dough into one long rectangle; seal seams and perforations. Cut into 48 pieces. Press onto bottom and up the sides of greased miniature muffin cups.

3. Fill each with about 2 teaspoons of sausage mixture. In a bowl, combine the eggs and cheeses. Spoon 2 teaspoonfuls over the sausage mixture. Sprinkle with the paprika.

4. Bake at 375° for 20-25 minutes or until a knife inserted in the center comes out clean. Cool for 5 minutes before removing from pans to wire racks. If desired, sprinkle with additional minced chives. Serve warm.

CRANBERRY-WHITE CHOCOLATE COOKIES

These classics are among my favorite Christmas cookies. I prepare the dough early in the holiday season and freeze it to pull out later as needed. The tartness of the berries perfectly balances the sweet white chocolate.

—Sherry Conley, Noel, Hants County, NS

Prep: 25 min.
Bake: 10 min./batch + cooling
Makes: about 7 dozen

    1   cup butter, softened
    ¾   cup sugar
    ¾   cup packed brown sugar
    2   large eggs
    ⅓   cup cranberry juice
    1   teaspoon vanilla extract
    3   cups all-purpose flour
    2   teaspoons baking powder
    ½   teaspoon salt
    2   cups dried cranberries
    2   cups vanilla or white chips
  GLAZE
    2   cups vanilla or white chips
    2   tablespoons plus
        1½ teaspoons shortening

1. In a large bowl, cream butter and sugars until light and fluffy. Beat in the eggs, cranberry juice and vanilla. Combine the flour, baking powder and salt; gradually add to creamed mixture and mix well. Fold in cranberries and vanilla chips.

2. Drop by rounded teaspoonfuls 2 in. apart onto greased baking sheets. Bake at 350° for 10-12 minutes or until edges begin to brown. Cool for 2 minutes before removing to wire racks to cool completely.

3. For glaze, microwave vanilla chips and shortening at 70% power until melted; stir until smooth. Drizzle over cookies.

SPRINGTIME BEIGNETS

I've always loved beignets, but I never thought I could make them myself. Turns out they're easy! Sometimes I'll even make a quick berry whipped cream and pipe it inside for a fun surprise.

—Kathi Hemmer, Grand Junction, CO

Prep: 25 min. + chilling • **Cook:** 25 min.
Makes: 4 dozen

    ¼   cup butter, room temperature
    ¾   cup granulated sugar
    ½   teaspoon salt
    ½   teaspoon ground cinnamon
    ½   cup plus 2 tablespoons warm
            water (120° to 130°), divided
    ½   cup evaporated milk
    1   package (¼ ounce)
            quick-rise yeast
    1   large egg
    3¼ to 3¾ cups all-purpose flour
            Oil for deep-fat frying
            Confectioners' sugar
            Berries and whipped topping,
            optional

1. Beat butter, sugar, salt and cinnamon until crumbly. Beat in ½ cup water and evaporated milk. In another bowl, dissolve yeast in remaining water; add to milk mixture. Beat in egg until blended.

2. Add 2 cups flour; mix until well blended. Stir in enough remaining flour to form a soft dough (dough will be sticky). Place in a greased bowl, turning once to grease the top. Cover; refrigerate 4 hours or overnight.

3. Bring dough to room temperature. On a floured surface, roll dough into a 16x12-in. rectangle. Cut into 2-in. squares. In an electric skillet or deep fryer, heat oil to 375°. Drop beignets, a few at a time, into hot oil. Fry until golden brown, about 1 minute per side. Drain on paper towels.

4. Dust with confectioners' sugar. If desired, serve with assorted berries and whipped topping.

CHOCOLATE-DIPPED MERINGUE SANDWICH COOKIES

Oh what fun it is to bite into this delectable combo of chocolate and crunchy meringue with sprinkles on top. We like to dip the cookies in garnishes that match the season or holiday.
—Donna Stelmach, Morristown, NJ

Prep: 1 hour + chilling
Bake: 40 min./batch + standing
Makes: 7 dozen

    4   large egg whites
    1   cup confectioners' sugar
    ½   cup almond flour
    ⅔   cup sugar

GANACHE

    6   ounces semisweet
        chocolate, chopped
    3   ounces unsweetened
        chocolate, chopped
    1¼ cups heavy whipping cream
    1   tablespoon light corn syrup

TOPPINGS

    ½   cup chocolate sprinkles
    ½   cup sliced almonds, finely
        chopped and toasted
    ½   cup sweetened shredded coconut,
        finely chopped and toasted

1. Place egg whites in a large bowl; let stand at room temperature 30 minutes.
2. Preheat oven to 225°. In a small bowl, whisk confectioners' sugar and almond flour until blended. Beat egg whites on medium speed until foamy. Gradually add sugar, 1 tablespoon at a time, beating on high after each addition until sugar is dissolved. Continue beating until stiff glossy peaks form. Fold in confectioners' sugar mixture.
3. Cut a small hole in the tip of a pastry bag or in a corner of a food-safe plastic bag; insert #805 round pastry tip. Fill bag with meringue. Pipe 1-in.-diameter cookies 1 in. apart onto parchment paper-lined baking sheets. Using a finger moistened with water, smooth tops of cookies.
4. Bake 40-45 minutes or until firm to the touch. Turn oven off (do not open oven door); leave cookies in oven for 1 hour. Remove from oven; cool completely on baking sheets.
5. For ganache, place semisweet and unsweetened chocolates in a small bowl. In a small saucepan, combine cream and corn syrup; bring just to a boil. Pour over chocolate; stir with a whisk until smooth. Remove 1 cup ganache to another bowl; refrigerate 25-30 minutes or until the mixture is thick enough to pipe, stirring occasionally. Reserve remaining ganache for dipping; let stand, covered, at room temperature, stirring occasionally.
6. Cut a small hole in the tip of a pastry bag or in a corner of a food-safe plastic bag; insert #802 round pastry tip. Fill bag with chilled ganache. Pipe onto bottoms of half of the cookies; cover with remaining cookies. (Ganache may soften as it warms. If necessary, return ganache to refrigerator until firm enough to pipe.)
7. Place toppings in separate shallow bowls. Dip each sandwich cookie halfway in room temperature ganache; allow excess to drip off. (If necessary, warm ganache in microwave for 10 seconds to thin slightly.) Dip in toppings as desired; place on waxed paper and let stand until set. Store in airtight containers at room temperature.

MAKE-AHEAD VEGGIE SALAD

Assemble this colorful mix of vegetables and let it soak up the sweet-sour dressing overnight. The next day, you'll be ready to hit the party with a refreshing and delicious salad that tastes extraordinary!
—Shirley Glaab, Hattiesburg, MS

Prep: 35 min. + marinating
Makes: 30 servings (½ cup each)

- 1 package (24 ounces) frozen shoepeg corn, thawed
- 1 package (16 ounces) frozen peas, thawed
- 1 package (16 ounces) frozen French-style green beans, thawed
- 1 large red onion, chopped
- 4 celery ribs, thinly sliced
- 2 medium carrots, thinly sliced
- 1 medium green pepper, chopped
- 1 medium sweet red pepper, chopped
- 1 jar (4½ ounces) sliced mushrooms, drained
- 1 jar (4 ounces) diced pimientos, drained
- ½ cup sugar
- ½ cup olive oil
- ½ cup red wine vinegar
- ¾ teaspoon salt
- ¼ teaspoon pepper

In a very large bowl, combine the first 10 ingredients. Place remaining ingredients in a jar with a tight-fitting lid; shake well. Pour over vegetable mixture; toss to coat. Refrigerate, covered, 8 hours or overnight, stirring occasionally.

SMOKY BEANS FOR A BUNCH

These beans are a perfect side to any potluck meal. The recipe is sized right for really big reunions.
—Pat Turner, Seneca, SC

Prep: 20 min. • **Bake:** 45 min.
Makes: 90-95 servings

- 3 pounds sliced bacon, diced
- 3 medium sweet onions, chopped
- 6 cans (28 ounces each) baked beans, undrained
- 6 cans (16 ounces each) kidney beans, rinsed and drained
- 6 cans (16 ounces each) butter beans, rinsed and drained
- 4 packages (12 ounces each) miniature smoked sausages, cut in thirds
- 3 cups packed brown sugar
- 1½ cups ketchup
- 1½ cups cider vinegar
- 1 tablespoon garlic powder
- 1 tablespoon ground mustard

1. In a Dutch oven, cook bacon over medium heat until crisp. Using a slotted spoon, remove to paper towels; drain, reserving 3 tablespoons drippings. Saute onions in reserved drippings until tender.
2. In a very large bowl, combine the beans, sausages, bacon and onions. Combine the remaining ingredients; stir into the bean mixture.
3. Pour into four greased 13x9-in. baking dishes. Bake, uncovered, at 350° for 45-55 minutes or until heated through.

MAKE-AHEAD SAUSAGE PINWHEELS

Filled with sausage, sweet pepper and cream cheese, these roll-ups are excellent for unexpected visitors, a cocktail party or a halftime snack. Besides being easy to make, they can be done way ahead and kept in the freezer. All you have to do is pop them into a hot oven, and you're all set.

—Cindy Nerat, Menominee, MI

Prep: 1 hour + freezing • **Bake:** 15 min.
Makes: about 6½ dozen

1 pound bulk regular or
   spicy pork sausage
½ cup diced sweet red pepper
1 green onion, chopped
1 package (8 ounces)
   cream cheese, cubed
2 tubes (8 ounces each)
   refrigerated crescent rolls

1. Preheat oven to 350°. In a large skillet, cook and crumble sausage over medium-high heat until no longer pink, 5-7 minutes; drain. Add pepper and green onion; cook and stir 2 minutes. Transfer to a bowl; cool 10 minutes. Stir in cream cheese until blended; cool completely.
2. Unroll one can of crescent dough and separate into four rectangles; pinch perforations to seal. Press each rectangle to 6x4½ in.; spread each with ⅓ cup filling to within ¼ in. of edges. Roll up jelly-roll style, starting with a short side; pinch seam to seal. Roll gently to make logs smooth. Place on a waxed paper-lined baking sheet, seam side down. Repeat with remaining crescent dough. Freeze, covered, until firm, about 1 hour.

3. Cut each log into 10 slices. Bake on parchment paper-lined baking sheets until golden brown, 15-18 minutes.
Freeze option: Freeze pinwheels in freezer containers, separating layers with waxed paper. To use, bake frozen pinwheels as directed, increasing time by 3-5 minutes.

FRENCH CANADIAN TOURTIERES

This recipe comes from my big sister. Each fall, we get together and make about 20 of these pies to serve at Christmas, give as gifts or save in the freezer for unexpected company.

—Pat Menee, Carberry, MB

Prep: 1¼ hours • **Bake:** 40 min.
Makes: 4 pies (8 servings each)

4 celery ribs
4 medium carrots
2 large onions
2 garlic cloves, peeled
4 pounds ground pork
2 pounds ground veal
2 pounds bulk pork sausage
1 can (14½ ounces) chicken broth
½ cup minced fresh parsley
1 tablespoon salt
1 teaspoon pepper
1 teaspoon dried basil
1 teaspoon dried rosemary, crushed
1 teaspoon cayenne pepper
1 teaspoon ground mace
1 teaspoon ground cloves
1 cup dry bread crumbs
   Pastry for four double-crust pies
   (9 inches)

1. Coarsely chop the celery, carrots and onions; place in a food processor with garlic. Cover and process until finely chopped; set aside.

2. In a stockpot or two Dutch ovens, cook vegetables, pork, veal and sausage until the meat is no longer pink; drain. Stir in broth, parsley and seasonings. Cover and cook over low heat 20 minutes. Stir in bread crumbs.
3. Preheat oven to 400°. Line four 9-in. pie plates with bottom crusts; trim pastry even with edges. Fill each with about 4 cups filling. Roll out remaining pastry to fit tops of pies; place over filling. Trim, seal and flute edges. Cut slits in pastry.
4. Cover edges of pies loosely with foil. Bake for 25 minutes. Reduce heat to 350°. Remove foil and bake pies 15-20 minutes longer or until crusts are golden brown.
Freeze option: Cover and freeze unbaked pies. To use, remove from freezer 30 minutes before baking (do not thaw). Preheat oven to 400°. Place pie on a baking sheet; cover edges loosely with foil. Bake 25 minutes. Reduce heat to 350°. Remove foil. Bake pie 50-60 minutes longer or until crust is golden brown and a thermometer inserted in center reads 165°.

★ ★ ★ ★ ★ **READER REVIEW**

"I made this recipe for the first time for my church brunch and everyone raved about it. Very good, did not change a thing."

LBW50 TASTEOFHOME.COM

COFFEE-GLAZED DOUGHNUTS

The coffee-flavored glaze on these tasty doughnuts makes them a perfect start to any morning. You'll find that the recipe is a delectable way to use up leftover potatoes, too.

—Pat Siebenaler, Random Lake, WI

Prep: 25 min. + rising
Cook: 5 min./batch
Makes: about 4 dozen

- 2 packages (¼ ounce each) active dry yeast
- ¼ cup warm water (110° to 115°)
- 2 cups warm 2% milk (110° to 115°)
- ½ cup butter, softened
- 1 cup hot mashed potatoes (without added milk and butter)
- 3 large eggs
- ½ teaspoon lemon extract, optional
- 1 cup sugar
- 1½ teaspoons salt
- ½ teaspoon ground cinnamon
- 9¼ to 9¾ cups all-purpose flour

COFFEE GLAZE
- 6 to 8 tablespoons cold 2% milk
- 1 tablespoon instant coffee granules
- 2 teaspoons vanilla extract
- ¾ cup butter, softened
- 6 cups confectioners' sugar
- ½ teaspoon ground cinnamon
  Dash salt
  Oil for deep-fat frying

1. In a large bowl, dissolve yeast in warm water. Add milk, butter, potatoes, eggs and, if desired, extract. Add sugar, salt, cinnamon and 3 cups flour. Beat until smooth. Stir in enough remaining flour to form a soft dough. Cover and let rise in a warm place until doubled, about 1 hour.

2. Stir down dough. On a well-floured surface, roll out to ½-in. thickness. Cut with a floured 2½-in. doughnut cutter. Place on greased baking sheets; cover and let rise for 45 minutes.

3. Meanwhile, for the glaze, combine 6 tablespoons milk, coffee and vanilla; stir to dissolve coffee. In a large bowl, beat butter, sugar, cinnamon and salt. Gradually add milk mixture; beat until smooth, adding milk to reach a good dipping consistency.

4. In an electric skillet or deep-fat fryer, heat oil to 375°. Fry doughnuts, a few at a time, about 1½ minutes per side or until golden. Drain on paper towels. Dip tops in glaze while warm.

Cinnamon-Sugar Doughnuts: Omit glaze. Gently roll warm doughnuts in a mixture of 2 cups sugar and 1 teaspoon ground cinnamon.

Poppy Seed Doughnuts: Add ¼ cup poppy seeds to dough along with the sugar. Substitute vanilla glaze for coffee glaze. In a saucepan, bring ½ cup sugar, ¼ cup 2% milk and ¼ cup butter to a boil. Cook and stir for 1 minute. Remove from heat; cool completely. Stir in ½ cup confectioners' sugar and ¼ teaspoon each salt and vanilla until smooth. Drizzle over doughnuts.

ALMOND COCONUT KRINGLES

My mom was well-known for her delicious kringle. She made it from memory, and when she passed away, we didn't have the recipe to carry on this tradition. We searched through her recipes, and we found what we believe was her original starting recipe. So that's where we began. The dough remains the same, but I adjusted the filling ingredients until it came out just right. Try this flaky, tender pastry with its almonds and coconut filling, and you'll be hooked on it the way we are!
—Deborah Richmond
Trabuco Canyon, CA

Prep: 1 hour + chilling
Bake: 25 min. + cooling
Makes: 4 kringles (9 slices each)

- 2 cups all-purpose flour
- 1 cup cold butter, cubed
- 1 cup (8 ounces) sour cream

FILLING
- 1¼ cups butter, softened
- 1 cup packed brown sugar
- 3 cups sliced almonds, toasted
- 1½ cups sweetened shredded coconut, toasted

GLAZE
- 1 cup confectioners' sugar
- 1 tablespoon butter, softened
- 1 teaspoon vanilla extract
- 4 to 6 teaspoons 2% milk

1. Place flour in a large bowl; cut in butter until crumbly. Stir in sour cream. Wrap in plastic. Refrigerate overnight.
2. Preheat oven to 375°. In a small bowl, cream butter and brown sugar until light and fluffy. Stir in almonds and coconut.
3. Divide dough into four portions. On a lightly floured surface, roll one portion into a 12x10-in. rectangle. (Keep the

remaining dough refrigerated until ready to use.) Spread 1 cup filling lengthwise down the center. Fold in sides of pastry to meet in the center; pinch seam to seal. Repeat with the remaining dough and filling. Transfer to two ungreased baking sheets. Bake until lightly browned, 23-27 minutes. Remove to wire racks to cool completely.
4. Meanwhile, combine the confectioners' sugar, butter, vanilla and enough milk to achieve desired consistency; drizzle over the kringles.

SWEET & SALTY PARTY MIX

These crunchy munchies are sure to rank high with your family and friends. The combination of sweet and salty flavors is just right.
—Candice Lumley, Charles City, IA

Prep: 10 min. • **Bake:** 1¼ hours + cooling
Makes: about 10 quarts

- 1 package (12 ounces) Corn Chex
- 1 package (10 ounces) Cheerios
- 1 package (10 ounces) Honeycomb cereal
- 1 package (10 ounces) pretzel sticks
- 1¾ cups sugar
- 1½ cups canola oil
- 1¼ cups butter, melted
- 3 tablespoons soy sauce
- 2 tablespoons garlic salt

1. Preheat oven to 275°. In a very large bowl, combine cereals and pretzels. In another bowl, mix the remaining ingredients until sugar is dissolved. Pour over cereal mixture; toss to coat.
2. Transfer to a large roasting pan. Bake, uncovered, 1¼ hours or until cereal is crisp, stirring every 15 minutes. Cool completely. Store in an airtight container.

CHOCOLATE MINT BROWNIES

One of the best things about this recipe is that the brownies get moister if you leave them in the refrigerator for a day or two. The problem at our house is that no one can leave them alone for that long!
—Helen Baines, Elkton, MD

....

Prep: 20 min. • **Bake:** 30 min. + chilling
Makes: 5-6 dozen

- ½ cup butter, softened
- 1 cup sugar
- 4 large eggs
- 1 can (16 ounces) chocolate syrup
- 1 teaspoon vanilla extract
- 1 cup all-purpose flour
- ½ teaspoon salt

FILLING
- ½ cup butter, softened
- 2 cups confectioners' sugar
- 1 tablespoon water
- ½ teaspoon mint extract
- 3 drops green food coloring

TOPPING
- 1 package (10 ounces) mint chocolate chips
- ½ cup plus 1 tablespoon butter, cubed

1. Preheat oven to 350°. In a large bowl, cream butter and sugar until light and fluffy. Add eggs, one at a time, beating well after each addition. Beat in syrup and vanilla. Add flour and salt; mix well.
2. Pour into a greased 13x9-in. baking pan. Bake 30 minutes (top of brownies will still appear wet). Cool on a wire rack.
3. For filling, in a small bowl, cream butter and confectioners' sugar; add water, extract and food coloring until blended. Spread over cooled brownies. Refrigerate until set.
4. For topping, melt the chocolate chips and butter. Cool 30 minutes, stirring occasionally. Spread over filling. Chill. Cut into bars. Store in refrigerator.
Note: If mint chocolate chips are not available, place 2 cups (12 ounces) semisweet chocolate chips and ¼ teaspoon peppermint extract in a plastic bag; seal and toss to coat. Allow chips to stand for 24-48 hours.

CONTEST-WINNING GRILLED CORN SALSA

This is a super way to use up summer's garden bounty. I prepare the veggies anytime I'm grilling something else, then whip up the salad and put it in the fridge to marinate.
—Teri Kman, Laporte, CO

....

Prep: 30 min.
Grill: 10 min. per batch + chilling
Makes: 7½ cups

- 8 medium ears sweet corn, husks removed
- 2 small yellow summer squash, cut into ½-inch slices
- 1 medium sweet red pepper, cut into four wedges
- 1 medium red onion, cut into ½-inch rings
- 1 medium tomato, seeded and chopped

BASIL VINAIGRETTE
- ½ cup olive oil
- ⅓ cup white balsamic or cider vinegar
- 12 fresh basil leaves, chopped
- 1 teaspoon salt
- 1 teaspoon garlic powder
- 1 teaspoon dried oregano

1. Fill a soup kettle two-thirds full with water; bring to a boil. Add the corn. Reduce heat; cover and simmer for 5 minutes or until crisp-tender. Remove corn; cool slightly.
2. On an oiled grill rack, grill the corn, squash, red pepper and onion, covered, over medium heat for 8-10 minutes or until lightly browned, turning occasionally.
3. Cut corn from cobs; cut the squash, red pepper and onion into bite-size pieces. Place grilled vegetables in a large bowl; add the tomato.
4. In a small bowl, whisk the vinaigrette ingredients. Pour over vegetables; toss to coat. Cover and refrigerate until chilled. Serve with a slotted spoon.

1. Cook noodles according to package directions. Meanwhile, in a Dutch oven, cook beef over medium heat until no longer pink; drain. Stir in spaghetti sauce; set aside. In a large bowl, combine the eggs, ricotta cheese, 4½ cups mozzarella cheese, parsley, salt and pepper.

2. Drain noodles. Spread 1 cup meat sauce in each of two greased 13x9-in. baking dishes. Layer each with three noodles, 1 cup ricotta mixture and 1½ cups meat sauce. Repeat layers twice. Top with Parmesan cheese and the remaining mozzarella cheese.

3. Cover and freeze one lasagna for up to 3 months. Cover and bake remaining lasagna at 375° for 45 minutes. Uncover; bake 10 minutes longer or until bubbly. Let stand for 10 minutes before cutting.

To use frozen lasagna: Thaw in the refrigerator overnight. Remove from the refrigerator 30 minutes before baking. Cover and bake at 375° for 60-70 minutes or until heated through. Uncover; bake 10 minutes longer or until bubbly. Let stand for 10 minutes before cutting.

TEST KITCHEN TIP
To keep lasagna from becoming soupy, be certain to drain the noodles well and pat them dry. Using a thick tomato sauce helps as well.

MAKE AHEAD
MAKE ONCE, EAT TWICE LASAGNA

Our family loves this recipe accompanied by a green salad and garlic bread. It's so handy to have an extra pan in the freezer for when unexpected guests drop in or when you need to take a main course to a charity event.
—Geri Davis, Prescott, AZ

Prep: 35 min. • **Bake:** 55 min. + standing
Makes: 2 lasagnas (12 servings each)

18 lasagna noodles
3 pounds ground beef
3 jars (26 ounces each) spaghetti sauce
2 large eggs, lightly beaten
1½ pounds ricotta cheese
6 cups (24 ounces) shredded part-skim mozzarella cheese, divided
1 tablespoon dried parsley flakes
1 teaspoon salt
½ teaspoon pepper
1 cup grated Parmesan cheese

MARBLED CHOCOLATE CHEESECAKE BARS

For success with these lovely bars, be sure to gently swirl the cheesecake layer into the batter. Too much mixing and you'll lose the pretty marbled effect.
—Elaine Hanson, Waite Park, MN

Prep: 20 min. • **Bake:** 20 min. + cooling
Makes: about 6 dozen

- ¾ cup water
- ½ cup butter
- 1½ ounces unsweetened chocolate
- 2 cups all-purpose flour
- 1½ cups packed brown sugar

- 1 teaspoon baking soda
- ½ teaspoon salt
- 2 large eggs
- ½ cup sour cream

CREAM CHEESE MIXTURE
- 1 package (8 ounces) cream cheese, softened
- ⅓ cup sugar
- 1 large egg, beaten
- 1 tablespoon vanilla extract
- 1 cup (6 ounces) semisweet chocolate chips

1. In a small saucepan, combine the water, butter and chocolate; cook and stir over low heat until smooth. Cool.

2. In a large bowl, combine the flour, brown sugar, baking soda and salt. Add eggs and sour cream; beat on low speed just until combined. Stir in chocolate mixture until smooth.

3. In another bowl, beat the cream cheese, sugar, egg and vanilla; set aside. Spread the chocolate batter into a greased 15x10x1-in. baking pan. Drop cream cheese mixture by tablespoonfuls over batter; cut through the batter with a knife to swirl. Sprinkle with chocolate chips.

4. Bake at 375° for 20-25 minutes or until a toothpick inserted near the center comes out clean. Cool on a wire rack. Cut into bars.

MINT MORSELS

Is it a cookie or a candy? No matter which answer folks choose, they find these minty morsels yummy. The recipe makes so many that you can whip up dozens of gifts at once.

—Adina Skilbred, Prairie du Sac, WI

Prep: 30 min. + chilling
Bake: 10 min. + cooling
Makes: about 10 dozen

⅓ cup shortening
⅓ cup butter, softened
¾ cup sugar
1 large egg
1 tablespoon 2% milk
1 teaspoon vanilla extract
1¾ cups all-purpose flour
⅓ cup baking cocoa
1½ teaspoons baking powder
¼ teaspoon salt
⅛ teaspoon ground cinnamon
PEPPERMINT LAYER
4 cups confectioners' sugar
6 tablespoons light corn syrup
6 tablespoons butter, melted
2 to 3 teaspoons peppermint extract
CHOCOLATE COATING
2 packages (11½ ounces each) milk chocolate chips
¼ cup shortening

1. In a large bowl, cream the shortening, butter and sugar until light and fluffy. Beat in the egg, milk and vanilla. Combine the flour, cocoa, baking powder, salt and cinnamon; gradually add to the creamed mixture. Cover and refrigerate for 8 hours or overnight.
2. On a lightly floured surface, roll dough to ⅛-in. thickness. Cut with a lightly floured 1½-in. round cookie cutter; place on ungreased baking sheets.
3. Bake at 375° for 6-8 minutes or until set. Cool for 2 minutes before removing to wire racks to cool completely.
4. In a large bowl, combine all the peppermint layer ingredients. Knead for 1 minute or until smooth. Shape into 120 balls, ½ in. each. Place a ball on each cookie and flatten to cover cookie. Place on waxed paper-lined baking sheets; refrigerate for 30 minutes.
5. In a microwave, melt chips and shortening; stir until smooth. Spread about 1 teaspoonful over each cookie. Chill until firm.

CHUCK WAGON BEANS

I followed the lead of cooks of the Old Western cattle ranges to come up with these savory beans. Sweet and smoky, they're made extra hearty by the addition of some sausage.

—Nancy Moore, Bucklin, KS

Prep: 15 min. • **Cook:** 8 hours
Makes: 24 servings (⅔ cup each)

2 cans (28 ounces each) baked beans
3 cans (16 ounces each) kidney beans, rinsed and drained
2 cans (15 ounces each) pinto beans, rinsed and drained
1 pound smoked kielbasa or Polish sausage, sliced
1 jar (12 ounces) pickled jalapeno slices, drained
1 medium onion, chopped
1 cup barbecue sauce
½ cup spicy brown mustard
¼ cup steak seasoning

In a greased 6-qt. slow cooker, combine all ingredients. Cover and cook on low for 8-10 hours or until heated through.
Note: This recipe was tested with McCormick's Montreal Steak Seasoning. Look for it in the spice aisle.

ZESTY MARINATED SHRIMP

These easy shrimp look impressive on a buffet table and taste even better! The zesty marinade has a wonderful spicy citrus flavor. I especially like this recipe because I can prepare it ahead of time.
—Mary Jane Guest, Alamosa, CO

Prep: 10 min. + chilling
Makes: about 4½ dozen pieces

- 12 **lemon or lime slices**
- ½ **cup thinly sliced red onion**
- 1 **tablespoon minced fresh parsley**
- ½ **cup canola oil**
- ½ **cup lime juice**
- ½ **teaspoon salt**
- ½ **teaspoon dill weed**
- ⅛ **teaspoon hot pepper sauce**
- 2 **pounds peeled and deveined cooked shrimp (26-30 per pound)**

Place first eight ingredients in a large bowl; toss with shrimp. Refrigerate, covered, for 4 hours, stirring occasionally. Drain before serving.

AU GRATIN PARTY POTATOES

When putting on a large party for their American Legion Post, my father and uncle prepared this yummy potato dish. I've used the recipe for smaller groups by making a half or quarter of it. It's simple to divide.
—Crystal Kolady, Henrietta, NY

Prep: 45 min. • **Bake:** 45 min.
Makes: about 60 servings (¾ cup each)

- 20 **pounds potatoes, peeled, cubed and cooked**
- 4 **cans (12 ounces each) evaporated milk**
- 3 **packages (16 ounces each) process cheese (Velveeta), cubed**

- 1 **cup butter, cubed**
- 2 **tablespoons salt**
- 2 **teaspoons pepper**
  Paprika, optional

1. Preheat oven to 350°. In several large bowls, combine potatoes, milk, cheese, butter, salt and pepper. Transfer to four greased 13x9-in. baking dishes.
2. Bake, uncovered, for 45-50 minutes or until bubbly. Sprinkle with paprika if desired.

HAM BALLS WITH BROWN SUGAR GLAZE

These smoky-sweet meatballs are truly a Pennsylvania Dutch specialty. I like setting them out when I'm expecting lots of friends.
—Janet Zeger, Middletown, PA

Prep: 30 min. • **Bake:** 30 min.
Makes: about 6 dozen

- 1 **pound fully cooked ham, cubed**
- 1 **pound ground pork**
- 1 **cup milk**
- 1 **cup crushed cornflakes**
- 1 **large egg, lightly beaten**
- ¼ **cup packed brown sugar**
- 1 **tablespoon ground mustard**
- ½ **teaspoon salt**

GLAZE
- 1 **cup packed brown sugar**
- ¼ **cup vinegar**
- 1 **tablespoon ground mustard**

1. Preheat oven to 350°. Pulse ham in batches in a food processor until finely ground. Combine with the next seven ingredients just until mixed. Shape into 1-in. balls; place in a single layer on greased 15x10-in. rimmed baking pans.
2. For glaze, cook and stir all ingredients in a small saucepan over medium heat until sugar is dissolved. Spoon over ham balls. Bake until ham balls are just beginning to brown, 30-35 minutes, rotating pans and carefully stirring halfway through. Gently toss in glaze. Serve warm.

1. In the bowl of a heavy-duty stand mixer, beat butter and ice cream until blended (mixture will appear curdled). Add flour and sugar; mix well. Divide dough into four portions; cover and refrigerate 2 hours or until easy to handle.

2. Preheat oven to 350°. On a lightly floured surface, roll one portion of dough into a 12x10-in. rectangle; cut into 2-in. squares. Place a teaspoonful of filling in the center of each square. Overlap two opposite corners of dough over filling; pinch tightly to seal. Place 2 in. apart on ungreased baking sheets. Repeat with remaining dough and filling.

3. Bake 11-14 minutes or until the bottoms are lightly browned. Cool 1 minute before removing cookies from pans to wire racks. Sprinkle with the confectioners' sugar if desired.

Note: This recipe was tested with Solo brand cake and pastry filling. Look for it in the baking aisle of your grocery store.

★ ★ ★ ★ ★ **READER REVIEW**

"I remember my mother making something similar, but I could never find a recipe until now. These are delicious! My family loved them and I wound up making another double batch a few days after baking the first batch. Definitely a keeper!"

KRISTINECHAYES TASTEOFHOME.COM

RICH PEANUT CLUSTERS

It's cheaper to make these bite-size morsels than it is to buy them in bulk at the store. Best of all, family and friends agree: These taste better!
—Janice Garvert, Plainville, KS

Prep: 20 min. + chilling
Makes: about 15 dozen

- 2 packages (12 ounces each) semisweet chocolate chips
- 2 packages (10 to 12 ounces each) vanilla or white chips
- 1 tablespoon shortening
- 1 teaspoon vanilla extract
- ½ teaspoon butter, softened
- 2 cans (12 ounces each) salted peanuts

1. In a microwave, melt chips and shortening; stir until smooth. Stir in the vanilla and butter. Add peanuts; mix well.

2. Drop by teaspoonfuls onto waxed paper-lined pans. Refrigerate until set. Store in an airtight container.

ICE CREAM KOLACHKES

These traditional pastries have Polish and Czech roots. The ice cream in the recipe offers a unique twist.
—Diane Turner, Brunswick, OH

Prep: 1 hour + chilling
Bake: 15 min./batch
Makes: 10 dozen

- 2 cups butter, softened
- 1 pint vanilla ice cream, softened
- 4 cups all-purpose flour
- 2 tablespoons sugar
- 2 cans (12 ounces each) apricot and/or raspberry cake and pastry filling
- 1 to 2 tablespoons confectioners' sugar, optional

Citrus-Herb
Pork Roast
page 189

Slow Cooker

Grab your slow cooker, because when it comes to
make-and-take success, there's no better travel partner.
Load up that little guy and create a savory crowd-pleaser that
simmers on its own. Then, pack it up and head off to the party!

SLOW COOKER CANDIED NUTS

I like giving spiced nuts as holiday gifts. This slow cooker recipe with ginger and cinnamon is so good, you just might use it all year long.

—Yvonne Starlin, Westmoreland, TN

Prep: 10 min. • **Cook:** 2 hours
Makes: 4 cups

- ½ cup butter, melted
- ½ cup confectioners' sugar
- 1½ teaspoons ground cinnamon
- ¼ teaspoon ground ginger
- ¼ teaspoon ground allspice
- 1½ cups pecan halves
- 1½ cups walnut halves
- 1 cup unblanched almonds

1. In a greased 3-qt. slow cooker, mix butter, confectioners' sugar and spices. Add nuts; toss to coat. Cook, covered, on low for 2-3 hours or until nuts are crisp, stirring once.

2. Transfer nuts to waxed paper to cool completely. Store in an airtight container.

SEAFOOD CIOPPINO

If you're looking for a great seafood recipe to create in your slow cooker, this classic fish stew is just the ticket. It's full to the brim with clams, crab, fish and shrimp and is fancy enough to be an elegant meal.

—Lisa Moriarty, Wilton, NH

Prep: 20 min. • **Cook:** 4½ hours
Makes: 8 servings (2½ quarts)

- 1 can (28 ounces) diced tomatoes, undrained
- 2 medium onions, chopped
- 3 celery ribs, chopped
- 1 bottle (8 ounces) clam juice
- 1 can (6 ounces) tomato paste
- ½ cup white wine or ½ cup vegetable broth
- 5 garlic cloves, minced
- 1 tablespoon red wine vinegar
- 1 tablespoon olive oil
- 1 to 2 teaspoons Italian seasoning
- 1 bay leaf
- ½ teaspoon sugar
- 1 pound haddock fillets, cut into 1-inch pieces
- 1 pound uncooked shrimp (41-50 per pound), peeled and deveined
- 1 can (6 ounces) chopped clams, undrained
- 1 can (6 ounces) lump crabmeat, drained
- 2 tablespoons minced fresh parsley

1. In a 4- or 5-qt. slow cooker, combine the first 12 ingredients. Cook, covered, on low 4-5 hours.

2. Stir in the fish and seafood. Cook, covered, 20-30 minutes longer or until fish just begins to flake easily with a fork and shrimp turn pink.

3. Remove bay leaf. Stir in parsley.

★ ★ ★ ★ ★ **READER REVIEW**

"I added bay scallops and crushed red pepper flakes to the mix. This was so good, and even better reheated the next day! I didn't have red wine vinegar, so I used more white wine."

ITSMESUSAN TASTEOFHOME.COM

SLOW COOKER HOT FUDGE CAKE

A cake baked in a slow cooker may seem unusual, but smiles around the dinner table prove how tasty it is! Sometimes, for a change of pace, I substitute butterscotch chips for chocolate.

—Marleen Adkins, Placentia, CA

Prep: 20 min. • **Cook:** 4 hours
Makes: 8 servings

1¾ cups packed brown sugar, divided
1 cup all-purpose flour
6 tablespoons baking cocoa, divided
2 teaspoons baking powder
½ teaspoon salt
½ cup 2% milk
2 tablespoons butter, melted
½ teaspoon vanilla extract
1½ cups semisweet chocolate chips
1¾ cups boiling water
Vanilla ice cream

1. In a small bowl, combine 1 cup brown sugar, flour, 3 tablespoons cocoa, baking powder and salt. Combine the milk, butter and vanilla; stir into dry ingredients just until combined.
2. Spread into a 3-qt. slow cooker coated with cooking spray. Sprinkle with the chocolate chips. In another bowl, combine the remaining brown sugar and cocoa; stir in boiling water. Slowly pour over batter (do not stir).
3. Cover and cook on high for 4-4½ hours or until a toothpick inserted in the center of the cake comes out clean. Serve warm with ice cream.

AFRICAN PEANUT SWEET POTATO STEW

When I was in college, my mom made an addicting sweet potato stew. I shared it with friends, and now we all serve it to our own kids. They love it just as much as we do.

—Alexis Scatchell, Niles, IL

Prep: 20 min. • **Cook:** 6 hours
Makes: 8 servings (2½ quarts)

1 can (28 ounces) diced tomatoes, undrained
1 cup fresh cilantro leaves
½ cup chunky peanut butter
3 garlic cloves, halved
2 teaspoons ground cumin
1 teaspoon salt
½ teaspoon ground cinnamon
¼ teaspoon smoked paprika
3 pounds sweet potatoes (about 6 medium), peeled and cut into 1-inch pieces
1 can (15 ounces) garbanzo beans or chickpeas, rinsed and drained
1 cup water
8 cups chopped fresh kale
Chopped peanuts and additional cilantro leaves, optional

1. Place the first eight ingredients in a food processor; process until pureed. Transfer to a 5-qt. slow cooker; stir in the sweet potatoes, garbanzo beans and water.
2. Cook, covered, on low 6-8 hours or until potatoes are tender, adding kale during the last 30 minutes. If desired, top each serving with chopped peanuts and additional cilantro.

SAVORY BEEF SANDWICHES

Before heading to work in the morning, I get this going in the slow cooker. Then it's all ready to serve—usually with hard rolls and potato salad—as soon as my husband and I walk in the door. It makes a lot, so if you have leftovers, simply pack them up for the freezer. Serve reheated beef on rolls with chips on the side.
—Lynn Williamson, Hayward, WI

Prep: 15 min. • **Cook:** 6 hours
Makes: 10 servings

1 tablespoon dried minced onion
2 teaspoons salt
2 teaspoons garlic powder
2 teaspoons dried oregano
1 teaspoon dried rosemary, crushed
1 teaspoon caraway seeds
1 teaspoon dried marjoram
1 teaspoon celery seed
¼ teaspoon cayenne pepper
1 boneless beef chuck roast
   (3 to 4 pounds), halved
10 sandwich rolls, split

Combine seasonings; rub over roast. Place in a 5-qt. slow cooker. Cover and cook on low for 6-8 hours or until meat is tender. Shred with a fork. Serve on sandwich rolls.

Note: No liquid is added to the slow cooker. The moisture comes from the roast.

CITRUS-HERB PORK ROAST

The genius combination of seasonings and citrus in this tender roast reminds us why we cherish tasty recipes.
—Laura Brodine, Colorado Springs, CO

Prep: 25 min. • **Cook:** 4 hours
Makes: 8 servings

- 1 boneless pork sirloin roast (3 to 4 pounds)
- 1 teaspoon dried oregano
- ½ teaspoon ground ginger
- ½ teaspoon pepper
- 2 medium onions, cut into thin wedges
- 1 cup plus 3 tablespoons orange juice, divided
- 1 tablespoon sugar
- 1 tablespoon white grapefruit juice
- 1 tablespoon steak sauce
- 1 tablespoon reduced-sodium soy sauce
- 1 teaspoon grated orange zest
- ½ teaspoon salt
- 3 tablespoons cornstarch
  Hot cooked egg noodles
  Minced fresh oregano, optional

1. Cut the roast in half. In a small bowl, combine the oregano, ginger and pepper; rub over pork. In a large nonstick skillet coated with cooking spray, brown roast on all sides. Transfer to a 4-qt. slow cooker; add onions.
2. In a small bowl, combine 1 cup orange juice, sugar, grapefruit juice, steak sauce and soy sauce; pour over top. Cover and cook on low for 4-5 hours or until meat is tender. Remove meat and onions to a serving platter; keep warm.
3. Skim fat from cooking juices; transfer to a small saucepan. Add orange zest and salt. Bring to a boil. Combine cornstarch and remaining orange juice until smooth. Gradually stir into the pan. Bring to a boil; cook and stir for 2 minutes or until thickened. Serve with pork and cooked egg noodles; if desired, sprinkle with minced fresh oregano.

MUSHROOM WILD RICE

This is one of my favorite side-dish recipes from my mother. With only seven ingredients, it's quick to assemble in the morning before I leave for work. By the time I get home, mouthwatering aromas have filled the house.
—Bob Malchow, Monon, IN

Prep: 5 min. • **Cook:** 3 hours
Makes: 16 servings

- 2¼ cups water
- 1 can (10½ ounces) condensed beef consomme, undiluted
- 1 can (10½ ounces) condensed French onion soup, undiluted
- 3 cans (4 ounces each) mushroom stems and pieces, drained
- ½ cup butter, melted
- 1 cup uncooked brown rice
- 1 cup uncooked wild rice

In a 3-qt. slow cooker, combine all ingredients. Cover and cook on low for 3-4 hours or until rice is tender.

GREEN CHILE CHICKEN CHILI

This easy chili is loaded with chicken and beans. You can always tame the spicy heat with a dollop or two of sour cream.

—Fred Lockwood, Plano, TX

Prep: 25 min. • **Cook:** 5 hours
Makes: 10 servings (3½ quarts)

- 4 **bone-in chicken breast halves (14 ounces each)**
- 2 **medium onions, chopped**
- 2 **medium green peppers, chopped**
- 1 **cup pickled jalapeno slices**
- 1 **can (4 ounces) chopped green chilies**
- 2 **jars (16 ounces each) salsa verde**
- 2 **cans (15½ ounces each) navy beans, rinsed and drained**
- 1 **cup (8 ounces) sour cream**
- ½ **cup minced fresh cilantro**
  Optional toppings: shredded Colby-Monterey Jack cheese, sour cream and crushed tortilla chips

1. Place the chicken, onions, peppers, jalapenos and chilies in a 5- or 6-qt. slow cooker. Pour salsa over top. Cover and cook on low for 5-6 hours or until chicken is tender.
2. Remove chicken; cool slightly. Shred chicken with two forks, discarding skin and bones; return meat to slow cooker. Stir in the navy beans, sour cream and fresh cilantro; heat through. Serve with toppings of your choice.
Freeze option: Before adding sour cream, cilantro and toppings, cool chili. Freeze in freezer containers. To use, partially thaw in refrigerator overnight. Heat through in a saucepan, stirring occasionally and adding a little water if necessary. Stir in sour cream and cilantro. Top as desired.
Note: Wear disposable gloves when cutting hot peppers; the oils can burn skin. Avoid touching your face.

EASY SLOW COOKER MAC & CHEESE

My sons say I'm the best mom in the world when I make this creamy crowd-pleaser. You simply can't beat a response like that, can you?

—Heidi Fleek, Hamburg, PA

Prep: 25 min. • **Cook:** 1 hour
Makes: 8 servings

- 2 **cups uncooked elbow macaroni**
- 1 **can (10¾ ounces) condensed cheddar cheese soup, undiluted**
- 1 **cup 2% milk**
- ½ **cup sour cream**
- ¼ **cup butter, cubed**
- ½ **teaspoon onion powder**
- ¼ **teaspoon white pepper**
- ⅛ **teaspoon salt**
- 1 **cup shredded cheddar cheese**
- 1 **cup shredded fontina cheese**
- 1 **cup shredded provolone cheese**

1. Cook macaroni according to package directions for al dente. Meanwhile, in a large saucepan, combine soup, milk, sour cream, butter and seasonings; cook and stir over medium-low heat until blended. Stir in cheeses until melted.
2. Drain macaroni; transfer to a greased 3-qt. slow cooker. Stir in cheese mixture. Cook, covered, on low 1-2 hours or until heated through.

10 uncooked bratwurst links
3 bottles (12 ounces each) light beer or nonalcoholic beer
1 large sweet onion, sliced
1 can (14 ounces) sauerkraut, rinsed and well-drained
¾ cup mayonnaise
¼ cup chili sauce
2 tablespoons ketchup
1 tablespoon finely chopped onion
2 teaspoons sweet pickle relish
1 garlic clove, minced
⅛ teaspoon pepper
10 hoagie buns, split
10 slices Swiss cheese

1. In a large skillet, brown bratwurst links in batches; drain. In a 5-qt. slow cooker, combine the beer, sliced sweet onion and sauerkraut; add bratwurst. Cook mixture, covered, on low for 7-9 hours or until sausages are cooked through.
2. Preheat oven to 350°. In a small bowl, mix mayonnaise, chili sauce, ketchup, chopped onion, relish, garlic and pepper until blended. Spread over cut sides of buns; top with cheese, bratwurst and sauerkraut mixture. Place on an ungreased baking sheet. Bake 8-10 minutes or until cheese is melted.

WARM FETA CHEESE DIP

We're huge fans of appetizers, and this super easy dip is a mashup of some of our favorite ingredients. It goes so well with a basket of crunchy tortilla chips or with toasted slices of French baguette.
—Ashley Lecker, Green Bay, WI

Prep: 5 min. • **Cook:** 2 hours
Makes: 2 cups

1 package (8 ounces) cream cheese, softened
1½ cups (6 ounces) crumbled feta cheese
½ cup chopped roasted sweet red peppers
3 tablespoons minced fresh basil or 2 teaspoons dried basil
    Sliced French bread baguette or tortilla chips

In a small bowl, beat cream cheese, feta cheese, peppers and basil until blended. Transfer to a greased 1½-qt. slow cooker; cook, covered, on low 2-3 hours or until heated through. Serve with baguette slices or chips.
Note: To prepare in the oven, preheat oven to 400°. In a small bowl, beat cream cheese, feta cheese, peppers and basil until blended. Transfer to a greased 3-cup baking dish. Bake 25-30 minutes or until bubbly.

SLOW-COOKED REUBEN BRATS

Sauerkraut gives these beer-simmered brats a big flavor boost, but it's the special chili sauce and melted cheese that put them over the top. I also recommend trying the sauce on your favorite burger; you won't be sorry.
—Alana Simmons, Johnstown, PA

Prep: 30 min. • **Cook:** 7¼ hours
Makes: 10 servings

SLOW-COOKED CHICKEN ENCHILADA SOUP

This recipe always delivers big bowls of comfort. Toppings like avocado, sour cream and tortilla strips are a must. It's a savory change of pace.
—Heather Sewell, Harrisonville, MO

Prep: 25 min. • **Cook:** 6 hours
Makes: 8 servings (3¼ quarts)

- 1 tablespoon canola oil
- 2 Anaheim or poblano peppers, finely chopped
- 1 medium onion, chopped
- 3 garlic cloves, minced
- 1 pound boneless skinless chicken breasts
- 1 carton (48 ounces) chicken broth
- 1 can (14½ ounces) Mexican diced tomatoes, undrained
- 1 can (10 ounces) enchilada sauce
- 2 tablespoons tomato paste
- 1 tablespoon chili powder
- 2 teaspoons ground cumin
- ½ teaspoon pepper
- ½ to 1 teaspoon chipotle hot pepper sauce, optional
- ⅓ cup minced fresh cilantro
  Optional toppings: shredded cheddar cheese, cubed avocado, sour cream and crispy tortilla strips

1. In a large skillet, heat oil over medium heat. Add peppers and onion; cook and stir 6-8 minutes or until tender. Add garlic; cook 1 minute longer. Transfer pepper mixture and chicken to a 5- or 6-qt. slow cooker. Stir in broth, tomatoes, enchilada sauce, tomato paste, seasonings and, if desired, pepper sauce. Cook, covered, on low 6-8 hours or until chicken is tender (a thermometer should read at least 165°).
2. Remove chicken from slow cooker. Shred with two forks; return to slow cooker. Stir in cilantro. Serve with toppings as desired.
Freeze option: Freeze cooled soup in freezer containers. To use, partially thaw in refrigerator overnight. Heat through in a saucepan, stirring occasionally and adding a little water if necessary.

SLOW COOKER SPICED POACHED PEARS

Some of the many reasons I love this dessert recipe are: It's on the healthy side; it's easy to make; the recipe can be mostly prepared in advance of company arriving; and the presentation is lovely.
—Jill Mant, Denver, CO

Prep: 25 min. • **Cook:** 4 hours
Makes: 8 servings

- 1½ cups dry red wine or cranberry juice
- ⅓ cup packed brown sugar
- 2 tablespoons dried cherries
- 1 tablespoon ground cinnamon
- 1 whole star anise
- 1 dried Sichuan peppercorn, optional
- 4 ripe Bosc pears
GANACHE
- 6 ounces bittersweet chocolate, chopped
- ¼ cup heavy whipping cream
TOPPINGS
- 2 tablespoons pine nuts
  Fresh blackberries
  Sweetened whipped cream, optional

1. In a 3-qt. slow cooker, mix wine, brown sugar, cherries, cinnamon, star anise and, if desired, peppercorn until blended. Peel and cut pears lengthwise in half. Remove cores, leaving a small well in the center of each. Arrange pears in wine mixture.
2. Cook, covered, on low for 4-5 hours or until pears are almost tender. Discard star anise and, if using, peppercorn.
3. Place chocolate in a small bowl. In a small saucepan, bring cream just to a boil. Pour over the chocolate; stir with a whisk until smooth.
4. To serve, remove pears to dessert dishes; drizzle with some of the poaching liquid. Spoon ganache into wells of pears. Top with pine nuts and blackberries. If desired, serve with whipped cream.

NORTH AFRICAN CHICKEN & RICE

I'm always looking to try recipes from different cultures, and this one is a huge favorite. We love the spice combinations. It cooks equally well in a pressure cooker.
—Courtney Stultz, Weir, KS

Prep: 10 min. • **Cook:** 4 hours
Makes: 8 servings

- 1 medium onion, diced
- 1 tablespoon olive oil
- 8 boneless skinless chicken thighs (about 2 pounds)
- 1 tablespoon minced fresh cilantro
- 1 teaspoon ground turmeric
- 1 teaspoon paprika
- 1 teaspoon sea salt
- ½ teaspoon pepper
- ½ teaspoon ground cinnamon
- ½ teaspoon chili powder
- 1 cup golden raisins
- ½ to 1 cup chopped pitted green olives
- 1 medium lemon, sliced
- 2 garlic cloves, minced
- ½ cup chicken broth or water
- 4 cups hot cooked brown rice

In a 3- or 4-qt. slow cooker, combine the onion and oil. Place chicken thighs on top; sprinkle with the next seven ingredients. Top with raisins, olives, lemon and garlic. Add broth. Cook, covered, on low until chicken is tender, 4-5 hours. Serve with hot cooked rice.

SLOW COOKER BERRY COBBLER

Enjoy the amazing flavor of homemade cobbler without heating up the kitchen. Whip up this yummy dessert for your friends and family at any time of year and you'll see what I mean.
—Karen Jarocki, Yuma, AZ

Prep: 15 min. • **Cook:** 1¾ hours
Makes: 8 servings

- 1¼ cups all-purpose flour, divided
- 2 tablespoons plus 1 cup sugar, divided
- 1 teaspoon baking powder
- ¼ teaspoon ground cinnamon
- 1 large egg
- ¼ cup fat-free milk
- 2 tablespoons canola oil
- ⅛ teaspoon salt
- 2 cups fresh or frozen raspberries, thawed
- 2 cups fresh or frozen blueberries, thawed
  Low-fat vanilla frozen yogurt, optional

1. In a bowl, whisk together 1 cup flour, 2 tablespoons sugar, baking powder and cinnamon. In another bowl, whisk together egg, milk and oil; add to dry ingredients, stirring just until moistened (batter will be thick). Spread onto the bottom of a 5-qt. slow cooker coated with cooking spray.
2. Mix salt and the remaining flour and sugar; toss with berries. Spoon over batter. Cook, covered, on high until berry mixture is bubbly, 1¾-2 hours. If desired, serve with frozen yogurt.

BRISKET FOR A BUNCH

This makes tender slices of delicious beef for a crowd. I make it a day ahead and set it in the refrigerator because it's easy to slice the brisket thin when it's chilled. Then, just reheat it in the savory juices.
—Dawn Fagerstrom, Warren, MN

Prep: 20 min. • **Cook:** 7 hours
Makes: 12 servings

- 1 fresh beef brisket (2½ pounds), cut in half
- 1 tablespoon canola oil
- ½ cup chopped celery
- ½ cup chopped onion
- ¾ cup beef broth
- ½ cup tomato sauce
- ¼ cup water
- ¼ cup sugar
- 2 tablespoons onion soup mix
- 1 tablespoon cider vinegar
- 12 split hamburger buns or garlic bread slices

1. In a large skillet, brown brisket in oil on both sides; transfer to a 3-qt. slow cooker. In the same skillet, saute celery and onion for 1 minute. Gradually add the broth, tomato sauce and water; stir to loosen the browned bits from pan. Add the sugar, soup mix and vinegar; bring to a boil. Pour over brisket.
2. Cover and cook on low for 7-8 hours or until the meat is tender. Let stand for 5 minutes before slicing. Skim fat from cooking juices. Serve with buns or bread and cooking juices.
Note: This is a fresh beef brisket, not corned beef.

PEPPERED MEATBALLS

Plenty of ground pepper gives these unique meatballs their irresistible zip. Double or triple the recipe for parties, or serve them over noodles as an entree.
—Darla Schroeder, Stanley, ND

Prep: 35 min. • **Cook:** 2 hours
Makes: 1½ dozen

- ½ cup sour cream
- 2 teaspoons grated Parmesan or Romano cheese
- 2 to 3 teaspoons pepper
- 1 teaspoon salt
- 1 teaspoon dry bread crumbs
- ½ teaspoon garlic powder
- 1½ pounds ground beef

SAUCE
- 1 can (10¾ ounces) condensed cream of mushroom soup, undiluted
- 1 cup (8 ounces) sour cream
- 2 teaspoons dill weed
- ½ teaspoon sugar
- ½ teaspoon pepper
- ¼ teaspoon garlic powder

1. In a large bowl, combine sour cream and cheese. Add the pepper, salt, bread crumbs and garlic powder. Crumble the meat over the mixture and mix well. Shape into 1-in. balls.
2. Place meatballs on a greased rack in a shallow baking pan. Bake at 350° for 20-25 minutes or until meat is no longer pink; drain.
3. Transfer to a 1½-qt. slow cooker. Combine the sauce ingredients; pour over meatballs. Cover and cook on high for 2-3 hours or until heated through.

EASY PORK POSOLE

Looking for a meal in a bowl? Sit down to a Mexican classic full of cubed pork, sliced sausage, hominy and more. It all goes into the slow cooker, so you can come home to a table-ready dinner or haul it off to a potluck.

—Greg Fontenot, The Woodlands, TX

Prep: 30 min. • **Cook:** 6 hours
Makes: 8 servings (2 quarts)

- 1 tablespoon canola oil
- ½ pound boneless pork shoulder butt roast, cubed
- ½ pound fully cooked andouille sausage links, sliced
- 6 cups reduced-sodium chicken broth
- 2 medium tomatoes, seeded and chopped
- 1 can (16 ounces) hominy, rinsed and drained
- 1 cup minced fresh cilantro
- 1 medium onion, chopped
- 4 green onions, chopped
- 1 jalapeno pepper, seeded and chopped
- 2 garlic cloves, minced
- 1 tablespoon chili powder
- 1 teaspoon ground cumin
- ½ teaspoon cayenne pepper
- ½ teaspoon coarsely ground pepper
  Optional ingredients: corn tortillas, chopped onion, minced fresh cilantro and lime wedges

1. In a large skillet, heat oil over medium-high heat. Brown pork and sausage; drain. Transfer to a 4-qt. slow cooker.
2. Stir in broth, tomatoes, hominy, cilantro, onion, green onions, jalapeno, garlic, chili powder, cumin, cayenne and pepper. Cook, covered, on low 6-8 hours or until meat is tender. If desired, serve with tortillas, onion, fresh cilantro and lime wedges.

Note: Wear disposable gloves when cutting hot peppers; the oils can burn skin. Avoid touching your face.

CRUNCHY CANDY CLUSTERS

Before I retired, I'd take these yummy peanut butter bites to work for special occasions. They're so simple! I still make them for big get-togethers, because my family looks forward to the coated cereal and marshmallow clusters.

—Faye O'Bryan, Owensboro, KY

Prep: 15 min. • **Cook:** 1 hour + standing
Makes: about 6½ dozen

- 2 pounds white candy coating, coarsely chopped
- 1½ cups peanut butter
- ½ teaspoon almond extract, optional
- 4 cups Cap'n Crunch cereal
- 4 cups crisp rice cereal
- 4 cups miniature marshmallows

1. Place candy coating in a 5-qt. slow cooker. Cover and cook on high for 1 hour. Add peanut butter. If desired, stir in extract.
2. In a large bowl, combine the cereals and marshmallows. Add the peanut butter mixture and stir until the cereal mixture is well-coated. Drop by tablespoonfuls onto waxed paper. Let stand until set. Store clusters at room temperature.

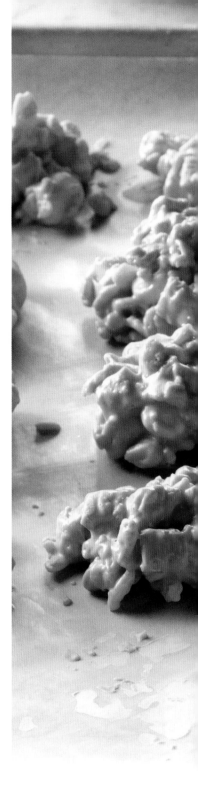

3 pounds lamb stew meat,
cut into 1½-inch cubes
1 teaspoon salt
1 teaspoon pepper
4 tablespoons olive oil, divided
6 medium carrots, sliced
2 medium onions, chopped
6 garlic cloves, minced
2 teaspoons grated lemon zest
¼ cup lemon juice
1 tablespoon minced
fresh gingerroot
1½ teaspoons ground cinnamon
1½ teaspoons ground cumin
1½ teaspoons paprika
2½ cups reduced-sodium
chicken broth
¼ cup sweet vermouth
¼ cup honey
½ cup pitted dates, chopped
½ cup sliced almonds, toasted

SLOW COOKER MEATBALL SANDWICHES

Our approach to meatball sandwiches is a simple one—cook the meatballs low and slow, load them into hoagie buns and top with provolone and pepperoncini. Enjoy!
—Stacie Nicholls, Spring Creek, NV

....

Prep: 5 min. • **Cook:** 3 hours
Makes: 8 servings

2 packages (12 ounces each)
frozen fully cooked Italian
meatballs, thawed
2 jars (24 ounces each)
marinara sauce
8 hoagie buns, split
8 slices provolone cheese
Sliced pepperoncini, optional

1. Place meatballs and sauce in a 3- or 4-qt. slow cooker. Cook, covered, on low 3-4 hours until the meatballs are heated through.
2. On each bun bottom, layer cheese, meatballs and, if desired, pepperoncini; replace tops.

TANGY LAMB TAGINE

I love lamb stew, but wanted to try something a little different, so I created this recipe that uses Moroccan spices. It's a wonderful way to use lamb, and it's easy to make in the slow cooker. If you ask me, the stew tastes even better served a day or two later.
—Bridget Klusman, Otsego, MI

....

Prep: 40 min. • **Cook:** 8 hours
Makes: 8 servings

1. Sprinkle lamb with salt and pepper. In a Dutch oven, brown meat in batches in 2 tablespoons oil. Using a slotted spoon, transfer to a 4- or 5-qt. slow cooker.
2. In the Dutch oven, saute the carrots, onions, garlic and lemon zest in remaining oil until crisp-tender. Add the lemon juice, ginger, cinnamon, cumin and paprika; cook and stir 2 minutes longer. Add to slow cooker.
3. Stir in the broth, vermouth, honey and pitted dates. Cover and cook on low for 8-10 hours or until lamb is tender. Sprinkle with almonds.

CREAMY BRATWURST STEW

I adapted a baked stew recipe from the newspaper to create a simple slow-cooked version. Rich and hearty, it's the best comfort food for cold winter nights. It's also great for a holiday open house.
—Susan Holmes, Germantown, WI

Prep: 20 min. • **Cook:** 6½ hours
Makes: 8 servings

- 1¾ pounds potatoes (about 4 medium), peeled and cubed
- 2 medium carrots, chopped
- 2 celery ribs, chopped
- 1 medium onion, chopped
- 1 medium green pepper, chopped
- 2 pounds uncooked bratwurst links
- ½ cup chicken broth
- 1 teaspoon salt
- 1 teaspoon dried basil
- ½ teaspoon pepper
- 2 cups half-and-half cream
- 1 tablespoon cornstarch
- 3 tablespoons cold water

1. Place the first five ingredients in a 5-qt. slow cooker; toss to combine. Top with bratwurst. Mix broth and seasonings; pour over top.

2. Cook, covered, on low until sausage is cooked through and vegetables are tender, 6-7 hours. Remove sausages from slow cooker; cut into 1-in. slices. Return to potato mixture; stir in cream.

3. Mix cornstarch and water until smooth; stir into stew. Cook, covered, on high until thickened, about 30 minutes.

SOUTHWESTERN NACHOS

Guests will go crazy when you serve two heaping pans of this cheesy nacho casserole, which features tender chunks of pork. You don't need to worry about filling the chip bowl because the tortilla chips are conveniently baked right into the dish! What a party pleaser!
—Kelly Byler, Goshen, IN

Prep: 40 min. • **Cook:** 7¼ hours
Makes: 30 servings

- 2 boneless whole pork loin roasts (3½ pounds each)
- 1 cup unsweetened apple juice
- 6 garlic cloves, minced
- 1 teaspoon salt
- 1 teaspoon liquid smoke, optional
- 2½ cups barbecue sauce
- ⅓ cup packed brown sugar
- 2 tablespoons honey
- 1 package (16 ounces) tortilla chips
- 1½ cups frozen corn
- 1 can (15 ounces) black beans, rinsed and drained
- 1 medium tomato, seeded and chopped
- 1 medium red onion, chopped
- ⅓ cup minced fresh cilantro
- 1 jalapeno pepper, seeded and chopped
- 2 teaspoons lime juice
- 1 package (16 ounces) process cheese (Velveeta), cubed
- ¼ cup 2% milk

1. Cut each roast in half; place in two 5-qt. slow cookers. Combine the apple juice, garlic, salt and, if desired, liquid smoke; pour over meat. Cover and cook on low 7-8 hours or until tender.
2. Preheat oven to 375°. Shred pork with two forks; place in a very large bowl. Stir in barbecue sauce, brown sugar and honey. Divide tortilla chips between two greased 13x9-in. baking dishes; top with pork mixture. Combine corn, beans, tomato, onion, cilantro, jalapeno and lime juice; spoon over the pork mixture. Bake, uncovered, for 15-20 minutes or until heated through.
3. Meanwhile, in a small saucepan, melt cheese with milk. Drizzle cheese sauce over nachos.

Note: Wear disposable gloves when cutting hot peppers; the oils can burn skin. Avoid touching your face.

MAKE AHEAD
BEER-BRAISED PULLED HAM

To jazz up leftover ham, I slow cook it with a beer sauce. Buns loaded with pickles, mustard and this ham are irresistible.
—Ann Sheehy, Lawrence, MA

Prep: 10 min. • **Cook:** 7 hours
Makes: 16 servings

- 2 bottles (12 ounces each) beer or nonalcoholic beer
- ¾ cup German or Dijon mustard, divided
- ½ teaspoon coarsely ground pepper
- 1 fully cooked bone-in ham (about 4 pounds)
- 4 fresh rosemary sprigs
- 16 pretzel hamburger buns, split
  Dill pickle slices, optional

1. In a 5-qt. slow cooker, whisk together beer and ½ cup mustard. Stir in pepper. Add ham and rosemary. Cook, covered, on low until tender, 7-9 hours.
2. Remove ham; cool slightly. Discard rosemary sprigs. Skim fat. When ham is cool enough to handle, shred meat with two forks. Discard bone. Return to slow cooker; heat through.
3. Using tongs, place shredded ham on pretzel buns; top with remaining mustard and, if desired, dill pickle slices.

Freeze option: Freeze cooled ham mixture in freezer containers. To use, partially thaw in the refrigerator overnight. Heat through in a covered saucepan, stirring gently and adding a little water if necessary.

Freeze option: Freeze cooled pork mixture in freezer containers. To use, partially thaw in the refrigerator overnight. Heat through in a covered saucepan, stirring gently and adding a little broth if necessary.

APPLE BETTY WITH ALMOND CREAM

I love making this treat for friends during the peak of apple season. I plan a quick meal of soup and bread so we can get right to the dessert!
—Elizabeth Godecke, Chicago, IL

Prep: 15 min. • **Cook:** 3 hours
Makes: 8 servings

- 3 pounds tart apples, peeled and sliced
- 10 slices cinnamon-raisin bread, cubed
- ¾ cup packed brown sugar
- ½ cup butter, melted
- 1 teaspoon almond extract
- ½ teaspoon ground cinnamon
- ¼ teaspoon ground cardamom
- ⅛ teaspoon salt

WHIPPED CREAM
- 1 cup heavy whipping cream
- 2 tablespoons sugar
- 1 teaspoon grated lemon zest
- ½ teaspoon almond extract

1. Place apples in an ungreased 4- or 5-qt. slow cooker. In a large bowl, combine the bread, brown sugar, butter, extract, cinnamon, cardamom and salt; spoon over apples. Cover and cook on low for 3-4 hours or until apples are tender.
2. In a small bowl, beat cream until it begins to thicken. Add the sugar, lemon zest and extract; beat until soft peaks form. Serve with apple mixture.

MAKE AHEAD
ASIAN SHREDDED PORK SANDWICHES

On cool-weather weeknights, the slow cooker is our friend. The addition of plums might be a surprise in these juicy pork sandwiches, but they add a little sweetness and make the meat extra tender. Yum!
—Holly Battiste, Barrington, NJ

Prep: 30 min. • **Cook:** 6 hours
Makes: 10 servings

- 1 can (15 ounces) plums, drained and pitted
- 1 tablespoon Sriracha Asian hot chili sauce
- 1 tablespoon hoisin sauce
- 1 tablespoon reduced-sodium soy sauce
- 1 tablespoon rice vinegar
- 1 tablespoon honey
- 2 garlic cloves, minced
- 1 teaspoon pepper
- 1 teaspoon sesame oil
- ½ teaspoon ground ginger
- ¼ teaspoon salt
- 2 tablespoons canola oil
- 1 boneless pork shoulder butt roast (3 pounds)
- 4 medium carrots, finely chopped
- 10 ciabatta rolls, split
  Shredded napa or other cabbage

1. Mix first 11 ingredients. In a large skillet, heat oil over medium-high heat. Brown roast on all sides.
2. Place the carrots in a 4- or 5-qt. slow cooker. Add roast; pour the plum mixture over the top. Cook, covered, on low until pork is tender, 6-8 hours.
3. Remove pork; shred with two forks. Skim fat from carrot mixture; stir in pork and heat through. Serve on rolls with shredded cabbage.

PROVENCAL HAM & BEAN SOUP

There is nothing quite like the wonderful feeling you get when you open the door and smell this delicious stew bubbling away in the slow cooker. To make preparation easy, I assemble the ingredients in the slow cooker the night before and set it in the fridge. Then, all I have to do is turn on the slow cooker in the morning.
—Lyndsay Wells, Ladysmith, BC

Prep: 15 min. + soaking • **Cook:** 7 hours
Makes: 10 servings (3½ quarts)

- 2 cups assorted dried beans for soup
- 1 can (28 ounces) whole plum tomatoes, undrained
- 2 cups cubed fully cooked ham
- 1 large Yukon Gold potato, peeled and chopped
- 1 medium onion, chopped
- 1 cup chopped carrot
- 1 celery rib, chopped
- 2 garlic cloves, minced
- 2 teaspoons herbes de Provence
- 1½ teaspoons salt
- 1 teaspoon pepper
- 1 carton (32 ounces) unsalted chicken stock
  French bread

1. Rinse and sort beans; soak according to package directions. Drain and rinse beans, discarding liquid.
2. Transfer beans to a 6-qt. slow cooker. Add tomatoes; crush with a wooden spoon until chunky. Stir in cooked ham, vegetables, garlic, seasonings and stock. Cook, covered, on low 7-9 hours or until beans are tender. Serve with bread.

GINGERBREAD PUDDING CAKE

Sweet spices and half a cup of molasses give my dessert delightful old-fashioned flavor. It's even homier topped with a dollop of whipped cream.
—Barbara Cook, Yuma, AZ

Prep: 20 min. • **Cook:** 2 hours + standing
Makes: 8 servings

- ½ cup molasses
- 1 cup water
- ¼ cup butter, softened
- ¼ cup granulated sugar
- 1 large egg white
- 1 teaspoon vanilla extract
- 1¼ cups all-purpose flour
- ¾ teaspoon baking soda
- ¼ teaspoon salt
- ½ teaspoon ground cinnamon
- ½ teaspoon ground ginger
- ¼ teaspoon ground allspice
- ⅛ teaspoon ground nutmeg
- ½ cup chopped pecans
- 6 tablespoons brown sugar
- ¾ cup hot water
- ⅔ cup butter, melted
  Sweetened whipped cream, optional

1. Mix molasses and 1 cup water. Cream softened butter and sugar until light and fluffy; beat in egg white and vanilla. In another bowl, whisk together flour, baking soda, salt and spices; add to creamed mixture alternately with molasses mixture, beating well after each addition. Fold in the pecans.
2. Pour into a greased 3-qt. slow cooker. Sprinkle with brown sugar. Mix hot water and melted butter; pour over batter (do not stir).
3. Cook, covered, on high until a toothpick inserted in the center comes out clean, 2-2½ hours. Turn off slow cooker; let stand for 15 minutes. If desired, serve pudding cake with whipped cream.

BROCCOLI & CHEESE

This crumb-topped side dish is quick to assemble and full of flavor. Since it simmers in a slow cooker, it frees up my oven for other things. This is a great help when I'm preparing several dishes for a big meal with lots of guests.
—Connie Slocum, Antioch, TN

Prep: 10 min. • **Cook:** 2¾ hours
Makes: 10 servings

- 6 cups frozen chopped broccoli, partially thawed
- 1 can (10¾ ounces) condensed cream of celery soup, undiluted
- 1½ cups shredded sharp cheddar cheese, divided
- ¼ cup chopped onion
- ½ teaspoon Worcestershire sauce
- ¼ teaspoon pepper
- 1 cup crushed butter-flavored crackers (about 25)
- 2 tablespoons butter

1. In a large bowl, combine broccoli, soup, 1 cup cheese, onion, Worcestershire sauce and pepper. Pour into a greased 3-qt. slow cooker. Sprinkle crackers on top; dot with butter.
2. Cover and cook on high for 2½-3 hours. Sprinkle with the remaining cheese. Cook for 10 minutes longer or until the cheese is melted.

TEST KITCHEN TIP
Unless a recipe directs you to add ingredients while cooking, do not lift the lid while the slow cooker is operating. Every time you lift the lid, steam escapes and you will need to add cooking time.

MAKE AHEAD
SAUCY CHICKEN & TORTELLINI

This heartwarming dish is something I threw together years ago for my oldest daughter. When she's having a rough day, I pull out the slow cooker and prepare this special recipe.
—Mary Morgan, Dallas, TX

Prep: 10 min. • **Cook:** 6¼ hours
Makes: 8 servings

- 1½ pounds boneless skinless chicken breasts, cut into 1-inch cubes
- ½ pound sliced fresh mushrooms
- 1 large onion, chopped
- 1 medium sweet red pepper, cut into ½-inch pieces
- 1 medium green pepper, cut into ½-inch pieces
- 1 can (2¼ ounces) sliced ripe olives, drained
- 1 jar (24 ounces) marinara sauce
- 1 jar (15 ounces) Alfredo sauce
- 2 packages (9 ounces each) refrigerated cheese tortellini
  Grated Parmesan cheese, optional
  Torn fresh basil, optional

1. In a 5-qt. slow cooker, combine first seven ingredients. Cook, covered, on low until chicken is tender, 6-8 hours.
2. Stir in Alfredo sauce and tortellini. Cook mixture, covered, until tortellini is tender, 15-20 minutes. If desired, top with grated Parmesan cheese and basil.

Freeze option: Place chicken and vegetables in freezer containers; top with sauce. Cool and freeze. To use, partially thaw in refrigerator overnight. Microwave, covered, on high in a microwave-safe dish or warm on stovetop until heated through, stirring gently and adding a little water if necessary.

CORN SPOON BREAD

My spoon bread is moister then corn pudding made in the oven, plus the cream cheese is a nice addition. It goes great with Thanksgiving turkey or Christmas ham.
—Tamara Ellefson, Frederic, WI

Prep: 15 min. • **Cook:** 3 hours
Makes: 8 servings

- 1 package (8 ounces) cream cheese, softened
- ⅓ cup sugar
- 1 cup 2% milk
- 2 large eggs
- 2 tablespoons butter, melted
- 1 teaspoon salt
- ¼ teaspoon ground nutmeg
  Dash pepper
- 2⅓ cups frozen corn, thawed
- 1 can (14¾ ounces) cream-style corn
- 1 package (8½ ounces) corn bread/muffin mix

1. In a large bowl, beat cream cheese and sugar until smooth. Gradually beat in milk. Beat in the eggs, butter, salt, nutmeg and pepper until blended. Stir in corn and cream-style corn. Stir in corn bread mix just until moistened.
2. Pour into a greased 3-qt. slow cooker. Cover and cook on high for 3-4 hours or until center is almost set.

POTATO SOUP

I decided to add some character to a basic potato chowder with roasted red peppers, sage and cilantro. The extra flavor gives a deliciously unique twist to this longtime staple.
—Mary Shivers, Ada, OK

Prep: 20 min. • **Cook:** 5½ hours
Makes: 12 servings (3 quarts)

- 3 pounds potatoes, peeled and cut into ½-inch cubes (8 cups)
- 1 large onion, chopped
- 1 jar (7 ounces) roasted sweet red peppers, drained and chopped
- 1 small celery rib, chopped
- 6 cups chicken broth
- ½ teaspoon garlic powder
- ½ teaspoon seasoned salt
- ½ teaspoon pepper
- ⅛ teaspoon rubbed sage
- ⅓ cup all-purpose flour
- 2 cups heavy whipping cream, divided
- 1 cup grated Parmesan cheese, divided
- 8 bacon strips, cooked and crumbled
- 2 tablespoons minced fresh cilantro

1. Place first nine ingredients in a 5- or 6-qt. slow cooker. Cook, covered, on low until potatoes are tender, 5-6 hours.
2. Mix flour and ½ cup cream until smooth; stir into soup. Stir in ¾ cup cheese, bacon, cilantro and remaining cream. Cook, covered, on low until slightly thickened, about 30 minutes. Serve with remaining Parmesan cheese.

FABULOUS FAJITAS

I've enjoyed cooking since I was a girl growing up in the Southwest. When friends call to ask me for new recipes to try, I suggest these flavorful fajitas. It's wonderful being able to put the beef in the slow cooker before church and come home to a hot, delicious main dish.
—Janie Reitz, Rochester, MN

Prep: 20 min. • **Cook:** 3 hours
Makes: 8 servings

- 1½ pounds beef top sirloin steak, cut into thin strips
- 2 tablespoons canola oil
- 2 tablespoons lemon juice
- 1 garlic clove, minced
- 1½ teaspoons ground cumin
- 1 teaspoon seasoned salt
- ½ teaspoon chili powder
- ¼ to ½ teaspoon crushed red pepper flakes
- 1 large green pepper, julienned
- 1 large onion, julienned
- 8 flour tortillas (8 inches)
  Shredded cheddar cheese, salsa, sour cream, lettuce and tomatoes, optional

1. In a large skillet, brown steak in oil over medium heat. Place steak and drippings in a 3-qt. slow cooker. Stir in the lemon juice, garlic, cumin, salt, chili powder and red pepper flakes.

2. Cover and cook on high until meat is almost tender, 2-3 hours. Add green pepper and onion; cover and cook until meat and vegetables are tender, 1 hour.

3. Warm tortillas according to package directions; spoon beef and vegetables down the center of tortillas. Top each with cheese, salsa, sour cream, lettuce and tomatoes if desired.

BUFFALO CHICKEN PASTA

Buffalo chicken is a favorite in our household. Combine it with pasta and you have the ultimate comfort food. For those who prefer less heat, the addition of sour cream, ranch dressing and mozzarella provides a creaminess that balances the spice.
—Kathy White, Henderson, NV

Prep: 10 min. • **Cook:** 4 hours
Makes: 8 servings

- 2 pounds boneless skinless chicken breasts, cut into 1-inch cubes
- 2 cans (10¾ ounces each) condensed cream of chicken soup, undiluted
- 1 cup Buffalo wing sauce
- 1 medium onion, finely chopped
- 1½ teaspoons garlic powder
- ½ teaspoon salt
- ½ teaspoon pepper
- 1 package (16 ounces) penne pasta
- 2 cups shredded part-skim mozzarella cheese
- 2 cups (16 ounces) sour cream
- ½ cup ranch salad dressing
  Finely chopped celery, optional

1. In a 5-qt. slow cooker, combine the first seven ingredients. Cook, covered, on low 4-5 hours or until chicken is tender. Cook pasta according to package directions for al dente; drain.

2. Remove slow cooker insert. Stir in the cheese until melted. Add the pasta, sour cream and ranch dressing. If desired, top with celery.

MAKE AHEAD

SWEET & TANGY CHICKEN WINGS

Here's a festive recipe that's perfect for parties. Put the wings in before you prepare for the event, and in a few hours you'll have wonderful appetizers!
—Ida Tuey, South Lyon, MI

Prep: 20 min. • **Cook:** 3¼ hours
Makes: about 2½ dozen

- 3 pounds chicken wingettes (about 30)
- ½ teaspoon salt, divided
  Dash pepper
- 1½ cups ketchup
- ¼ cup packed brown sugar
- ¼ cup red wine vinegar
- 2 tablespoons Worcestershire sauce
- 1 tablespoon Dijon mustard
- 1 teaspoon minced garlic
- 1 teaspoon liquid smoke, optional
  Sesame seeds, optional

1. Sprinkle chicken with a dash of salt and pepper. Broil 4-6 in. from the heat for 5-10 minutes on each side or until chicken is golden brown. Transfer to a greased 5-qt. slow cooker.
2. Combine the ketchup, brown sugar, vinegar, Worcestershire sauce, mustard, garlic, liquid smoke if desired and the remaining salt; pour over wings. Toss to coat.
3. Cover and cook on low for 3¼-3¾ hours or until chicken juices run clear. Sprinkle with sesame seeds if desired.
Freeze option: Freeze cooled, fully cooked wings in freezer containers. To use, partially thaw in refrigerator overnight. Reheat wings in a foil-lined 15x10x1-in. baking pan in a preheated 325° oven until heated through, covering if necessary to prevent browning. Serve as directed.

SLOW COOKER PEACH CRUMBLE

I look forward to going on my family's beach vacation every year, but I don't always relish the time spent cooking for everybody. This slow cooker breakfast (or dessert!) gives me more time for fun and relaxation.
—Colleen Delawder, Herndon, VA

Prep: 20 min. • **Cook:** 3 hours
Makes: 8 servings

- 1 tablespoon butter, softened
- 6 large ripe peaches, peeled and sliced (about 6 cups)
- 2 tablespoons light brown sugar
- 1 tablespoon lemon juice
- 1 tablespoon vanilla extract
- 2 tablespoons coconut rum, optional

TOPPING

- 1 cup all-purpose flour
- ¾ cup packed light brown sugar
- 1½ teaspoons baking powder
- 1 teaspoon ground cinnamon
- ½ teaspoon baking soda
- ⅛ teaspoon salt
- 1 cup old-fashioned oats
- 6 tablespoons cold butter, cubed

1. Grease a 6-qt. oval slow cooker with 1 tablespoon softened butter. Toss the peaches with brown sugar, lemon juice, vanilla and, if desired, rum; spread evenly in the slow cooker.
2. Whisk together the first six topping ingredients; stir in oats. Cut in butter until crumbly; sprinkle over peaches. Cook, covered, on low until peaches are tender, 3-4 hours.

SWEDISH MEATBALLS ALFREDO

I'm a big fan of this potluck-perfect dish. It only takes a few hours, unlike many other slow cooker recipes. Plus, it's easy. I'm all for easy!
—Carole Bess White, Portland, OR

Prep: 10 min. • **Cook:** 2 hours
Makes: 10 servings

  2 **jars (15 ounces each) roasted garlic Alfredo sauce**
  2 **cups heavy whipping cream**
  2 **cups (16 ounces) sour cream**
  ¾ **teaspoon hot pepper sauce**
  ½ **teaspoon garlic powder**
  ½ **teaspoon dill weed**
  ⅛ **teaspoon pepper**
  1 **package (32 ounces) frozen fully cooked Swedish meatballs, thawed**
      Paprika
      Hot cooked egg noodles

In a 5-qt. slow cooker, combine the first seven ingredients. Stir in meatballs. Cook, covered, on low 2-3 hours or until meatballs are heated through. Sprinkle with paprika. Serve with noodles.

SLOW-SIMMERED KIDNEY BEANS

My husband always signs us up for this side dish when we're invited to a potluck. Canned beans cut back on prep time, yet they get plenty of zip from bacon, apple, red pepper and onion. I like how the slow cooker blends the flavors and I don't have to stand over the stove.
—Sheila Vail, Long Beach, CA

Prep: 15 min. • **Cook:** 6 hours
Makes: 16 servings (¾ cup each)

  6 **bacon strips, diced**
  ½ **pound smoked Polish sausage or kielbasa, sliced**
  4 **cans (16 ounces each) kidney beans, rinsed and drained**
  1 **can (28 ounces) diced tomatoes, drained**
  2 **medium sweet red peppers, chopped**
  1 **large onion, chopped**
  1 **cup ketchup**
  ½ **cup packed brown sugar**
  ¼ **cup honey**
  ¼ **cup molasses**
  1 **tablespoon Worcestershire sauce**
  1 **teaspoon salt**
  1 **teaspoon ground mustard**
  2 **medium unpeeled red apples, cubed**

1. In a large skillet, cook bacon until crisp. Remove with a slotted spoon to paper towels. Add sausage to drippings; cook and stir for 5 minutes. Drain and set aside.
2. In a 6-qt. slow cooker, combine the beans, tomatoes, red peppers, onion, ketchup, brown sugar, honey, molasses, Worcestershire sauce, salt and mustard. Stir in the bacon and sausage. Cover and cook on low for 4-6 hours. Stir in the apples. Cover and cook 2 hours longer or until bubbly.

MAKE AHEAD
SLOW COOKER SWEET POTATO SOUP

I love that I can top this creamy soup with anything my heart desires, which means I can eat it several days in a row without ever having to have it the same way twice. You can substitute fresh onions and celery in this recipe if you prefer, but using the dried version makes it easy to throw together.
—Colleen Delawder, Herndon, VA

Prep: 15 min. • **Cook:** 5 hours
Makes: 8 servings (2½ quarts)

  3 **pounds sweet potatoes, peeled and cut into 1-inch cubes (about 8 cups)**
  2 **tablespoons butter**
  1 **tablespoon Worcestershire sauce**
  1 **teaspoon dried minced onion**
  1 **teaspoon dried celery flakes, optional**
  ½ **teaspoon salt**
  ½ **teaspoon pepper**
  ¼ **teaspoon dried thyme**
  ⅛ **teaspoon ground chipotle pepper**
  6 **cups reduced-sodium chicken broth**
      Sour cream and pepitas, optional

1. In a 4- or 5-qt. slow cooker, combine all ingredients except the sour cream and pepitas. Cook soup, covered, on low until the potatoes are tender, 5-6 hours.
2. Puree soup using an immersion blender. Or, cool slightly and puree soup in batches in a blender; return to slow cooker and heat through. If desired, top servings with sour cream and pepitas.
Freeze option: Freeze cooled soup in freezer containers. To use, partially thaw in refrigerator overnight. Heat through in a saucepan, stirring occasionally and adding a little broth or water if necessary.

Bittersweet
Chocolate
Cheesecake
page 237

The Sweetest Treats

Julia Child famously quipped, "A party without cake is just a meeting." Amen! These cakes, cookies, brownies and other decadent desserts would have made the great chef proud. They're guaranteed to make you (and guests) smile, too!

LAYERED PUMPKIN DESSERT

Pretty layers of cheesecake and pumpkin star in this prize-winning torte. It's not too heavy and is an especially nice way to end a big meal. There's never a morsel left!

—Ruth Ann Stelfox, Raymond, AB

Prep: 40 min. + cooling
Bake: 15 min. + chilling
Makes: 15 servings

- 1½ cups graham cracker crumbs
- ⅓ cup sugar
- 1 teaspoon ground cinnamon
- ⅓ cup butter, melted

CREAM CHEESE FILLING
- 12 ounces cream cheese, softened
- 1 cup sugar
- 3 large eggs

PUMPKIN FILLING
- 1 can (15 ounces) solid-pack pumpkin
- 3 large eggs, separated
- ¾ cup sugar, divided
- ½ cup 2% milk
- 2 teaspoons ground cinnamon
- ½ teaspoon salt
- 1 envelope unflavored gelatin
- ¼ cup cold water

TOPPING
- 1 cup heavy whipping cream
- 3 tablespoons sugar
- ¼ teaspoon vanilla extract

1. Preheat oven to 350°. In a large bowl, combine crumbs, sugar and cinnamon; stir in butter. Press into an ungreased 13x9-in. baking dish. In a large bowl, beat cream cheese until smooth. Beat in sugar and eggs until fluffy. Pour over the crust. Bake 15-20 minutes or until set. Cool on a wire rack.

2. In the top of a double boiler or a metal bowl over simmering water, combine pumpkin, egg yolks, ½ cup sugar, milk, cinnamon and salt. Cook and stir over low heat until a thermometer reads 160°; remove from heat. Transfer to a large bowl; wipe out double boiler.

3. In a small saucepan, sprinkle gelatin over cold water; let stand 1 minute. Heat over low heat, stirring until gelatin is completely dissolved. Stir into pumpkin mixture; cool.

4. In the double boiler, whisk egg whites and remaining sugar over low heat until temperature reaches 160°. Remove from heat; using a mixer, beat until stiff glossy peaks form and sugar is dissolved. Fold into pumpkin mixture. Pour over cream cheese layer. Cover and refrigerate for at least 4 hours or until set.

5. Just before serving, in a large bowl, beat cream until it begins to thicken. Add sugar and vanilla; beat until stiff peaks form. Spread over pumpkin layer.

CARAMEL TOFFEE BROWNIES

I love to create recipes using ingredients I'm craving, such as chocolate, toffee and caramel. The trio came together in this brownie for one sensational treat. I often bake these to add to care packages for family and friends.

—Brenda Caughell, Durham, NC

Prep: 30 min. • **Bake:** 40 min. + cooling
Makes: 2 dozen

CARAMEL LAYER
- ½ cup butter, softened
- ⅓ cup sugar
- ⅓ cup packed brown sugar
- 1 large egg
- ½ teaspoon vanilla extract
- 1 cup all-purpose flour
- ½ teaspoon baking soda
- ¼ teaspoon salt
- ½ cup caramel ice cream topping
- 2 tablespoons 2% milk
- 1 cup toffee bits

BROWNIE LAYER
- 1 cup butter, cubed
- 4 ounces unsweetened chocolate
- 4 large eggs, lightly beaten
- 2 cups sugar
- 2 teaspoons vanilla extract
- 2 cups all-purpose flour

1. Preheat oven to 350°. In a large bowl, cream butter and sugars until light and fluffy; beat in egg and vanilla. Combine flour, baking soda and salt; gradually add to creamed mixture and mix well. In a small bowl, combine caramel topping and milk; add to batter and mix well. Fold in toffee bits; set aside.

2. In a microwave, melt butter and chocolate. Beat in eggs, sugar and vanilla; gradually beat in flour.

3. Spread half of brownie batter into a greased 13x9-in. baking pan. Drop the caramel batter by spoonfuls onto brownie batter; swirl to combine. Drop remaining brownie batter on top.

4. Bake 40-45 minutes or until a toothpick inserted in center comes out clean. Cool on a wire rack.

ALMOND TORTE

Reduced-fat sour cream, egg whites and applesauce lighten up this gorgeous torte, while a creamy custard filling lends richness. It's a flavor combination that never goes out of season.
—Kathy Olsen, Marlborough, NH

Prep: 45 min. + chilling
Bake: 25 min. + cooling
Makes: 16 servings

⅓ cup sugar
1 tablespoon cornstarch
½ cup reduced-fat sour cream
3 large egg yolks
1 tablespoon butter
1 teaspoon vanilla extract
½ teaspoon almond extract

CAKE

4 large egg whites
⅓ cup butter, softened
1½ cups sugar, divided
2 large egg yolks
⅓ cup fat-free milk
¼ cup unsweetened applesauce
1 teaspoon vanilla extract
1 cup cake flour
1 teaspoon baking powder
⅛ teaspoon salt
½ cup sliced almonds
½ teaspoon ground cinnamon

1. In a double boiler or metal bowl over simmering water, constantly whisk the sugar, cornstarch, sour cream and egg yolks until mixture reaches 160° or is thick enough to coat the back of a spoon.

2. Remove from the heat; stir in butter and extracts until blended. Press waxed paper onto surface of custard. Refrigerate for several hours or overnight.

3. Place the egg whites in a large bowl; let them stand at room temperature for 30 minutes. Line two 8-in. round baking pans with waxed paper. Coat sides and paper with cooking spray; sprinkle with flour and set aside.

4. In a large bowl, beat the butter and ½ cup sugar until they are blended, for about 2 minutes. Add the egg yolks; mix well. Beat in the milk, applesauce and vanilla (mixture may appear curdled). Combine the flour, baking powder and salt; add to the butter mixture. Transfer to prepared pans; set aside.

5. Using clean beaters, beat egg whites on medium speed until soft peaks form. Gradually beat in the remaining sugar, 2 tablespoons at a time, on high until stiff glossy peaks form and sugar is dissolved. Spread evenly over batter; sprinkle with almonds and cinnamon.

6. Bake at 350° for 25-30 minutes or until meringue is lightly browned. Cool in pans on wire racks for 10 minutes (meringue will crack). Loosen edges of cakes from pans with a knife. Using two large spatulas, carefully remove one cake to a serving plate, meringue side up; remove the remaining cake to a wire rack, meringue side up. Cool cakes completely.

7. Carefully spread custard over cake on serving plate; top with remaining cake. Store in the refrigerator.

MINT-FROSTED CHOCOLATE CAKE

I often make a peanut butter version of this cake but wanted to switch things up by introducing a new flavor. I tinkered with the recipe and decided mint was my new go-to ingredient. My son came up with the idea for the frosting. The rest is delicious history! The cake is fragile, so I recommend freezing the layers beforehand for easier assembly.
—Melanie Cooksey, Monroe, GA

Prep: 25 min. + chilling
Bake: 30 min. + cooling
Makes: 16 servings

- 2 large eggs
- 1½ cups water
- 1 cup canola oil
- 1 cup (8 ounces) sour cream
- 2 tablespoons white vinegar
- 1 teaspoon vanilla extract
- 2½ cups sugar
- 2 cups all-purpose flour
- ¾ cup baking cocoa
- 2 teaspoons baking soda
- 1 teaspoon salt

MINT FROSTING
- 1 package (8 ounces) cream cheese, softened
- ½ cup butter, softened
- 5 cups confectioners' sugar
- ¾ teaspoon mint extract
- 2 to 3 drops green food coloring
- 24 mint Andes candies, chopped

CHOCOLATE GLAZE
- 8 ounces semisweet chocolate, coarsely chopped
- ½ cup half-and-half cream
- 2 tablespoons light corn syrup
  Additional mint Andes candies, chopped, optional

1. Preheat oven to 350°. Line bottom of three greased 8-in. round baking pans with parchment paper; grease paper.
2. In a large bowl, beat eggs, water, oil, sour cream, vinegar, and vanilla until well blended. In another bowl, whisk sugar, flour, cocoa, baking soda and salt; gradually beat into egg mixture.
3. Transfer to prepared pans. Bake 30-35 minutes or until a toothpick inserted in center comes out clean. Cool in pans 10 minutes before removing to wire racks; remove paper. Cool completely.
4. In a large bowl, beat cream cheese and butter until blended. Gradually beat in confectioners' sugar until smooth. Beat in mint extract and food coloring.
5. Place one cake layer on a serving plate; spread with ⅔ cup mint frosting. Sprinkle with half of the mints. Repeat layers. Top with remaining cake layer. Frost top and sides of cake with the remaining frosting. Refrigerate until set.
6. Place chocolate in a small bowl. In a small saucepan, bring cream just to a boil. Pour over chocolate; let stand 5 minutes. Stir with a whisk until smooth. Stir in corn syrup. Cool slightly, stirring occasionally. Pour over the cake and quickly spread to edges. If desired, top with additional mints. Refrigerate until serving.

BERRY CREAM PIE

I found this recipe in an old cookbook and made it for a family gathering. The pie was gone in no time. It's a perfect summertime treat.
—Sue Yaeger, Boone, IA

....

Prep: 15 min. • **Cook:** 15 min. + chilling
Makes: 6-8 servings

FILLING
½ cup sugar
3 tablespoons cornstarch
3 tablespoons all-purpose flour
½ teaspoon salt
2 cups 2% milk
1 large egg, lightly beaten
½ teaspoon vanilla extract
½ teaspoon almond extract, optional
½ cup heavy whipping cream
1 pastry shell (9 inches), baked

GLAZE
½ cup crushed strawberries
½ cup water
¼ cup sugar
2 teaspoons cornstarch
1½ cups quartered strawberries
1½ cups fresh raspberries

1. In a large saucepan, combine the sugar, cornstarch, flour and salt; gradually stir in milk until smooth. Cook and stir over medium-high heat until thickened and bubbly. Reduce heat; cook and stir 2 minutes more.
2. Remove from the heat and stir a small amount of hot filling into egg; return all to the saucepan, stirring constantly. Bring to a gentle boil; cook and stir for 2 minutes. Remove from the heat; gently stir in vanilla and almond extract if desired. Cool to room temperature.
3. In a small bowl, beat cream until stiff peaks form; fold into filling. Pour into pastry shell. Chill for at least 2 hours.
4. About 2 hours before serving, prepare the glaze. In a large saucepan, combine crushed strawberries and water; cook for 2 minutes. Combine sugar and cornstarch; gradually add to the pan. Cook and stir until thickened and clear; strain. Cool for 20 minutes.
5. Meanwhile, arrange quartered strawberries and raspberries over filling; pour glaze evenly over berries. Refrigerate for 1 hour.

WHITE CHOCOLATE CEREAL BARS

A friend gave me this sweet take on traditional crispy treats. My husband loves the white chocolate. They're so quick to make that you can prepare them during a TV commercial and you won't miss much of your program.
—Anne Powers, Munford, AL

....

Start to Finish: 15 min.
Makes: about 3 dozen

4 cups miniature marshmallows
8 ounces white baking chips (about 1⅓ cups)
¼ cup butter, cubed
6 cups Rice Krispies

1. Using a Dutch oven, combine the marshmallows, baking chips and butter. Cook and stir over medium-low heat until melted. Remove from heat. Add the Rice Krispies; stir to coat.
2. Transfer to a greased 13x9-in. pan; gently press mixture evenly into pan. Cut into bars.

LINZER TARTS

With a creamy chocolate and hazelnut filling, these decadent Christmas cookies look and taste amazing. Guests will never guess how easy they are to make.
—Mary Maddox, Bellmore, NY

....

Prep: 30 min. + chilling
Bake: 10 min./batch + cooling
Makes: about 2 dozen

- 1   cup butter, softened
- 1   cup confectioners' sugar
- 1   large egg
- 3   cups all-purpose flour
- ¼   teaspoon salt
     Additional confectioners' sugar
- ½   cup Nutella

1. In a large bowl, cream the butter and confectioners' sugar until light and fluffy. Beat in egg. Combine flour and salt; gradually add to creamed mixture and mix well. Divide dough in thirds. Shape each into a ball, then flatten into a disk. Wrap in plastic and refrigerate for 30 minutes.
2. Preheat oven to 350°. On a lightly floured surface, roll one portion of dough to ⅛-in. thickness. Cut with floured 2½-in. holiday cookie cutters. Using floured 1-in. shaped cookie cutters, cut out the centers of half of the cookies.
3. Place solid and window cookies 1 in. apart on greased baking sheets. Repeat with remaining portions of dough. Bake 8-10 minutes or until set. Remove to wire racks to cool completely.
4. Sprinkle window cookies with additional confectioners' sugar. Spread 1 teaspoon Nutella on the bottom of each solid cookie; place window cookies over filling.

BLACK BOTTOM CUPCAKES

This recipe has been in our family for years. I always double or triple the ingredients because these cupcakes get eaten up fast. You'll see what I mean when you try them—I can't remember anyone who's tried them for the first time and not asked for a second.
—Julie Briceland, Windsor, PA

....

Prep: 20 min. • **Bake:** 20 min. + cooling
Makes: 20-24 cupcakes

FILLING
- 1   package (8 ounces) cream cheese, softened
- ⅓   cup sugar
- 1   large egg
- ⅛   teaspoon salt
- 1   cup (6 ounces) semisweet chocolate chips

CUPCAKES
- 1   cup sugar
- 1   cup water
- ⅓   cup vegetable oil
- 1   large egg
- 1   tablespoon white vinegar
- 1   teaspoon vanilla extract
- 1½ cups all-purpose flour
- ¼   cup baking cocoa
- 1   teaspoon baking soda
- ½   teaspoon salt

TOPPING
     Sugar
     Chopped almonds, optional

1. In a small bowl, beat the cream cheese, sugar, egg and salt until smooth. Stir in chips; set aside.
2. For cupcakes, in a large bowl, beat the sugar, water, oil, egg, vinegar and vanilla until well blended. Combine the flour, cocoa, baking soda and salt; gradually beat into egg mixture until blended.
3. Fill paper-lined muffin cups half full with chocolate batter. Drop a heaping tablespoonful of cheese mixture in center of batter of each cupcake. Sprinkle with sugar and chopped almonds if desired.
4. Bake at 350° for 18-20 minutes or until a toothpick inserted in the cake portion comes out clean. Cool in pans for 10 minutes before removing to racks to cool completely. Refrigerate leftovers.

CHOCOLATE PEANUT BUTTER CUPCAKES

I enjoy experimenting with different flavors and textures in my baking. Peanut butter and chocolate are a classic pairing, so I decided to try them in cupcakes. After just one taste, I knew I had a winner.

—Ronda Schabes, Vicksburg, MI

Prep: 55 min. • **Bake:** 20 min. + cooling
Makes: 2 dozen

- 2 cups sugar
- 1¾ cups all-purpose flour
- ¾ cup baking cocoa
- ½ teaspoon salt
- ½ teaspoon baking soda
- ½ teaspoon baking powder
- 1 cup buttermilk
- 1 cup strong brewed coffee, room temperature
- ½ cup canola oil
- 2 large eggs
- 1 teaspoon vanilla extract

FILLING
- ½ cup creamy peanut butter
- 3 tablespoons unsalted butter, softened
- 1 cup confectioners' sugar
- 2 to 4 tablespoons 2% milk

GANACHE
- 2 cups (12 ounces) semisweet chocolate chips
- ½ cup heavy whipping cream

PEANUT BUTTER FROSTING
- 1 cup packed brown sugar
- 4 large egg whites
- ¼ teaspoon salt
- ¼ teaspoon cream of tartar
- 1 teaspoon vanilla extract
- 2 cups unsalted butter, softened
- ⅓ cup creamy peanut butter

1. Preheat oven to 350°. In a large bowl, combine first six ingredients. Whisk buttermilk, coffee, oil, eggs and vanilla until blended; add to the dry ingredients until combined. (Batter will be very thin.) Fill paper-lined muffin cups two-thirds full.
2. Bake 18-20 minutes or until a toothpick inserted in the center comes out clean. Cool 10 minutes before removing from pans to wire racks to cool completely.
3. In a small bowl, cream peanut butter, butter, confectioners' sugar and enough milk to achieve piping consistency. Cut a small hole in the corner of a pastry or plastic bag; insert a small round tip. Fill with peanut butter filling. Insert tip into the top center of each cupcake; pipe about 1 tablespoon filling into each.
4. Place chocolate chips in a small bowl. In a small saucepan, bring cream just to a boil. Pour over chocolate; whisk until smooth. Dip the top of each cupcake into ganache; place on wire racks to set.
5. In a large heavy saucepan, combine brown sugar, egg whites, salt and cream of tartar over low heat. With a hand mixer, beat on low speed 1 minute. Continue beating on low over low heat until frosting reaches 160°, about 8-10 minutes. Pour into a large bowl; add vanilla. Beat on high until stiff peaks form, about 5 minutes.
6. Add butter, 1 tablespoon at a time, beating well after each addition. If mixture begins to look curdled, place frosting bowl in another bowl filled with hot water for a few seconds. Continue adding butter and beating until smooth. Beat in peanut butter 1-2 minutes or until smooth.
7. Place the frosting in a pastry or plastic bag with a large star tip; pipe onto each cupcake. Store in an airtight container in the refrigerator. Let it stand at room temperature before serving.

BERRY MINI CHEESECAKES

Life's too short to pass up dessert. These little bites of rich, velvety cheesecake are worth every bite.

—*Taste of Home* Test Kitchen

Prep: 20 min. Bake 15 min. + chilling
Makes: 1½ dozen

- 1 cup graham cracker crumbs
- 3 tablespoons butter, melted
- 8 ounces cream cheese, softened
- ⅓ cup sugar
- 1 teaspoon vanilla extract
- 1 large egg, lightly beaten
- 18 fresh raspberries

1. Preheat oven to 350°. In a small bowl, combine graham cracker crumbs and butter. Press gently onto the bottom of 18 paper-lined miniature muffin cups. In another small bowl, beat cream cheese, sugar and vanilla until smooth. Add egg; beat on low speed just until combined. Spoon over crusts.
2. Bake 12-14 minutes or until centers are set. Cool for 10 minutes before removing from pan to wire rack to cool completely. Refrigerate at least 1 hour.
3. To serve, remove paper liners; top cheesecakes with raspberries.

CHOCOLATE STRAWBERRY PUNCH BOWL TRIFLE

I threw this dessert together when I needed something quick to take to my in-laws' house. Everyone thought I fussed because it looks so impressive. But I'm proud to say that it's easy, and since it makes a lot, it's perfect for potlucks and large get-togethers.
—Kristi Judkins, Morrison, TN

Prep: 20 min. • **Bake:** 20 min.
Makes: 24-28 servings

- 1 package chocolate cake mix (regular size)
- 1 quart fresh whole strawberries, sliced
- 1 carton (13½ ounces) strawberry glaze
- 2 cartons (12 ounces each) frozen whipped topping, thawed, divided
- 1 cup chocolate frosting
  Shaved chocolate, optional

1. Prepare and bake cake according to package directions, using a 13x9-in. baking pan. Cool completely on a wire rack. Cut cake into 1-in. cubes. Place half of the cubes in a 6-qt. glass punch bowl. Top with half of the sliced strawberries; drizzle with half of the strawberry glaze. Spread with 3½ cups whipped topping.
2. In a microwave-safe bowl, heat frosting on high for 20-30 seconds or until it is pourable, stirring often; cool slightly. Drizzle half over the whipped topping. Repeat layers of cake, berries, glaze and whipped topping. If desired, drizzle with remaining frosting and sprinkle with shaved chocolate.

CHOCOLATE MAPLE BARS

My family runs a maple syrup operation, and I'm always looking for new ways to incorporate maple syrup into my cooking and baking. These bars are delicious!
—Cathy Schumacher, Alto, MI

Prep: 20 min. • **Bake:** 25 min. + cooling
Makes: 3 dozen

- ½ cup shortening
- ¾ cup maple syrup
- ½ cup sugar
- 3 large eggs
- 3 tablespoons milk
- 1 teaspoon vanilla extract
- 1¼ cups all-purpose flour
- ¼ teaspoon baking powder
- ¼ teaspoon salt
- 1½ ounces unsweetened chocolate, melted
- ½ cup chopped pecans
- ½ cup sweetened shredded coconut

FROSTING
- ¼ cup butter, softened
- 1 cup confectioners' sugar
- ½ cup baking cocoa
- ½ cup maple syrup
- 1 cup miniature marshmallows

1. In a large bowl, cream the shortening, syrup and sugar until light and fluffy. Beat in the eggs, milk and vanilla. Combine the flour, baking powder and salt; add it to creamed mixture and mix well. Remove half of the batter to another bowl.
2. Combine melted chocolate and pecans; stir into one bowl. Spread into a greased 13x9-in. baking pan. Add coconut to remaining batter. Spread carefully over chocolate batter.
3. Bake at 350° for 25 minutes or until a toothpick inserted in the center comes out clean. Cool completely on a wire rack.
4. For frosting, in a small bowl, beat the butter until smooth. Gradually add the confectioners' sugar and cocoa. Gradually add syrup, beating until smooth. Fold in marshmallows. Frost bars.

CHOCOLATE MACAROON CUPCAKES

A delightful coconut and ricotta cheese filling is hidden inside these cupcakes.
—Dolores Skrout, Summerhill, PA

Prep: 20 min. • **Bake:** 30 min. + cooling
Makes: 1½ dozen

- 2 large egg whites
- 1 large egg
- ⅓ cup unsweetened applesauce
- 1 teaspoon vanilla extract
- 1¼ cups all-purpose flour
- 1 cup sugar
- ⅓ cup baking cocoa
- ½ teaspoon baking soda
- ¾ cup buttermilk

FILLING

- 1 cup reduced-fat ricotta cheese
- ¼ cup sugar
- 1 large egg white
- ⅓ cup sweetened shredded coconut
- ½ teaspoon coconut or almond extract
   Confectioners' sugar

1. Preheat oven to 350°. Coat 18 muffin cups with cooking spray.
2. Beat first four ingredients until well blended. In another bowl, whisk together the flour, sugar, cocoa and baking soda; gradually beat into egg mixture alternately with buttermilk.
3. For filling, beat ricotta cheese, sugar and egg white until blended. Stir iin the coconut and extract.
4. Fill the prepared cups with half of the batter. Drop filling by tablespoonfuls into center of each cupcake; cover with remaining batter.
5. Bake until a toothpick inserted in the cupcake portion comes out clean, 28-33 minutes. Cool 10 minutes before removing from pans to wire racks; cool completely. Dust with confectioners' sugar.

CHOCOLATE PECAN PIE BARS

These yummy pecan bars start out with a homemade pastry crust before piling on lots of semisweet chocolate.
They're perfect for a holiday bake sale or casual get-together.
—Heather Biedler, Martinsburg, WV

Prep: 30 min. + chilling
Bake: 50 min. + cooling
Makes: 3 dozen

- 1¾ cups all-purpose flour
- ¼ teaspoon salt
- ¾ cup cold butter
- ¼ to ½ cup ice water

FILLING

- 4 large eggs
- 2 cups sugar
- ½ teaspoon salt
- 1 cup all-purpose flour
- 1 cup butter, melted and cooled
- 4 teaspoons vanilla extract
- 2⅔ cups (16 ounces) semisweet chocolate chips
- 1⅓ cups chopped pecans

1. In a small bowl, mix flour and salt; cut in butter until crumbly. Gradually add ice water, tossing with a fork until dough holds together when pressed. Shape into a disk; wrap in plastic. Refrigerate 1 hour or overnight.
2. Preheat the oven to 350°. On a lightly floured surface, roll dough to fit bottom of a 13x9-in. baking pan; press into pan. Refrigerate while preparing filling.
3. In a large bowl, beat eggs, sugar, and salt on high speed 2 minutes. Stir in the flour, melted butter and vanilla. Fold in the chocolate chips. Pour over pastry; sprinkle with pecans.
4. Cover loosely with foil. Place on a lower oven rack; bake for 20 minutes. Then bake, uncovered, 30 minutes longer or until the top is golden brown and a knife inserted in the center comes out clean.
5. Cool in pan on a wire rack. Cut into bars. Refrigerate leftovers.

APPLE CRANBERRY SLAB PIE

My husband loves pie. This one made with apples, raspberries and cranberries is so good, I bend the rules and let him and our grandkids enjoy it for breakfast.
—Brenda Smith, Curran, MI

Prep: 45 min. • **Bake:** 40 min. + cooling
Makes: 15 servings

> Pastry for two double-crust pies (9 inches)
> 1½ cups sugar
> ¼ cup all-purpose flour
> 4 medium tart apples, peeled and sliced (about 4½ cups)
> 4 cups frozen or fresh raspberries
> 2 cups fresh or frozen cranberries
> 2 teaspoons grated orange peel
> ½ cup orange juice
> 1 teaspoon ground nutmeg
> 1 teaspoon ground cinnamon
>   Additional orange juice and sugar, optional

1. Divide pastry dough into two portions so that one is slightly larger than the other; wrap each portion in plastic wrap. Refrigerate 1 hour or overnight.
2. In a Dutch oven, mix sugar and flour; stir in fruit, orange peel, orange juice and spices. Bring to a boil over medium-high heat. Reduce heat; simmer, uncovered, 10-12 minutes or until apples are tender and the juices are thickened, stirring occasionally. Cool slightly.
3. Preheat oven to 375°. Roll out larger portion of pastry dough between two pieces of waxed paper into a 16x12-in. rectangle. Remove top sheet of waxed paper; place a 13x9-in. baking pan upside down over pastry. Lifting with waxed paper, carefully invert pastry into pan. Remove waxed paper; press pastry onto bottom and up sides of pan. Add filling.
4. On a well-floured surface, roll remaining dough into a 14x10-in. rectangle; cut into ¾-in.-wide strips. Arrange the strips over filling, sealing ends to bottom pastry. If desired, brush the pastry with additional orange juice and sprinkle it with some additional sugar.
5. Bake 40-50 minutes or until crust is golden brown and filling is bubbly. Cool on a wire rack.

Pastry for two double-crust pies (9 inches): In a large bowl, combine 4½ cups all-purpose flour, 1 tablespoon sugar and 2 teaspoons. salt; cut in 1¾ cups shortening until crumbly. Whisk 1 large egg, 1 tablespoon white vinegar and ½ cup ice water; gradually add to flour mixture, tossing with a fork until dough holds together when pressed.

ELEGANT ORANGE BLOSSOM CHEESECAKE

The aroma of orange zest hints at how heavenly this delicate cheesecake tastes. Gingersnap cookie crumbs make a distinctive crust, while glazed orange slices become a blossomlike topping.
—Sharon Delaney-Chronis
South Milwaukee, WI

Prep: 40 min. • **Bake:** 70 min. + chilling
Makes: 16 servings

> 3 cups crushed gingersnap cookies (about 60 cookies)
> 2 teaspoons plus 2 tablespoons grated orange peel, divided
> ⅓ cup butter, melted
> 1½ cups orange juice
> ⅓ cup sliced fresh gingerroot
> 4 packages (8 ounces each) cream cheese, softened
> ⅔ cup sugar
> 6 ounces white baking chocolate, melted
> 1 tablespoon vanilla extract
> 4 large eggs, lightly beaten

CANDIED ORANGE SLICES
> 3 cups water
> 1½ cups sugar
> 2 small navel oranges, thinly sliced

1. Place a greased 9-in. springform pan on a double thickness of heavy-duty foil (about 18 in. square). Securely wrap foil around pan.
2. In a large bowl, combine cookie crumbs, 2 teaspoons orange peel and butter. Press onto bottom and 2-in. up the sides of prepared pan.
3. In a large saucepan, combine orange juice and ginger; bring to a boil. Reduce heat and simmer, stirring occasionally, until syrupy and reduced to about 3 tablespoons. Strain and discard ginger.
4. In a large bowl, beat cream cheese and sugar until smooth. Beat in ginger syrup, melted chocolate, vanilla and remaining orange peel. Add eggs; beat on low speed just until combined. Pour into crust. Place springform pan in a large baking pan; add 1 in. of hot water to larger pan.
5. Bake at 325° for 70-80 minutes or until the center is just set and top appears dull. Remove springform pan from water bath; remove the foil. Cool on a wire rack for 10 minutes. Carefully run a knife around the edge of pan to loosen; cool 1 hour longer. Refrigerate overnight.
6. For candied orange slices, in a large skillet, combine water and sugar. Cook and stir over medium heat until sugar is completely dissolved. Add orange slices. Bring to a boil. Reduce heat; simmer for 45 minutes or until translucent. Drain the oranges on a wire rack; arrange in a single layer on waxed paper to dry.
7. Remove sides of pan. Top cheesecake with candied orange slices. Refrigerate the leftovers.

HONEY-PECAN SQUARES

When we left Texas to move north, a neighbor gave me so many pecans from his trees that the trunk of my car was bulging at the seams. So I brought these treats for him when we went back to visit. He loved them!

—Lorraine Caland, Shuniah, ON

Prep: 15 min. • **Bake:** 30 min.
Makes: 2 dozen

- 1 cup unsalted butter, softened
- ¾ cup packed dark brown sugar
- ½ teaspoon salt
- 3 cups all-purpose flour

FILLING
- ½ cup unsalted butter, cubed
- ½ cup packed dark brown sugar
- ⅓ cup honey
- 2 tablespoons sugar
- 2 tablespoons heavy whipping cream
- ¼ teaspoon salt
- 2 cups chopped pecans, toasted
- ½ teaspoon maple flavoring or vanilla extract

1. Preheat oven to 350°. Line a 13x9-in. baking pan with parchment paper, letting the ends extend up the sides of the pan. In a large bowl, cream the butter, brown sugar and salt until it is light and fluffy. Gradually beat in flour. Press onto bottom of prepared pan. Bake for 16-20 minutes or until lightly browned.

2. In a small saucepan, combine the first six filling ingredients; bring to a boil. Cook 1 minute. Remove from the heat; stir in the pecans and maple flavoring. Pour over the crust.

3. Bake for 10-15 minutes or until bubbly. Cool in pan on a wire rack. Lifting with parchment paper, transfer to a cutting board; cut into bars.

Note: To toast nuts, bake in a shallow pan in a 350° oven for 5-10 minutes or until lightly browned, stirring occasionally.

AMISH SUGAR COOKIES

These easy-to-make cookies melt in your mouth. I've passed the recipe to many friends. After I gave the recipe to my sister, she entered the cookies in a local fair and won the best of show prize.

—Sylvia Ford, Kennett, MO

Prep: 10 min. • **Bake:** 10 min./batch
Makes: about 5 dozen

- 1 cup butter, softened
- 1 cup vegetable oil
- 1 cup sugar
- 1 cup confectioners' sugar
- 2 large eggs
- 1 teaspoon vanilla extract
- 4½ cups all-purpose flour
- 1 teaspoon baking soda
- 1 teaspoon cream of tartar

1. In a large bowl, beat the butter, oil and sugars. Beat in eggs until well blended. Beat in vanilla. Combine the flour, baking soda and cream of tartar; gradually add to creamed mixture.

2. Drop by small teaspoonfuls onto ungreased baking sheets. Bake at 375° until lightly browned, 8-10 minutes. Remove to wire racks to cool.

1. In a small heavy saucepan, combine the sugar, cornstarch and salt. Stir in milk and cream until smooth. Cook and stir over medium-high heat until thickened and bubbly. Reduce heat to low; cook and stir 2 minutes longer.

2. Remove from the heat. Stir a small amount of hot mixture into egg yolk; return all to the pan, stirring constantly. Bring to a gentle boil; cook and stir 2 minutes longer. Remove from the heat. Stir in vanilla. Cool for 15 minutes, stirring occasionally. Transfer to a small bowl. Press waxed paper onto surface of custard. Refrigerate for 2-3 hours.

3. In a large bowl, cream butter and sugar until light and fluffy. Beat in the egg yolks, egg, vanilla and lemon peel. Combine the cake flour, all-purpose flour, baking soda and salt; gradually add to the creamed mixture alternately with buttermilk and mix well.

4. Drop by rounded teaspoonfuls 2 in. apart onto greased baking sheets. Bake at 400° for 5-7 minutes or until firm to the touch. Remove cookies to wire racks to cool completely.

5. Spread custard over the bottoms of half of the cookies; top with the remaining cookies.

6. For glaze, place chocolate and butter in a small bowl. In a small saucepan, bring cream just to a boil. Pour over chocolate and butter; whisk until smooth. Stir in confectioners' sugar. Spread over cookies; let dry completely. Store in refrigerator.

To Make Ahead: Package cookies in an airtight container, separating layers with waxed paper and freeze for up to 1 month. Thaw in a single layer before assembling.

MAKE AHEAD

BOSTON CREAM PIE COOKIES

Here, a homemade vanilla custard is sandwiched between two tender cookies. With their shiny chocolate glaze, these bite-size gems remind me of classic Boston cream pie.
—Evangeline Bradford, Erlanger, KY

Prep: 70 min. + chilling
Bake: 5 min./batch + cooling
Makes: 4 dozen

- 6 **tablespoons sugar**
- 3 **tablespoons cornstarch**
- ¼ **teaspoon salt**
- 1 **cup 2% milk**
- 6 **tablespoons heavy whipping cream**
- 1 **large egg yolk, beaten**
- 2 **teaspoons vanilla extract**

COOKIES
- 9 **tablespoons butter, softened**
- 1 **cup sugar**
- 2 **large egg yolks**
- 1 **large egg**
- 2 **teaspoons vanilla extract**
- ½ **teaspoon grated lemon peel**
- 1 **cup plus 2 tablespoons cake flour**
- 1 **cup all-purpose flour**
- ¾ **teaspoon baking soda**
- ½ **teaspoon salt**
- ½ **cup plus 2 tablespoons buttermilk**

GLAZE
- 2 **ounces unsweetened chocolate, chopped**
- 4 **teaspoons butter**
- ½ **cup whipping cream**
- 1 **cup confectioners' sugar**

1. Place egg whites in a large bowl; let stand at room temperature 30 minutes. Preheat oven to 350°. Line bottoms of two greased 9-in. round baking pans with parchment paper; grease paper.

2. In a large bowl, cream the butter, shortening and sugar until light and fluffy. Beat in the extract. In another bowl, whisk the flour, baking powder, baking soda and salt; add to creamed mixture alternately with buttermilk, beating well after each addition.

3. With clean beaters, beat egg whites on medium speed until stiff peaks form. Fold into batter.

4. Transfer batter to prepared pans. Bake for 20-25 minutes or until a toothpick inserted in center comes out clean and edges are golden.

5. Cool in pans for 10 minutes before removing to wire racks; remove paper. Cool completely. In a large bowl, beat shortening and butter until combined. Beat in confectioner's sugar alternately with extract and enough milk to reach a spreading consistency.

6. Using a long serrated knife, cut each cake horizontally in half. Place one cake layer on a serving plate; spread with half of the preserves. Top with another cake layer and ¾ cup frosting. Place third cake layer over frosting; spread with remaining preserves. Top with remaining cake layer.

7. Frost the top and sides of cake with 1 cup frosting, forming a crumb coating. Refrigerate cake until frosting is set, about 30 minutes. Remove from refrigerator and cover with remaining frosting. Top with raspberries.

SPECIAL RASPBERRY TORTE

With raspberry preserves, a burst of lemon and a homemade buttercream frosting, this berry-topped cake always gets rave reviews. It's my mom's favorite dessert.
—Lori Daniels, Beverly, WV

Prep: 45 min. + chilling
Bake: 20 min. + cooling
Makes: 12 servings

- 5 large egg whites
- ½ cup butter, softened
- ½ cup shortening
- 2 cups sugar
- 1 teaspoon lemon extract
- 3 cups all-purpose flour
- 2 teaspoons baking powder
- ½ teaspoon baking soda
- ⅛ teaspoon salt
- 1½ cups buttermilk

FROSTING
- ¾ cup shortening
- ⅓ cup butter, softened
- 4½ cups confectioners' sugar
- 1½ teaspoons lemon extract
- 5 to 6 tablespoons 2% milk
- 1 jar (10 ounces) seedless raspberry preserves
  Fresh raspberries

LEMON CHEESECAKE TARTS

These adorable tarts are fantastic made with pie pastry, but to make them even quicker, add the filling to store-bought phyllo tart shells.
—Sarah Gilbert, Beaverton, OR

Prep: 30 min. • **Bake:** 10 min. + cooling
Makes: 2 dozen

- 1 **package (14.1 ounces) refrigerated pie pastry**
FILLING
- 1 **package (8 ounces) cream cheese, softened**
- 1 **teaspoon vanilla extract**
- 1 **jar (10 ounces) lemon curd, divided**
- 1 **container (8 ounces) frozen whipped topping, thawed**
- 1 **cup fresh blueberries Confectioners' sugar, optional**

1. Preheat the oven to 450°. On a work surface, unroll the pastry sheets. Cut 24 circles with a floured 3-in. scalloped round cookie cutter, rerolling scraps as necessary. Press circles onto bottoms and partway up sides of ungreased muffin cups, smoothing edges. Prick bottoms generously with a fork.
2. Bake 5-7 minutes or until light golden brown. Remove from pans to wire racks to cool completely.
3. In a large bowl, beat cream cheese and vanilla until blended; beat in ¼ cup lemon curd. Fold in a third of the whipped topping, then fold in remaining topping.
4. Spoon 2 tablespoons cream cheese mixture into each tart shell; top each with 1 teaspoon lemon curd. Top with blueberries; refrigerate until serving. If desired, dust with confectioners' sugar.

CHOCOLATE FUDGE BROWNIES

My walnut-studded brownies are so rich and fudgy they don't need icing.
—Hazel Fritchie, Palestine, IL

Prep: 15 min. • **Bake:** 35 min. + cooling
Makes: 16 servings

- 1 **cup butter, cubed**
- 6 **ounces unsweetened chocolate, chopped**
- 4 **large eggs**
- 2 **cups sugar**
- 1 **teaspoon vanilla extract**
- ½ **teaspoon salt**
- 1 **cup all-purpose flour**
- 2 **cups chopped walnuts Confectioners' sugar, optional**

1. Preheat the oven to 350°. In a small saucepan, melt butter and chocolate over low heat. Cool slightly.
2. In a large bowl, beat eggs, sugar, vanilla and salt until blended. Stir in chocolate mixture. Add the flour, mixing well. Stir in the walnuts.
3. Spread into a greased 9-in. square baking pan. Bake 35-40 minutes or until a toothpick inserted in center comes out with moist crumbs (do not overbake).
4. Cool completely in pan on a wire rack. If desired, dust with confectioners' sugar. Cut into bars.

PEANUT BUTTER PUDDING DESSERT

Here's a fun, layered dessert that will appeal to all ages. If you want it even nuttier, you can use chunky peanut butter, and if you're not a fan of cashews, substitute your favorite nut.
—Barbara Schindler, Napoleon, OH

Prep: 25 min. • **Bake:** 25 min. + chilling
Makes: 16 servings

- 1 cup all-purpose flour
- ½ cup cold butter, cubed
- 1½ cups chopped cashews, divided
- 1 package (8 ounces) cream cheese, softened
- ⅓ cup creamy peanut butter
- 1 cup confectioners' sugar
- 1 carton (12 ounces) frozen whipped topping, thawed, divided
- 2⅔ cups cold milk
- 1 package (3.9 ounces) instant chocolate pudding mix
- 1 package (3.4 ounces) instant vanilla pudding mix
- 1 milk chocolate candy bar (1.55 ounces), coarsely chopped

1. Place the flour and butter in a food processor; cover and process until the mixture resembles coarse crumbs. Add 1 cup cashews; pulse a few times until combined.
2. Press into a greased 13x9-in. baking dish. Bake at 350° for 25-28 minutes or until golden brown. Cool completely on a wire rack.
3. In a small bowl, beat the cream cheese, peanut butter and confectioners' sugar until smooth. Fold in 1 cup whipped topping. Spoon over crust.
4. In another bowl, whisk milk and both pudding mixes for 2 minutes. Let stand for 2 minutes or until soft-set. Spread over the cream cheese layer. Top with the remaining whipped topping. Sprinkle with chopped candy bar and the remaining cashews. Cover and refrigerate for at least 1 hour before serving.

TOFFEE BROWNIE TRIFLE

This decadent combination of pantry items in a terrific way to dress up a brownie mix. Try it with other flavors of pudding or substitute your favorite candy bar. It tastes great with low-fat and sugar-free products, too.
—Wendy Bennett, Sioux Falls, SD

Prep: 20 min. • **Bake:** 25 min. + cooling
Makes: 16 servings

- 1 package fudge brownie mix (13x9-in. pan size)
- 2½ cups cold milk
- 1 package (3.4 ounces) instant cheesecake or vanilla pudding mix
- 1 package (3.3 ounces) instant white chocolate pudding mix
- 1 carton (8 ounces) frozen whipped topping, thawed
- 2 to 3 Heath candy bars (1.4 ounces each), chopped

1. Prepare and bake brownies according to the package directions for cake-like brownies, using a greased 13x9-in. baking pan. Cool completely on a wire rack.
2. In a large bowl, beat milk and pudding mixes on low speed for 2 minutes. Let stand for 2 minutes or until soft-set. Fold in whipped topping.
3. Cut the brownies into 1-in. cubes; place half in a 3-qt. glass trifle bowl or serving dish. Cover with half of the pudding. Repeat layers. Sprinkle with chopped candy bars. Refrigerate leftovers.

PEANUT BUTTER CHOCOLATE TART

I've been submitting recipes to Taste of Home contests for years, but never dreamed I would win! Everyone who loves peanut butter cups will be in heaven when they bite into this rich, sensational tart. While it looks spectacular, it is actually very easy to put together.
—Mary Ann Lee, Clifton Park, NY

Prep: 40 min. + chilling
Makes: 16 servings

- 1 package (9 ounces) chocolate wafers
- ½ cup peanut butter chips
- 2 tablespoons sugar
- ½ cup butter, melted

FILLING

- 1 cup creamy peanut butter
- ½ cup butter, softened
- 4 ounces cream cheese, softened
- 1 cup confectioners' sugar
- ¼ cup light corn syrup
- 1 teaspoon vanilla extract

GANACHE

- ¾ cup semisweet chocolate chips
- ½ cup heavy whipping cream
- 1½ teaspoons sugar
- 1½ teaspoons light corn syrup
- ¼ cup chopped salted peanuts

1. In a food processor, place the wafers, peanut butter chips and sugar; cover and process until finely crushed. Stir in melted butter. Press onto the bottom and up the sides of an ungreased 9-in. fluted tart pan with removable bottom. Refrigerate for 30 minutes.

2. For filling, in a large bowl, beat peanut butter, butter and cream cheese until they are fluffy. Add the confectioners' sugar, corn syrup and vanilla; beat until smooth. Pour into crust. Refrigerate while making the ganache.

3. Place chocolate chips in a small bowl. In a small saucepan, bring the cream, sugar and corn syrup just to a boil. Pour over chips; whisk until melted and smooth. Pour over filling. Sprinkle with peanuts. Refrigerate for at least 2 hours.

FROSTED MAPLE COOKIES

Living in New England, I've come to appreciate the unique qualities of our area. Many people here enjoy the flavor of maple in their recipes, and I love this adaptation of an old favorite.
—Connie Borden, Marblehead, MA

Prep: 20 min. + chilling
Bake: 10 min./batch + cooling
Makes: 4 dozen (2½-inch cookies)

- ½ cup shortening
- 1½ cups packed brown sugar
- 2 large eggs
- 1 cup (8 ounces) sour cream
- 1 tablespoon maple flavoring
- 2¾ cups all-purpose flour
- 1 teaspoon salt
- ½ teaspoon baking soda
- 1 cup chopped nuts

FROSTING

- ½ cup butter
- 2 cups confectioners' sugar
- 2 teaspoons maple flavoring
- 2 to 3 tablespoons hot water

1. In a large bowl, cream shortening and brown sugar until light and fluffy. Add eggs, one at a time, beating well after each addition. Stir in sour cream and maple flavoring. Combine the flour, salt and baking soda; add to creamed mixture and mix well. Stir in nuts. Cover and refrigerate for 1 hour.

2. Drop dough by rounded tablespoonfuls 2 in. apart onto greased baking sheets. Bake at 375° for 8-10 minutes or until the edges are lightly browned. Cool completely on wire racks.

3. For frosting, in a small saucepan, heat butter over low heat until golden brown. Remove from the heat; blend in the confectioners' sugar, maple flavoring and enough water to achieve spreading consistency. Frost cookies.

BITTERSWEET CHOCOLATE CHEESECAKE

While it's common for one generation to pass a cherished recipe to the next, sometimes there's one that's so good it goes the other way! That's the case here: I'm a great-grandmother, and I received this recipe from my niece. My whole family enjoys this dessert.

—Amelia Gregory, Omemee, ON

Prep: 20 min. • **Bake:** 1 hour + chilling
Makes: 16 servings

- 1 cup chocolate wafer crumbs
- ½ cup finely chopped hazelnuts, toasted
- ⅓ cup butter, melted
- 3 packages (8 ounces each) cream cheese, softened
- 1 cup sugar
- 12 ounces bittersweet chocolate, melted and cooled
- 1 cup (8 ounces) sour cream
- 1½ teaspoons vanilla extract
- ½ teaspoon almond extract
  Dash salt
- 3 large eggs, lightly beaten

GLAZE
- 4 ounces bittersweet chocolate, chopped
- ¼ cup heavy whipping cream
- 1 teaspoon vanilla extract
  Whipped cream and additional toasted hazelnuts, optional

1. Preheat oven to 350°. Mix wafer crumbs, hazelnuts and melted butter; press onto bottom of an ungreased 9-in. springform pan.
2. Beat cream cheese and sugar until smooth. Beat in cooled chocolate, then sour cream, extracts and salt. Add eggs; beat on low speed just until blended. Pour over crust. Place pan on a baking sheet.
3. Bake until center is almost set, 60-65

minutes. Cool on a wire rack 10 minutes. Loosen sides from pan with a knife; cool 1 hour longer. Refrigerate 3 hours.
4. For the glaze, in a microwave, melt the chocolate with the cream; stir it until it is smooth. Stir in the vanilla. Spread over chilled cheesecake. Refrigerate, covered, overnight. Remove the rim from pan. If desired, served with whipped cream and additional hazelnuts.
Note: Semisweet baking chocolate may be substituted for the bittersweet chocolate.

GERMAN SPICE COOKIES

These chewy spice cookies are great with coffee and taste even better the next day. The recipe has been a family favorite for more than 40 years.

—Joan Tyson, Bowling Green, OH

Start to Finish: 20 min.
Makes: 3½ dozen

- 3 large eggs
- 2 cups packed brown sugar
- 1 teaspoon ground cloves
- 1 teaspoon ground cinnamon
- ½ teaspoon pepper
- 2 cups all-purpose flour
- ½ teaspoon baking soda
- ½ teaspoon salt
- 1 cup raisins
- 1 cup chopped walnuts

1. In a large bowl, beat eggs. Add the brown sugar, cloves, cinnamon and pepper. Combine the flour, baking soda and salt; gradually add to the egg mixture. Stir in raisins and walnuts.
2. Drop by tablespoonfuls 2 in. apart onto lightly greased baking sheets. Bake at 400° for 8-10 minutes or until surface cracks. Remove to wire racks to cool.
Note: This recipe contains no butter or shortening.

BLACK BEAN BROWNIES

You'd never guess these rich, velvety chocolate treats contain a can of black beans. This recipe does not call for flour, so it's a great choice for anyone on a gluten-restricted diet.
—Kathy Hewitt, Cranston, RI

Prep: 15 min. • **Bake:** 20 min. + cooling
Makes: 1 dozen

- 1 can (15 ounces) black beans, rinsed and drained
- ½ cup semisweet chocolate chips, divided
- 3 tablespoons canola oil
- 3 large eggs
- ⅔ cup packed brown sugar
- ½ cup baking cocoa
- 1 teaspoon vanilla extract
- ½ teaspoon baking powder
- ⅛ teaspoon salt

1. Place the beans, ¼ cup chocolate chips and oil in a food processor; cover and process until blended. Add eggs, brown sugar, cocoa, vanilla, baking powder and salt; cover and process until smooth.
2. Transfer to a parchment paper-lined 8-in. square baking pan. Sprinkle with remaining chocolate chips. Bake at 350° for 20-25 minutes or until a toothpick inserted in center comes out clean. Cool on a wire rack. Cut into bars.

★ ★ ★ ★ ★ **READER REVIEW**

"Served these as an after-dinner dessert with a scoop of low-fat ice cream and everyone loved them!"

MARYROSE90 TASTEOFHOME.COM

BILLIE'S SOUTHERN SWEET POTATO CAKE

I made this cake for my kids when they were small, and they told me in their sweet, tender voices, "Mommy, you're the best baker." Little did they know it was my first attempt at homemade cake!
—Billie Williams-Henderson, Bowie, MD

Prep: 25 min. • **Bake:** 40 min. + cooling
Makes: 20 servings

- 4 large eggs
- 2 cups sugar
- 2 cups canola oil
- 2 teaspoons vanilla extract
- 2 cups all-purpose flour
- 2 teaspoons baking soda
- 2 teaspoons ground cinnamon
- ½ teaspoon ground ginger
- ½ teaspoon ground allspice
- ½ teaspoon salt
- 3 cups shredded peeled sweet potatoes (about 2 medium)
- 1 cup finely chopped walnuts

FROSTING

- 1 package (8 ounces) cream cheese, softened
- ½ cup butter, softened
- 1 teaspoon vanilla extract
- 2 cups confectioners' sugar

1. Preheat oven to 350°. Grease a 13x9-in. baking pan.
2. In a large bowl, beat eggs, sugar, oil and vanilla until well blended. In another bowl, whisk flour, baking soda, spices and salt; gradually beat into the egg mixture. Stir in sweet potatoes and walnuts.
3. Transfer to prepared pan. Bake 40-45 minutes or until a toothpick inserted in center comes out clean. Cool completely in pan on a wire rack.
4. In a small bowl, beat the cream cheese, butter and vanilla until they are blended. Gradually beat in the confectioners' sugar until smooth. Spread over the cooled cake. Refrigerate leftovers.

MRS. THOMPSON'S CARROT CAKE

I received this recipe from the mother of a patient I cared for back in 1972 in St. Paul, MN. It was, and still is, the best carrot cake I have ever tasted.
—Becky Wachob, Laramie, WY

Prep: 30 min. • **Bake:** 35 min.
Makes: 15 servings

- 3 cups shredded carrots
- 1 can (20 ounces) crushed pineapple, well drained
- 2 cups sugar
- 1 cup canola oil
- 4 large eggs
- 2 cups all-purpose flour
- 2 teaspoons baking soda
- 2 teaspoons ground cinnamon

FROSTING
- 1 package (8 ounces) cream cheese, softened
- ¼ cup butter, softened
- 2 teaspoons vanilla extract
- 3¾ cups confectioners' sugar

1. In a large bowl, beat first five ingredients until well blended. In another bowl, mix the flour, baking soda and cinnamon; gradually beat into the carrot mixture.
2. Transfer mixture to a greased 13x9-in. baking pan. Bake at 350° for 35-40 minutes or until a toothpick inserted in center comes out clean. Cool completely in pan on a wire rack.
3. For frosting, in a large bowl, beat the cream cheese, butter and vanilla until blended. Gradually beat in the confectioners' sugar until smooth. Spread over cake. Store in the refrigerator.

PUMPKIN PIE SQUARES

My husband and daughters love this dessert. It has all of the spicy pumpkin goodness of the traditional pie without the fuss of a pastry crust. The pecans on top add a nice crunch.
—Denise Goedeken, Platte Center, NE

Prep: 15 min.
Bake: 1 hour 20 min. + cooling
Makes: 16-20 servings

- 1 cup all-purpose flour
- ½ cup quick-cooking oats
- ½ cup packed brown sugar
- ½ cup cold butter

FILLING
- 2 cans (15 ounces each) solid-pack pumpkin
- 2 cans (12 ounces each) evaporated milk
- 4 large eggs
- 1½ cups granulated sugar
- 2 teaspoons ground cinnamon
- 1 teaspoon ground ginger
- ½ teaspoon ground cloves
- 1 teaspoon salt

TOPPING
- ½ cup packed brown sugar
- ½ cup chopped pecans
- 2 tablespoons butter, softened
  Sweetened whipped cream, optional

1. Preheat oven to 350°. Combine the flour, oats and brown sugar. Cut in butter until the mixture is crumbly. Press into a greased 13x9-in. pan. Bake until golden brown, about 20 minutes.
2. Meanwhile, beat filling ingredients until smooth; pour over crust. Bake 45 minutes.
3. Combine topping ingredients; sprinkle over filling. Bake until a knife inserted in the center comes out clean, about 15-20 minutes longer. Cool, then refrigerate until serving. If desired, serve with whipped cream.

FRESH BERRY & ALMOND TARTS

We hosted a party for friends who enjoy trying new foods. Every dish was a Taste of Home recipe. These tarts were the big hit of the evening!
—Sheila Wyum, Rutland, ND

Prep: 15 min. • **Bake:** 10 min. + cooling
Makes: 16 tarts

- 1 package (14.1 ounces) refrigerated pie pastry
- 1 package (8 ounces) cream cheese, softened
- ¼ cup confectioners' sugar
- ¼ teaspoon almond extract
- 2 cups fresh blueberries
- 2 cups fresh raspberries
- ¼ cup sliced almonds, toasted
  Additional confectioners' sugar, optional

1. Preheat the oven to 400°. On a lightly floured surface, unroll pastry sheets. Roll dough to ⅛-inch thickness. Cut each with a floured 3-in. cookie cutter to make eight circles or other shapes. Now transfer to ungreased baking sheets; prick holes in pastries with a fork.

2. Bake for 8-10 minutes or until golden brown. Remove from pans to wire racks to cool completely.

3. Meanwhile, in a small bowl, mix cream cheese, confectioners' sugar and almond extract until blended. Spread over cooled pastries. Top with berries, pressing lightly to adhere. Sprinkle with almonds and, if desired, confectioners' sugar. Refrigerate the leftovers.

Note: To toast nuts, bake in a shallow pan in a 350° oven for 5-10 minutes or cook in a skillet over low heat until lightly browned, stirring occasionally.

MARSHMALLOW-FILLED BANANA CUPCAKES

A friend gave me this recipe when I first moved into my neighborhood 40 years ago. It might look time-consuming, but it's easy and the results are incredible.
—Monique Caron, Greensboro, NC

Prep: 40 min. • **Bake:** 20 min. + cooling
Makes: 1½ dozen

- ¾ cup shortening
- 1½ cups sugar
- 2 large eggs
- 1 cup mashed ripe bananas (about 2 medium)
- 1 teaspoon vanilla extract
- 2 cups all-purpose flour
- 1 teaspoon baking soda
- ¼ teaspoon salt
- ¼ cup buttermilk

FILLING
- 1 cup butter, softened
- 2 cups marshmallow creme
- 1½ cups confectioners' sugar
  Additional confectioners' sugar

1. Preheat oven to 375°. Line 18 muffin cups with paper or foil liners.

2. In a large bowl, cream shortening and sugar until light and fluffy. Add the eggs, one at a time, beating well after each addition. Beat in the bananas and vanilla. In another bowl, whisk the flour, baking soda and salt; add to the creamed mixture alternately with buttermilk, beating well after each addition.

3. Fill prepared cups two-thirds full. Bake 18-22 minutes or until a toothpick inserted in center comes out clean. Cool in pans 10 minutes before removing to wire racks to cool completely.

4. For filling, in a large bowl, beat butter, marshmallow creme and confectioners' sugar until smooth. Using a sharp knife, cut a 1-in. circle, 1 in. deep, in top of each cupcake. Carefully remove cut portion and set aside. Fill cavity with about 1 teaspoon filling. Replace tops, pressing down lightly. Dollop or pipe remaining filling over tops. Dust with additional confectioners' sugar.

LUSCIOUS ALMOND CHEESECAKE

Almonds and almond extract give a traditional sour cream-topped cheesecake a tasty twist.
—Brenda Clifford, Overland Park, KS

....

Prep: 15 min. • **Bake:** 55 min. + chilling
Makes: 14-16 servings

- 1¼ cups crushed vanilla wafers (about 40 wafers)
- ¾ cup finely chopped almonds
- ¼ cup sugar
- ⅓ cup butter, melted

FILLING
- 4 packages (8 ounces each) cream cheese, softened
- 1¼ cups sugar
- 4 large eggs, lightly beaten
- 1½ teaspoons almond extract
- 1 teaspoon vanilla extract

TOPPING
- 2 cups (16 ounces) sour cream
- ¼ cup sugar
- 1 teaspoon vanilla extract
- ⅛ cup toasted sliced almonds

1. In a bowl, combine the wafer crumbs, almonds and sugar; stir in the butter and mix well. Press into bottom of a greased 10-in. springform pan; set aside.
2. In a large bowl, beat cream cheese and sugar until smooth. Add eggs; beat on low speed just until combined. Stir in extracts. Pour into crust. Place on a baking sheet.
3. Bake at 350° for 50-55 minutes or until center is almost set. Remove from the oven; let stand for 5 minutes (leave oven on). Combine the sour cream, sugar and vanilla. Spoon around edge of cheesecake; carefully spread over the filling. Bake for 5 minutes longer. Cool on a wire rack for 10 minutes. Carefully run a knife around edge of pan to loosen; cool 1 hour longer. Refrigerate overnight.

4. Just before serving, sprinkle with almonds and remove sides of pan. Refrigerate leftovers.

MAPLE-GLAZED CINNAMON CHIP BARS

Cinnamon chips and a maple glaze add fabulous flavor. When I make these, the kitchen smells like Christmas. The glaze fancies them up a bit.
—Lyndi Pilch, Springfield, MO

....

Prep: 20 min. • **Bake:** 20 min.
Makes: 2 dozen

- 1 cup butter, softened
- 2 cups packed brown sugar
- 2 teaspoons vanilla extract
- 2 large eggs
- 2⅔ cups all-purpose flour
- 2 teaspoons baking powder
- 1 teaspoon salt
- ¾ cup cinnamon baking chips
- 1 tablespoon cinnamon sugar

GLAZE
- ½ cup confectioners' sugar
- 3 tablespoons maple syrup
- ½ teaspoon vanilla extract

1. Preheat oven to 350°. In a large bowl, cream butter and brown sugar until well blended. Beat in vanilla and eggs, one at a time. In another bowl, whisk together flour, baking powder and salt; gradually beat into creamed mixture. Stir in the cinnamon chips. Spread into a greased 13x9-in. baking pan. Sprinkle top with cinnamon sugar.
2. Bake until golden brown and a toothpick inserted in the center comes out clean, 20-25 minutes. Cool completely in the pan on a wire rack.
3. In a small bowl, mix all glaze ingredients until smooth; drizzle over top. Cut into bars. Store in an airtight container.

1. Place egg whites in a small bowl; let stand at room temperature 30 minutes.
2. Preheat oven to 350°. Line bottoms of three greased 9-in. round baking pans with parchment paper; grease paper.
3. In a large bowl, cream butter and sugar until light and fluffy. Add egg yolks, one at a time, beating well after each addition. Beat in the vanilla. In another bowl, whisk the flour, baking soda and salt; add this to the creamed mixture alternately with the buttermilk, beating well after each addition. Fold in coconut and pecans.
4. With clean beaters, beat egg whites on medium speed until stiff peaks form. Gradually fold into the batter. Transfer to prepared pans. Bake 20-25 minutes or until a toothpick inserted in center comes out clean. Cool in pans 10 minutes before removing to wire racks; remove paper. Cool completely.
5. For frosting, in a large bowl, beat cream cheese and butter until smooth. Beat in vanilla. Gradually beat in confectioners' sugar and enough of the cream to reach spreading consistency. Spread frosting between layers and over top and sides of cake. Sprinkle with pecans and, if desired, coconut. Refrigerate leftovers.

Note: To toast pecans and coconut, spread each, one at a time, in a 15x10x1-in. baking pan. Bake at 350° for 5-10 minutes or until lightly browned, stirring occasionally.

COCONUT ITALIAN CREAM CAKE

I'd never tasted an Italian Cream Cake before moving to Colorado. Now I bake for people in the area, and this beauty is one of my most-requested desserts.
—Ann Bush, Colorado City, CO

Prep: 50 min. • **Bake:** 20 min. + cooling
Makes: 16 servings

- 5 large eggs, separated
- 1 cup butter, softened
- 1⅔ cups sugar
- 1½ teaspoons vanilla extract
- 2 cups all-purpose flour
- ¾ teaspoon baking soda
- ½ teaspoon salt
- 1 cup buttermilk
- 1⅓ cups sweetened shredded coconut
- 1 cup chopped pecans, toasted

FROSTING
- 12 ounces cream cheese, softened
- 6 tablespoons butter, softened
- 2¼ teaspoons vanilla extract
- 5⅔ cups confectioners' sugar
- 3 to 4 tablespoons heavy whipping cream
- ½ cup chopped pecans, toasted
- ¼ cup toasted sweetened shredded coconut, optional

1. Preheat oven to 375°. Line 18 muffin cups with paper liners.
2. In a large bowl, cream butter and sugar until light and fluffy. Add eggs, one at a time, beating well after each addition. Split vanilla beans lengthwise; using the tip of a sharp knife, scrape seeds from the center into creamed mixture. In another bowl, whisk flour, baking powder and salt; add to creamed mixture alternately with milk, beating well after each addition.
3. Fill prepared cups three-fourths full. Bake 16-18 minutes or until a toothpick inserted in center comes out clean. Cool in pans 10 minutes before removing to wire racks to cool completely.
4. In a large bowl, beat cream cheese, butter and vanilla until blended. Gradually beat in confectioners' sugar until smooth. Frost cupcakes. Decorate with candies and coarse sugar as desired. Refrigerate the leftovers.

Freeze option: Freeze cooled cupcakes in resealable plastic freezer bags. To use, thaw at room temperature. Frost as directed.

MAKE AHEAD

VANILLA BEAN CUPCAKES

My young son loves these cupcakes. Flecks of vanilla bean in the moist, tender cake and a sprinkle of sugar on top gives them special-occasion status.
—Alysha Braun, St. Catharines, ON

Prep: 30 min. • Bake: 20 min. + cooling
Makes: 1½ dozen

- ¾ cup unsalted butter, softened
- 1¼ cups sugar
- 2 large eggs
- 2 vanilla beans
- 2 cups cake flour
- 2 teaspoons baking powder
- ½ teaspoon salt
- ⅔ cup whole milk
FROSTING
- 1 package (8 ounces) cream cheese, softened
- 6 tablespoons unsalted butter, softened
- 1½ teaspoons vanilla extract
- 3 cups confectioners' sugar
  Assorted candies and coarse sugar

MAKE AHEAD

MINI PEANUT BUTTER SANDWICH COOKIES

Peanut butter lovers go nuts for these rich little sandwich cookies. To cool down on a hot day, sandwich ice cream between the cookies instead of frosting.
—Keri Wolfe, Nappanee, IN

Prep: 25 min.
Bake: 15 min./batch + cooling
Makes: about 3½ dozen

- 1 cup shortening
- 1 cup creamy peanut butter
- 1 cup sugar
- 1 cup packed brown sugar
- 3 large eggs
- 1 teaspoon vanilla extract
- 3½ cups all-purpose flour
- 2 teaspoons baking soda
- ½ teaspoon salt
FILLING
- ¾ cup creamy peanut butter
- ½ cup 2% milk
- 1½ teaspoons vanilla extract
- 4 cups confectioners' sugar

1. Preheat oven to 350°. In a large bowl, cream shortening, peanut butter and sugars until blended. Beat in eggs and vanilla. In another bowl, whisk the flour, baking soda and salt; gradually beat into the creamed mixture.
2. Shape into 1-in. balls; place 2 in. apart on ungreased baking sheets. Bake 11-13 minutes or until set. Remove from pans to wire racks to cool completely.
3. In a small bowl, beat the peanut butter, milk and vanilla until blended. Beat in the confectioners' sugar until smooth. Spread filling on bottoms of half of the cookies; cover with remaining cookies.

Freeze option: Freeze the unfilled cookies in freezer containers. To use, thaw cookies and fill as directed.

Note: Reduced-fat peanut butter is not recommended for this recipe.

ALMOND-COCONUT LEMON BARS

Give traditional lemon bars a tasty twist with the addition of almonds and coconut.
—*Taste of Home* Test Kitchen

Prep: 10 min. • **Bake:** 40 min. + cooling
Makes: 2 dozen

1½ cups all-purpose flour
½ cup confectioners' sugar
⅓ cup blanched almonds, toasted
1 teaspoon grated lemon peel
¾ cup cold butter, cubed

FILLING
3 large eggs
1½ cups sugar
½ cup sweetened shredded coconut
¼ cup lemon juice
3 tablespoons all-purpose flour
1 teaspoon grated lemon peel
½ teaspoon baking powder
Confectioners' sugar

1. In a food processor, combine the flour, confectioners' sugar, almonds and lemon peel; cover and process until nuts are finely chopped. Add butter; pulse just until the mixture is crumbly. Press into a greased 13x9-in. baking dish. Bake at 350° for 20 minutes.
2. Meanwhile, in a large bowl, whisk eggs, sugar, coconut, lemon juice, flour, lemon peel and baking powder; pour over the hot crust. Bake until light golden brown, 20-25 minutes. Cool on a wire rack. Dust with confectioners' sugar. Cut into squares.

LEMON-BLUEBERRY POUND CAKE

Pair a slice of this moist cake with a scoop of vanilla ice cream. It's a staple at our family barbecues.
—Rebecca Little, Park Ridge, IL

Prep: 25 min. • **Bake:** 55 min. + cooling
Makes: 12 servings

⅓ cup butter, softened
4 ounces cream cheese, softened
2 cups sugar
3 large eggs
1 large egg white
1 tablespoon grated lemon peel
2 teaspoons vanilla extract
2 cups fresh or frozen unsweetened blueberries
3 cups all-purpose flour, divided
1 teaspoon baking powder
½ teaspoon baking soda
½ teaspoon salt
1 cup (8 ounces) lemon yogurt

GLAZE
1¼ cups confectioners' sugar
2 tablespoons lemon juice

1. Preheat oven to 350°. Grease and flour a 10-in. fluted tube pan. In a large bowl, cream the butter, cream cheese and sugar until blended. Add eggs and egg white, one at a time, beating well after each addition. Beat in lemon peel and vanilla.
2. Toss blueberries with 2 tablespoons of flour. In another bowl, mix the remaining flour with baking powder, baking soda and salt; add to creamed mixture alternately with the yogurt, beating after each addition just until it is combined. Fold in the blueberry mixture.
3. Transfer batter to prepared pan. Bake for 55-60 minutes or until a toothpick inserted in center comes out clean. Cool in pan 10 minutes before removing to wire rack; cool completely.
4. In a small bowl, mix confectioners' sugar and lemon juice until smooth. Drizzle over the cake.
Note: For easier removal of cake, use solid shortening when greasing a fluted or plain tube pan.

PEACH MELBA TRIFLE

This dream of a dessert tastes extra good on a busy day because you can make it ahead of time. If you don't have fresh peaches handy, use the canned ones.
—Christina Moore, Casar, NC

....

Prep: 20 min. + chilling
Makes: 12 servings

- 2 packages (12 ounces each) frozen unsweetened raspberries, thawed
- 1 tablespoon cornstarch
- 1½ cups (12 ounces) fat-free peach yogurt
- ⅛ teaspoon almond extract
- 1 carton (8 ounces) frozen reduced-fat whipped topping, thawed
- 2 prepared angel food cakes (8 to 10 ounces each), cut into 1-inch cubes (about 8 cups)
- 4 small peaches, peeled and sliced (about 2 cups)

1. In a large saucepan, mix raspberries and cornstarch until blended. Bring to a boil; cook and stir for 1-2 minutes or until thickened. Strain the seeds; cover and refrigerate.
2. In a large bowl, mix yogurt and extract; fold in whipped topping. In a 4-qt. bowl, layer half of the cake cubes, yogurt mixture and peaches. Repeat layers. Refrigerate, covered, at least 3 hours before serving. Serve with raspberry sauce.

STRAWBERRY-RHUBARB CREAM DESSERT

A neighbor shared this recipe with me, and I created my own variation using garden-fresh rhubarb and strawberries. The cookie crust and creamy sweet-tart layers went over big at a family party... not a crumb was left!
—Sara Zignego, Hartford, WI

....

Prep: 1 hour + chilling
Makes: 12 servings

- 2 cups all-purpose flour
- 1 cup chopped pecans
- 1 cup butter, melted
- ¼ cup sugar

TOPPING
- 1 cup packed brown sugar
- 3 tablespoons cornstarch
- 5 cups chopped fresh or frozen rhubarb
- 1 cup sliced fresh strawberries
- 1 package (8 ounces) cream cheese, softened
- 1 cup confectioners' sugar
- 1¼ cups heavy whipping cream, whipped, divided
   Additional brown sugar, optional

1. In a small bowl, combine the flour, pecans, butter and sugar. Press into a greased 13x9-in. baking dish. Bake at 350° for 18-20 minutes or until golden brown. Cool on a wire rack.
2. In a large saucepan, combine brown sugar and cornstarch. Stir in rhubarb until combined. Bring to a boil over medium heat, stirring often. Reduce the heat; cook and stir for 4-5 minutes or until thickened. Remove from the heat; cool. Stir in the strawberries.
3. In a large bowl, beat cream cheese and confectioners' sugar until smooth. Fold in 1 cup whipped cream. Spread over crust; top with rhubarb mixture. Spread with remaining whipped cream. Refrigerate for 3-4 hours before serving. Garnish with additional brown sugar if desired.

★ ★ ★ ★ ★ **READER REVIEW**
"I have made this recipe several times. It is without a doubt my absolute favorite dessert."
MOONFROST TASTEOFHOME.COM

1. Preheat oven to 350°. Grease and flour a 10-in. fluted tube pan. Chop 1 cup of hazelnuts. Place remaining hazelnuts in a food processor; pulse until finely ground.
2. In a large bowl, cream butter and sugar until light and fluffy. Add eggs, one at a time, beating well after each addition. Beat in extracts.
3. In another bowl, whisk flour, salt, baking soda and ground hazelnuts; add to the creamed mixture alternately with ricotta cheese, beating after each addition just until combined. Fold in the pears and chopped hazelnuts.
4. Transfer batter to prepared pan. Bake for 55-65 minutes or until a toothpick inserted in center comes out clean. Cool in pan 10 minutes before removing to a wire rack to cool completely.
5. For glaze, in a small heavy saucepan, melt butter over medium heat. Heat 5-7 minutes or until golden brown, stirring constantly. Transfer to a bowl. Stir in milk, vanilla and enough confectioners' sugar to reach desired consistency. Drizzle over cooled cake.

Note: To remove cakes easily, use solid shortening to grease plain and fluted tube pans. To toast whole hazelnuts, spread hazelnuts in a 15x10x1-in. baking pan. Bake in a 350° oven 7-10 minutes or until fragrant and lightly browned, stirring occasionally. To remove skins, wrap hazelnuts in a tea towel; rub with towel to loosen skins.

HAZELNUT PEAR CAKE

From the hazelnuts to the yummy brown butter glaze, this cake is a little different from an everyday pound cake.
—Elisabeth Larsen, Pleasant Grove, UT

Prep: 30 min. • **Bake:** 55 min. + cooling
Makes: 16 servings

1½ cups whole hazelnuts, toasted and skins removed
1 cup unsalted butter, softened
2 cups sugar
4 large eggs
2 teaspoons vanilla extract
1 teaspoon almond extract
2½ cups all-purpose flour
½ teaspoon salt
½ teaspoon baking soda
1 cup ricotta cheese
3 ripe medium pears, peeled and chopped (about 2 cups)

BROWNED BUTTER GLAZE
½ cup butter, cubed
3 tablespoons 2% milk
1 teaspoon vanilla extract
1¾ to 2 cups confectioners' sugar

CHOCOLATE-STRAWBERRY CREAM CHEESE TART

Sure to impress, this dessert features velvety cream cheese, red strawberries and a drizzle of fudge piled on a crunchy chocolate almond crust.

—Priscilla Yee, Concord, CA

Prep: 20 min. • **Bake:** 15 min. + chilling
Makes: 12 servings

- ¾ cup all-purpose flour
- ½ cup finely chopped almonds, toasted
- 6 tablespoons butter, melted
- ⅓ cup baking cocoa
- ¼ cup packed brown sugar

FILLING

- 16 ounces cream cheese, softened
- 1 cup confectioners' sugar
- 1 teaspoon vanilla extract
- 3 cups halved fresh strawberries
- 3 tablespoons hot fudge ice cream topping

1. Preheat oven to 375 °. In a small bowl, combine the first five ingredients; press onto the bottom and up the sides of an ungreased 9-in. fluted tart pan with a removable bottom. Bake 12-15 minutes or until crust is set. Cool on a wire rack.
2. In another small bowl, beat cream cheese, confectioners' sugar and vanilla until smooth. Spread over bottom of prepared crust. Arrange strawberry halves, cut side down, over filling. Cover and refrigerate at least 1 hour.
3. Just before serving, drizzle fudge topping over tart. Refrigerate leftovers.

CHOCOLATE-PEANUT BUTTER SHEET CAKE

I love peanut butter and chocolate, so this sheet cake is a favorite. The chopped peanuts on top add a nice crunch. Serve with vanilla ice cream if you like.

—Lisa Varner, El Paso, TX

Prep: 25 min. • **Bake:** 25 min. + cooling
Makes: 15 servings

- 2 cups all-purpose flour
- 2 cups sugar
- 1 teaspoon baking soda
- ½ teaspoon salt
- 1 cup water
- ½ cup butter, cubed
- ½ cup creamy peanut butter
- ¼ cup baking cocoa
- 3 large eggs
- ½ cup sour cream
- 2 teaspoons vanilla extract

FROSTING

- 3 cups confectioners' sugar
- ½ cup creamy peanut butter
- ½ cup 2% milk
- ½ teaspoon vanilla extract
- ½ cup chopped salted or unsalted peanuts

1. Preheat oven to 350°. Grease a 13x9-in. baking pan.
2. In a large bowl, whisk the flour, sugar, baking soda and salt. In a small saucepan, combine the water, butter, peanut butter and cocoa; bring just to a boil, stirring it occasionally. Add to flour mixture, stirring just until moistened.
3. In a small bowl, whisk eggs, sour cream and vanilla until blended; add to the flour mixture, whisking constantly. Transfer to prepared pan. Bake for 25-30 minutes or until a toothpick inserted in center comes out clean.
4. To prepare frosting, in a large bowl, beat confectioners' sugar, peanut butter, milk and vanilla until the blend is smooth.
5. Remove cake from oven; place on a wire rack. Immediately spread with frosting; sprinkle with peanuts. Cool completely.

CHEWY GOOD OATMEAL COOKIES

Here's a great oatmeal cookie with all my favorite extras: dried cherries, white chocolate chips and macadamia nuts.
—Sandy Harz, Spring Lake, MI

Prep: 20 min. • **Bake:** 10 min./batch
Makes: 3½ dozen

- 1 cup butter, softened
- 1 cup packed brown sugar
- ½ cup sugar
- 2 large eggs
- 1 tablespoon honey
- 2 teaspoons vanilla extract
- 2½ cups quick-cooking oats
- 1½ cups all-purpose flour
- 1 teaspoon baking soda
- ½ teaspoon salt
- ½ teaspoon ground cinnamon
- 1⅓ cups dried cherries
- 1 cup white baking chips
- 1 cup (4 ounces) chopped macadamia nuts

1. Preheat oven to 350°. In a large bowl, cream butter and sugars until light and fluffy. Beat in the eggs, honey and vanilla. In another bowl, mix the oats, flour, baking soda, salt and cinnamon; gradually beat into creamed mixture. Then stir in the remaining ingredients.

2. Drop dough by rounded tablespoonfuls 2 in. apart onto greased baking sheets. Bake 10-12 minutes or until golden brown. Cool on pan 2 minutes; remove to wire racks to cool.

Chewy Cranberry Oatmeal Cookies: Substitute dried cranberries for the dried cherries.

Chewy Oatmeal Chip Cookies: Omit the cinnamon, dried cherries and macadamia nuts. Add 1 cup each semisweet chocolate chips and butterscotch chips with the white baking chips.

ORANGE-CRANBERRY NUT TARTS

My friend gave me a recipe for orange cookies. I decided to turn it into tarts and add cranberry sauce, nuts and a white chocolate drizzle.
—Nancy Bruce, Big Timber, MT

Prep: 50 min. + chilling • **Bake:** 10 min./batch + cooling
Makes: 4 dozen

- ½ cup butter, softened
- 1 cup sugar
- 1 large egg
- 4 teaspoons grated orange peel
- ¼ cup orange juice
- 2 tablespoons evaporated milk or 2% milk
- 3 cups all-purpose flour
- 3 teaspoons baking powder
- ¼ teaspoon salt

FILLING
- 1 can (14 ounces) whole-berry cranberry sauce
- ½ cup sugar
- 2 tablespoons orange juice
- 1 cup chopped walnuts
- 4 ounces white baking chocolate, melted

1. In a large bowl, cream butter and sugar until light and fluffy. Beat in egg until blended. Beat in orange peel, orange juice and milk. In another bowl, whisk flour, baking powder and salt; gradually beat into creamed mixture.

2. Divide dough into three portions. On a lightly floured surface, shape each into a 10-in.-long roll. Wrap in plastic; refrigerate overnight or until firm.

3. For filling, in a small saucepan, combine cranberry sauce, sugar and orange juice. Bring to a boil, stirring constantly; cook and stir 2 minutes. Remove from heat; cool completely. Stir in walnuts.

4. Preheat oven to 375°. Unwrap each portion of dough and cut crosswise into 16 slices. Press onto bottoms and up the sides of greased mini-muffin cups. Fill each with 2 teaspoons cranberry mixture.

5. Bake 8-10 minutes or until edges are light golden. Cool in pans 10 minutes. Remove to wire racks to cool completely. Drizzle with melted white chocolate; let stand until set.

Alphabetical Index

CHOCOLATE STRAWBERRY PUNCH BOWL TRIFLE PAGE 225